The History of American Trotskyism

James P. Cannon in 1938

The History of American Trotskyism

Report of a participant

James P. Cannon

PATHFINDER

New York ◆ London ◆ Montreal ◆ Sydney

Copyright © 1944, 1972, 1995 by Pathfinder Press
Copyright renewed 1973

ISBN 0-87348-814-8 paper; ISBN 0-87348-815-6 cloth
Library of Congress Catalog Card Number 72-78439
Manufactured in the United States of America

First edition, 1944
Second edition, 1972
Third edition, 1995

Cover painting:
Patrick Heron, *Green and Mauve Horizontals: January 1958,* oil on canvas,
121.9 x 55.9 cm © 1995 Patrick Heron / Licensed by VAGA, New York, NY

Editorial preparation by Sara Lobman
Cover design by Toni Gorton

Pathfinder

410 West Street, New York, NY 10014, U.S.A.
Fax: (212) 727-0150 • CompuServe: 73321,414
• Internet: pathfinder@igc.apc.org

Pathfinder distributors around the world:

Australia (and Asia and the Pacific):
    Pathfinder, 19 Terry St., Surry Hills, Sydney, N.S.W. 2010
    Postal address: P.O. Box K879, Haymarket, N.S.W. 2000

Britain (and Europe, Africa except South Africa, and Middle East):
    Pathfinder, 47 The Cut, London, SE1 8LL

Canada:
    Pathfinder, 4581 rue St-Denis, Montreal, Quebec, H2J 2L4

Iceland:
    Pathfinder, Klapparstíg 26, 2d floor, 101 Reykjavík
    Postal address: P. Box 233, 121 Reykjavík

New Zealand:
    Pathfinder, La Gonda Arcade, 203 Karangahape Road, Auckland
    Postal address: P.O. Box 8730, Auckland

Sweden:
    Pathfinder, Vikingagatan 10, S-113 42, Stockholm

United States (and Caribbean, Latin America, and South Africa):
    Pathfinder, 410 West Street, New York, NY 10014

To Vincent R. Dunne
(1889-1970)
whose faith and works
contributed mightily to the making
of the history herein recorded

Contents

Preface   *1*
by Jack Barnes, July 2, 1995

Introduction to the first edition   *5*
by Joseph Hansen, June 24, 1944

1
The first days of American Communism   *13*
Trotskyism defined • continuity of Marxist movement • Socialist Party • influence of Russian revolution • formation of Left Wing • Foreign Language Federations • faction struggles • two Communist Parties • driven underground • ultraleftism • United Communist Party • struggle for legality • Workers Party

2
Factional struggles in the old Communist Party   *34*
Ideological superiority of Communist Party • trade union gains • Farmer-Labor Party adventure • Communist press • labor defense • factional struggles • social composition • consolidation of leadership • role of Communist International • origin of Trotskyist movement

3
The beginning of the Left Opposition   57

Marxism vs. Stalinism • Russian Left Opposition • national narrow-mindedness of American Communists • campaign against Trotskyism • Sixth World Congress • Cannon and Spector become Trotskyists • "trial" and expulsion of Cannon, Shachtman, and Abern • appeal to party • publication of the *Militant* • growth of faction

4
The Left Opposition under fire   79

Regeneration of American Communism • propaganda by correspondence • Spector in Canada • Stalinist ostracism, slander, gangsterism • appeal to plenum of Central Committee of CP • public meetings • publication of Trotskyist platform • first national conference of Left Opposition • Communist League of America launched

5
The dog days of the Left Opposition   102

Program and tasks • Lovestone group • Russian question • trade union question • a faction of the party and the Comintern • Albert Weisbord • Stalinist "left turn" • isolation • "lunatic fringe" • factionalism • publications • poverty • internationalism • "Tenacity! Tenacity! Tenacity!"

6
The break with the Comintern   126

Internationalism • unemployed work • trade union work • German events • capitulation of German Communist Party • bankruptcy of Third International • trends in Socialist Party • Conference for Progressive Labor Action • turn to mass work • sectarian opposition • American Workers Party • campaign for new party

7

The turn to mass work *146*

What to do next? • Paterson strike • hotel workers strike • B.J. Field • Minneapolis coal yard strike • negotiations with American Workers Party • Lovestone-Cannon debate • Trotskyism on the march

8

The great Minneapolis strikes *170*

Strike wave of 1934 • Auto-Lite strike in Toledo • role of unemployed • Minneapolis truck drivers strike • Bill Brown • "Organizing Committee" • Farrell Dobbs • "The Battle of Deputies Run" • July strike • federal mediators • *Daily Organizer* • Floyd Olson • arrest of Cannon and Shachtman • raid on strike headquarters • "Haas-Dunnigan Plan" • victory

9

The fusion with the Musteites *204*

Unity negotiations with American Workers Party • A.J. Muste • Salutsky (J.B.S. Hardman) • Louis Budenz • Ludwig Lore • organizational concessions by League • "Declaration of Principles" • plenum of Executive Committee of International Communist League in Paris • visit to Trotsky • Oehler-Stamm opposition to "French turn" • fusion of Communist League and American Workers Party • Workers Party launched

10

The struggle against sectarianism   227

Socialist Party "Militants" • pressure of Stalinists • Spanish experience • Oehlerites • Sacramento "criminal-syndicalism" trial • Active Workers Conference • Joseph Zack • financial trouble • June 1935 plenum • Abern clique • Oehler-Muste-Abern faction • October plenum • expulsion of Oehlerites

11

The 'French Turn' in America   258

Politics vs. organization • split in Socialist Party • negotiation with "Militants" • conditions of entry • convention of March 1936 • Stalinist agents in Allentown • entry into Socialist Party

12

The Trotskyists in the Socialist Party   278

Tendencies in SP • world situation • Spanish civil war • Moscow trials • French events • Trotsky Defense Committee • Socialist Party of California • *Socialist Appeal* • *Labor Action* • "Socialist Appeal Conference" • Prohibition of *Socialist Appeal* • "Gag" law • expulsion of Trotskyists • "National Committee of Expelled Branches" • Chicago convention • Socialist Workers Party launched

Index   304

Preface

In this sequence of twelve public talks given in 1942 in New York City, James P. Cannon recounts a formative—and heroic—chapter in the effort to build a proletarian party in the United States.

Beginning with three talks summarizing the initial efforts to found a communist party that aspired to emulate the Bolsheviks in the years following the Russian revolution, Cannon concentrates in this book on the period following the expulsion from the Workers (Communist) Party of America in 1928 of those veteran communists who opposed the growing Stalinization of the party leadership and supported the fight led by Russian revolutionary Leon Trotsky to continue V.I. Lenin's communist course. Cannon takes the story up to New Year's 1938, when the communist organization in the United States took the name Socialist Workers Party.

Two decades after he gave these talks, in *The First Ten*

Years of American Communism Cannon returned to a more detailed account of the earlier period in the history of the Marxist movement in the United States, once again from the standpoint of a leading participant. Published in 1962, *The First Ten Years of American Communism* traces in greater detail the years from the Bolshevik-led revolution of 1917 until 1928. In the process, Cannon reaffirms the summary conclusions on the roots of the communist movement in the United States and the character of its pioneers first presented in these 1942 lectures.

Cannon was born in Rosedale, Kansas, in 1890 and joined the Socialist Party at the age of eighteen. A traveling organizer for the Industrial Workers of the World before and during World War I and a leader of the working-class left wing of the Socialist Party, he became a founding leader of the communist movement in the United States following the Russian revolution. He was a member of the presidium of the executive committee of the Communist International in Moscow and then a delegate to the Fourth Congress of the Communist International during the seven months he was in Soviet Russia from June 1922 to January 1923. He later served as executive secretary of the International Labor Defense, a committee in the United States that fought for the release of prisoners framed-up for their militancy in the working-class movement. Cannon was a founding leader in 1928 of the Communist League of America, which evolved into the Socialist Workers Party in 1938. He served as SWP national secretary until 1953, when he became the party's national chairman, and then, in 1972, national chairman emeritus until the time of his death in 1974.

On December 8, 1941, just a few months before he presented these talks, Cannon and seventeen other leaders and cadres of the Socialist Workers Party and of Local 544-CIO (formerly Teamsters Local 544) had been sentenced to prison on frame-up charges in a federal court in Minneapolis, Minnesota, because of their active opposition within the U.S. labor movement to Washington's joining in the imperialist slaughter of World War II. The U.S. Court of Appeals upheld the verdict and sentences in late 1943. Cannon was imprisoned for sixteen months in the federal penitentiary at Sandstone, Minnesota, and was released in early 1945. The appeals court also affirmed the convictions of the other seventeen defendants, all of whom were imprisoned for similar terms.

Readers of *The History of American Trotskyism* will be interested in *The Left Opposition in the U.S., 1928–31* and *The Communist League of America, 1932–34*, which include writings and speeches by Cannon from a substantial portion of the period covered in this book. Other writings by Cannon include *The Struggle for a Proletarian Party, Notebook of an Agitator, Socialism on Trial, Letters from Prison, The Socialist Workers Party in World War II, Speeches to the Party,* and *Speeches for Socialism.* All these titles, as well as *The First Ten Years of American Communism*, are available from Pathfinder.

*   *   *

This fiftieth anniversary edition of *The History of American Trotskyism* restores Cannon's original subtitle "Report of a participant" and includes the original 1944 introduction by Socialist Workers Party leader Joseph Hansen. The text has been scanned and reset for this third edition.

Cannon's account is an essential companion not only to his *First Ten Years of American Communism,* but also to the article "Their Trotsky and Ours: Communist Continuity Today," published in 1983 in the inaugural issue of the Marxist magazine *New International.* All three of these works take as their starting point the Bolshevik perspective Cannon stated in the opening sentences of these 1942 talks: "Trotskyism is not a new movement, a new doctrine, but the restoration, the revival, of genuine Marxism as it was expounded and practiced in the Russian revolution and in the early days of the Communist International."

Jack Barnes
July 2, 1995

Introduction to the First Edition

In order to understand any process which occurs in nature, or in society, or in the human mind it is indispensable first to gain a clear grasp of its history, that is, to learn how a particular process came into being, through what paths it took growth, what changes it underwent, and how it developed. Once this is known, then—and only then—is the road clear for genuine knowledge. This, of course, holds likewise true for the understanding of the complex and scientific system of ideas represented by Trotskyism.

However, what has hitherto been lacking is precisely a history of Trotskyism. Cannon's book, which deals with the inception, growth, and development of the Trotskyist movement in the United States, thus supplies a long-felt want. And what is more, supplies it in a way that makes the most essential features of the history of American Trotskyism accessible not merely to trained students but to any advanced worker anxious and willing to learn. Cannon's exposition begins with the inception of the Communist movement in the United States after the first world war and acquaints the reader with the various stages of the development of the Trotskyist movement from the expulsion of the original Trotskyist cadre from the Communist Party in 1928 to the formation of the Socialist Workers Party in 1938.

The informal style of *The History of American Trotskyism*, originally delivered in the spring of 1942 as a series of lectures in New York City, might meet with objections on the part of pedants or philistines but no serious student will permit himself to be misled thereby.

Historians of the future, writing the definitive history of American and world Trotskyism, will undoubtedly round out Cannon's history with additional material delved from original sources; but, while there is no pretension to exhaustive research or extensive documentation in this work, future historians utilizing it as source material will find that they must likewise depend heavily upon it as a guidepost.

Of the few attempts to write a history of American Communism, not a single one, previous to the appearance of the present work, can be said to have achieved objectivity. In the tendentious account appearing over the signature of Benjamin Gitlow (*I Confess,* by Benjamin Gitlow), for instance, the founders of American Communism are made to appear as petty connivers and rascals who, under cover of professed belief in the future Communist society, devoted their main energies to unprincipled struggles and sordid intrigues for personal position and factional advantage. Not only does Gitlow fail to dwell upon the progressive significance of the founding of a native American Communist movement, but he even fails to contrast these leaders (including himself) with the rest of their generation who, at the expense of every progressive interest of their time, sold themselves and their services to the gangrenous capitalist system.

In contrast to the shallow approach of Gitlow and others of the same subjective school, Cannon is the first to offer a rational and valid explanation from the political point of view of the intense internal conflicts which marked the growth of the young Communist Party. He reveals the ideological and political issues that lay below the surface clash of personalities. It is this concern for ideas, principles, and political issues and their outcome which distinguishes Cannon's approach and gives it complete objectivity. Following a principled political criterion, he is relieved of the necessity of superficially and falsely explaining the development of American Communism by the good or bad traits of certain individuals.

In characterizing the many well-known figures of working-class politics with whom he once worked or came into contact, Cannon could be said to have been guided by the advice of Othello, "nothing extenuate, nor set down aught in malice."

It is no secret that a line of blood separates Cannon from his former associates still in the so-called Communist Party; yet he refrains from labeling these men in a derogatory way when he deals in the opening lectures with the early days of the Communist movement in the United States. They were the pioneer Communists "whom he once valued highly." He "did not wish to pass cursory judgment upon them despite all that happened in subsequent years." There is not a subjective word in these pages. In Cannon's opinion, "the men who founded the American Communist movement and carried it through its first years were indubitably among the most qualified, talented, and able people of their generation. The twenties witnessed the heyday of American capitalism; while all the bright young men were making their fortunes, the leaders of the American Communist Party of all the factions slaved away at less than mechanic's wages trying to build a new society."

Cannon gives full justice to the early Communist Party and its leaders. "All the factions had good in them," in his opinion. "With proper international leadership they could have been integrated. In the days of Lenin and Trotsky, for instance, the internal problems of the American Communist Party upon being taken to Moscow for advice and guidance found their natural solution." The party in those days was bound tighter together and advanced appreciably toward its goal. Internal democracy was not violated. Under the regime of Stalinism, however, the difficulties and growing pains of the young American Communist Party were artificially fostered and magnified to malignant proportions. The system of ideas and practices represented by Stalinism is principally responsible for the degeneration of the American Communist Party, not the particular weakness of individual leaders in the United States.

In considering this early period of American Communism, Cannon mentions only those figures who were significant as representatives of the main ideological currents within the movement. Those who were prominent in those days in the movement receive due prominence in this history. The names of adventitious figures, obscure shadows, who later were projected on the political screen by Stalin to act as his foreign agents, are not mentioned by Cannon, because in the heroic founding days of American Communism no one knew them.

Later, in dealing with certain leaders of the Socialist Party and others who impinged upon the rising movement of American Trotskyism, he does not hesitate to make concrete judgments. He presents for instance a rounded portrait of one Salutsky-Hardman. Cannon's reasons for this are not at all obscure or subjective. Although the founders of American Communism with all their faults were worthy of more detailed treatment, he devotes time to Salutsky-Hardman because he is a typical *"half-and-half"* man. Cannon's objective is to utilize the figure of Salutsky-Hardman in steeling the younger generation against the paralyzing weakness which made this man representative of a most dangerous political type.

As for the leaders of the Socialist Party "Militants" who at one time occupied a somewhat prominent position in left-wing politics, Cannon deals with them in detail in order to inoculate the young generation against the malignant disease of *dabbling* and *dilettantism.*

The leaders of the petty-bourgeois opposition within the Socialist Workers Party who turned traitor to Trotskyism upon the outbreak of the second world war are likewise treated with scrupulous fairness as in the case of all the figures who appear in the history.

The outstanding figures in this history are the pioneer Trotskyists. A great debt is owed to comrades such as those in

Minneapolis and those who stood at their posts in the national office when days not infrequently passed without barest subsistence. In recognizing these impeccable fighters, Cannon is acknowledging for the whole Trotskyist movement the place they have earned. Despite their own poverty, the Minneapolis comrades contributed every dollar they could scrape together to keep the party on its feet. Of just as great value was their moral support. In hard years such as those, even the strongest could not have continued to bear the pressure of all world reaction without the encouragement and moral support of those behind them. Moreover, whenever danger threatened from an unprincipled clique or irresponsible faction they were invariably to be found in the front ranks fighting to save the party.

The dedication to Vincent R. Dunne, who is now serving a prison sentence together with Cannon and sixteen others for their Trotskyist beliefs, is a fitting tribute to one of the foremost Trotskyist pioneers.

Along with the two companion volumes already published—*In Defense of Marxism,* by Leon Trotsky and *The Struggle for a Proletarian Party,* by James P. Cannon—this history provides what is in essence the balance sheet of the experience in the United States of building with the methods of Lenin a proletarian party—the fundamental instrument for the emancipation of the working class and for the socialist reorganization of society. These three volumes will undoubtedly become the handbooks of party builders and organizers in the United States. Moreover, just as the American Trotskyists have learned from the experiences of Fourth Internationalists elsewhere, those of China, Western Europe, Latin America, and in particular the Trotskyists of the Soviet Union, so in turn our cothinkers throughout the world can draw valuable conclusions from the developments and conditions of struggle for Trotskyism within the mightiest bastion of capitalism. We are sure that those who bring a receptive mind and a willingness to assimilate will find themselves amply rewarded in studying the lessons which are recorded in the history written by Comrade Cannon.

Joseph Hansen
June 24, 1944
New York

1

The First Days of American Communism

It seems rather appropriate, Comrades, to give a course of lectures on the history of American Trotskyism in this Labor Temple. It was right here in this auditorium at the beginning of our historic fight in 1928 that I made the first public speech in defense of Trotsky and the Russian Opposition. The speech was given not without some difficulties, for the Stalinists tried to break up our meeting by physical force. But we managed to get through with it. Our public speaking activity as avowed Trotskyists really began here in this Labor Temple, thirteen, nearly fourteen, years ago.

No doubt, in reading the literature of the Trotskyist movement in this country, you frequently noted the repeated statements that we have no new revelation: Trotskyism is not a new movement, a new doctrine, but the restoration, the revival, of genuine Marxism as it was expounded and practiced in the Russian revolution and in the early days of the Communist International.

Bolshevism itself was also a revival, a restoration, of genuine Marxism after this doctrine had been corrupted by the opportunists of the Second International, who culminated their betrayal of the proletariat by supporting the imperialist governments in the World War of 1914–18. When you study the particular period I am going to speak about in this course—the last thirteen years—or any other period since the time of Marx and Engels, one thing is observable. That is, the uninterrupted continuity of the revolutionary Marxist movement.

Marxism has never lacked authentic representatives. Despite all perversions and betrayals which have disoriented the movement from time to time, a new force has always arisen, a new element has come forward to put it back on the right course; that is, on the course of orthodox Marxism. This was so in our case, too.

We are rooted in the past. Our movement which we call Trotskyism, now crystallized in the Socialist Workers Party, did not spring full-blown from nowhere. It arose directly from the Communist Party of the United States. The Communist Party itself grew out of the preceding movement, the Socialist Party, and, in part, the Industrial Workers of the World. It grew out of the movement of the revolutionary workers in America in the pre-war and wartime period.

The Communist Party, which took organizational form in 1919, was originally the Left Wing of the Socialist Party. It was from the Socialist Party that the great body of Communist troops came. As a matter of fact, the formal launching of the Party in September 1919 was simply the organizational culmination of a protracted struggle inside the Socialist

Party. There the program had been worked out and there, within the Socialist Party, the original cadres were shaped. This internal struggle eventually led to a split and the formation of a separate organization, the Communist Party.

In the first years of the consolidation of the Communist movement—that is, you may say, from the Bolshevik revolution of 1917 until the organization of the Communist Party in this country two years later, and even for a year or two after that—the chief labor was the factional struggle against opportunist socialism, then represented by the Socialist Party. That is almost always the case when a workers political organization deteriorates and at the same time gives birth to a revolutionary wing. The struggle for the majority, for the consolidation of forces within the party, almost invariably limits the initial activity of a new movement to a rather narrow, intraparty struggle which does not end with the formal split.

The new party continues to seek proselytes in the old. It takes time for the new party to learn how to stand firmly on its own feet. Thus even after the formal split had taken place in 1919, through the force of inertia and habit and also because the fight was not really ended, the factional struggle continued. People remained in the Socialist Party who were undecided and who were the most likely candidates for the new party organization. The Communist Party concentrated its activity in the first year or so to the fight to clarify doctrine and win over additional forces from the Socialist Party. Of course, as is almost invariably the case in such historical developments, this factional phase eventually gave way to direct activity in the class struggle, to recruitment of new forces and the development of the new organization on an entirely independent basis.

The Socialist Party Left Wing, which later became the Communist Party, was directly inspired by the Bolshevik revolution of 1917. Prior to that time American militants had very little opportunity to acquire a genuine Marxist education. The leaders of the Socialist Party were not Marxists. The literature of Marxism printed in this country was quite meager and confined almost solely to the economic side of the doctrine. The Socialist Party was a heterogeneous body; its political activity, its agitation and propagandistic teachings were a terrible hodgepodge of all kinds of radical, revolutionary, and reformist ideas. In those days before the last war, and even during the war, young militants coming to the party looking for a clear programmatic guide had a hard time finding it. They couldn't get it from the official leadership of the party, which lacked serious knowledge of such things. The prominent heads of the Socialist Party were American counterparts of the opportunist leaders of the Social Democratic parties of Europe, only more ignorant and more contemptuous of theory. Consequently, despite their revolutionary impulses and spirit, the great mass of young militants of the American movement were able to learn little Marxism; and without Marxism it is impossible to have a consistent revolutionary movement.

The Bolshevik revolution in Russia changed everything almost overnight. Here was demonstrated in action the conquest of power by the proletariat. As in every other country, the tremendous impact of this proletarian revolutionary victory shook our movement in America to its very foundation.

The inspiration alone of the deed enormously strengthened the revolutionary wing of the party, gave the workers new hope, and aroused new interest in those theoretical problems of revolution which had not received proper recognition before that time.

We soon discovered that the organizers and leaders of the Russian revolution were not merely revolutionists of action. They were genuine Marxists in the field of doctrine. Out of Russia, from Lenin, Trotsky, and the other leaders, we received for the first time serious expositions of the revolutionary politics of Marxism. We learned that they had been engaged in long years of struggle for the restoration of unfalsified Marxism in the international labor movement. Now, thanks to the great authority and prestige of their victory in Russia, they were finally able to get a hearing in all countries. All the genuine militants rallied around them and began studying their writings with an interest and eagerness we had never known before. The doctrine they expounded had a tenfold authority because it had been verified in practice. Furthermore, month by month, year by year, despite all the power that world capitalism mobilized against them, they showed a capacity to develop the great revolution, create the Red Army, hold their own, make gains. Naturally, Bolshevism became the authoritative doctrine among revolutionary circles in all the workers political movements of the world, including our own here.

On that basis was formed the Left Wing of the Socialist Party. It had publications of its own; it had organizers, speakers, and writers. In the spring of 1919—that is, four or five months before the Communist Party was formally organized—we held in New York the first National Conference of the Left Wing faction. I was a delegate to this conference, coming at that time from Kansas City. It was at this conference that the faction virtually took shape as a party within a party in preparation for the later split. The official organ of the Left Wing was called the *Revolutionary Age*. This paper brought to the workers of America the first authentic explanation of the doctrines of Lenin and Trotsky. Its editor was the first one in this country to expound and popularize the doctrines of the Bolshevik leaders. Thereby, he must be historically recognized as the founder of American Communism. This editor was a man named Louis C. Fraina. His heart was not as strong as his head. He succumbed in the struggle and became a belated convert to bourgeois "democracy" in the period of its death agony. But that is only his personal misfortune. What he did in those early days retains all its validity, and neither he nor anybody else can undo it.

Another prominent figure of the movement in those days was John Reed. He was no leader, no politician. But his moral influence was very great. John Reed was the American socialist journalist who went to Russia, took part in the revolution, truthfully reported it, and wrote a great book about it, *Ten Days that Shook the World*.

The bulk of the membership in the early Left Wing of the Socialist Party were foreign-born. At that time, more than twenty years ago, a very large section of the basic proletariat in America were foreign-born. Prior to the war the doors of immigration had been wide open, as it served the needs of American capital to accumulate a great labor reserve. Many of these immigrants came to America with socialist sentiments from their home countries. Under the impact of the Russian revolution the foreign-language socialist movement grew by leaps and bounds. The foreign-born were organized into language federations, practically autonomous bodies affiliated to the Socialist Party. There were as many as eight or nine thousand members in the Russian Federation, five or six thousand among the Poles, three or four thousand Ukrainians, about twelve thousand Finns, etc.—an enormous mass of foreign-born members in the party. The great majority rallied to the slogans of the Russian revolution and after the split from the Socialist Party constituted the bulk of the members of the early Communist Party.

The leaders of these Federations aspired to control the new party and did in fact control it. By virtue of these blocs of foreign-language workers whom they represented, they exercised an inordinate influence in the early days of the Communist movement. This was good in some ways because for the greater part they were earnest Communists and helped inculcate the doctrines of Bolshevism.

But their domination was very bad in other respects. Their minds were not really in the United States but in Russia. They gave the movement a sort of unnatural formation and afflicted it at the start with an exotic sectarianism. The dominant leaders of the party—dominant, that is, in the sense that they had the real power because of the blocs of members behind them— were people absolutely unfamiliar with the American economic and political scene. They didn't understand the psychology of the American workers and didn't pay them too much attention. As a result, the early movement suffered from excesses of unrealism and had even a tinge of romanticism which removed the party in many of its activities and thoughts from the actual class struggle in the United States. Strangely enough, these leaders of the Foreign Language Federations were convinced, many of them, of their messianic mission. They were determined to control the movement in order to keep it in the pure faith.

From its very beginning in the Left Wing of the Socialist Party and later in the Communist Party, the American Communist movement was wracked by tremendous factional struggles, "struggles for control" they were called. The domination of foreign-born leaders created a paradoxical situation. You know, normally in the life of a big imperialist country like this, foreign-language immigrant workers occupy the position of a national minority and have to wage a constant struggle for equality, for their rights, without ever fully getting them. But in the Left Wing of the Socialist Party and in the early Communist Party this relationship was reversed. Each of the Slavic languages was very heavily represented. Russians, Lithuanians, Poles, Letts, Finns, etc., had the majority. They were the overwhelming majority, and we native Americans, who thought we had some ideas about the way the movement ought to be led, were in the minority. From the start we waged the struggle of a persecuted minority. In the early days we had very little success.

I belonged to the faction first in the Left Wing of the Socialist Party and later in the independent Communist movement that wanted an American leadership, an American direction for the movement. We were convinced that it was impossible to build a movement in this country without a leadership in control more intimately acquainted with and related to the native movement of the American workers. They for their part were equally convinced, many of them, that it was impossible for an American to be a real simon-pure Bolshevik. They wanted us and appreciated us—as their "English expression"—but thought they had to remain in control in order to keep the movement from becoming opportunist and centrist. Over the years a great deal of time was spent fighting out that fight which, for the foreign-language leaders, could only be a losing fight. In the long run the movement had to find native leadership, otherwise it could not survive.

The struggle for control assumed the shape of a struggle over organization forms. Should the foreign-language groups be organized in autonomous federations? Or should they be organized into local branches without a national structure or autonomous rights? Should we have a centralized party or a federated party? Naturally the conception of a centralized party was a Bolshevik conception. However, in a centralized party the foreign-language groups couldn't be mobilized so easily in solid blocs; whereas in a federated party it was possible for the Federation leaders to confront the party with solid blocs of voting supporters in conventions, etc.

This struggle disrupted the Left Wing Conference at New York in 1919. By the time we got to Chicago in September 1919, that is, at the National Convention of the Socialist Party where the split took place, the forces of the Left Wing were already split among themselves. The Communists at the moment of their break with the Socialist Party were incapable of organizing a united party of their own. They announced to the world a few days later that they had organized not one

Communist Party, but two. One holding the majority was the Communist Party of the United States, dominated by the Foreign Language Federations; the other was the Communist Labor Party, representing the minority faction, which I have mentioned, with its larger proportion of natives and Americanized foreigners. Naturally there were variations and individual fluctuations, but this was the main line of demarcation.

Such was the inauspicious beginning of the independent Communist movement—two parties in the field with identical programs, fiercely battling against each other. To make matters worse our divided ranks faced terrific persecution. That year, 1919, was the year of great reaction in this country, the postwar reaction. After the masters finished the war to "make the world safe for democracy," they decided to write a supplementary chapter to make the U.S. safe for the open shop. They began a furious patriotic drive against all the workers organizations. Thousands of workers were arrested on a nationwide scale. The new Communist parties bore the brunt of this attack. Almost every local organization from coast to coast was raided; practically every leader of the movement, national or local, put under arrest, indicted for one thing or another. Wholesale deportations of foreign-born militants took place. The movement was persecuted to such an extent that it was driven underground. The leaders of both parties thought it impossible to continue open, legal functioning. So, in the very first year of American Communism we not only had the disgrace and scandal and organizational catastrophe of two separate and rival Communist parties, but we also had both parties, after a few months, functioning in underground groups and branches.

The movement remained underground from 1919 until early 1922. After the first shock of the persecutions passed over, and the groups and branches settled down to their underground existence, the elements in the leadership who tended toward unrealism gained strength, inasmuch as the movement was then completely isolated from public life and from the labor organizations of the country.

Factional strife between the two parties continued to consume an enormous amount of time; refinements of doctrine, hairsplitting, became quite a pastime. Then I, for my part, realized for the first time the full malignancy of the sickness of ultraleftism. It seems to be a peculiar law that the greater a party's isolation from the living labor movement, the less contact it has with the mass movement, and the less correction it can get from the impact of the mass movement, all the more radical it becomes in its formulations, its program, etc. Whoever wants to study the history of the movement closely should examine some of the party literature issued during those days. You see, it didn't cost any more to be extra radical because nobody paid any attention anyhow. We didn't have public meetings; we didn't have to talk to workers or see what their reactions were to our slogans. So the loudest shouters at shut-in meetings became more and more dominant in the leadership of the movement. Phrasemongering "radicalism" had a field day. The early years of the Communist movement in this country were pretty much consecrated to ultraleftism.

During the 1920 presidential elections the movement was underground and couldn't devise any means of having its own candidate. Eugene V. Debs was the candidate of the

Socialist Party, but we were engaged in a fierce factional fight
with that party and mistakenly thought we couldn't support
him. So the movement decided on a very radical program: It
issued a ringing proclamation calling the workers to boycott
the elections! You might think that we could have just said,
"We have no candidate; we can't do anything about it." That
was the case, for example, with the Socialist Workers Party,
the Trotskyists, in 1940; because of technical, financial, and
organizational difficulties, we weren't able to get on the bal-
lot. We didn't find it possible to support any of the candidates, so we just let the matter pass. The Communist Party in
those days, however, never let anything pass without issuing
a proclamation. If I quite often show indifference to procla-
mations it is because I saw so many of them in the early days
of the Communist Party. I lost entirely the idea that every occasion must have a proclamation. It is better to get along with
fewer; to issue them on the more important occasions. They
then have more weight. Well, in 1920 a leaflet was issued
calling for boycott of the elections, but nothing came of it.

A strong antiparliamentary tendency grew up in the
movement, a lack of interest in elections which took years
and years to overcome. In the meantime we read Lenin's
pamphlet, *The Infantile Sickness of Left Communism*. Everybody recognized—theoretically—the necessity of participating in elections, but there was no disposition to do anything
about it, and several years were to elapse before the party developed any serious electoral activity.

Another ultraradical idea gained predominance in the
early underground Communist movement: The conception
that it is a revolutionary principle to remain underground.

For the past two decades we have enjoyed the advantages of legality. Practically all the comrades of the Socialist Workers Party have known no form of existence other than that of a legal party. It is quite possible that a legalistic bias has grown up among them. Such comrades can get some rude shocks in time of persecution because the party has to be able to carry on its activities regardless of the attitude of the ruling class. It is necessary for a revolutionary party to know how to operate even in underground formations. But this should be done only from necessity, never from choice.

After a person experiences both underground and open political organization, he can easily convince himself that the most economical, the most advantageous is the open one. It is the easiest way of coming in contact with workers, the easiest way of making converts. Consequently, a genuine Bolshevik, even in the times of sharpest persecution, tries always to grasp and utilize every possibility to function in the open. If he can't say everything he wants to say openly, he will say as much as he can—and supplement legal propaganda by other methods.

In the early Communist movement, before we had properly assimilated the writings and teachings of the leaders of the Russian revolution, a tendency grew up to regard the underground party as a principle. As time went on and the wave of reaction receded, possibilities for legal activities opened up. But tremendous factional struggles were necessary before the party took the slightest step in the direction of legalizing itself. The absolutely incredible idea that the party can't be revolutionary unless it is illegal was actually accepted by the majority in the Communist movement in 1921 and early 1922.

On the trade union question "radicalism" held sway, too. It is a terrible virus, this ultraleftism. It thrives best in an isolated movement. That's always where you find it at its worst —in a movement that is isolated from the masses, gets no corrective from the masses. You see it in these split-offs from the Trotskyist movement—our own "lunatic fringe." The less people listen to them, the less effect their words have on the course of human events, the more extreme and unreasonable and hysterical they become in their formulations.

The trade union question was on the agenda of the first underground convention of the Communist movement. This convention celebrated a split and a unification too. A faction headed by Ruthenberg had split away from the Communist Party, dominated by the foreign-language groups. The Ruthenberg faction met in joint convention with the Communist Labor Party to form a new organization called the United Communist Party in May 1920 at Bridgeman, Michigan. (This is not to be confused with another convention at Bridgeman in August 1922 which was raided by the police.) The United Communist Party gained the upper hand and merged with the remaining half of the original Communist Party a year later.

The 1920 Convention, I remember very distinctly, adopted a resolution on the trade union question. In the light of what has been learned in the Trotskyist movement, it would make your hair stand on end. This resolution called for "boycott" of the American Federation of Labor. It stated that a party member who "is compelled by job necessity" to belong to the AFL should work there in the same way that a Communist works in a bourgeois Congress—not to build it up but to blow it up from within. That nonsense was later corrected along with many other things. Many people who committed these stupidities later learned and did better in the political movement.

Following the Russian revolution the young generation, revolting against opportunist betrayals of the Social Democrats, took radicalism in too big doses. Lenin and Trotsky led the "Right Wing"—that is what they demonstratively called their tendency—at the Third World Congress of the Communist International in 1921. Lenin wrote his pamphlet, *The Infantile Sickness of Left Communism*, directed against the German leftists, taking up questions of parliamentarianism, trade unionism, etc. This pamphlet, together with the Congress decisions, did a great deal in the course of time to liquidate the leftist tendency in the early Comintern.

I don't at all want to picture the founding of American Communism as a circus, as the sideline philistines do. It wasn't, by any means. There were positive sides to the movement, and the positive sides predominated. It was composed of thousands of courageous and devoted revolutionists willing to make sacrifices and take risks for the movement. In spite of all their mistakes, they built a party the like of which had never been seen in this country before; that is, a party founded on a Marxist program, with a professional leadership and disciplined ranks. Those who went through the period of the underground party acquired habits of discipline and learned methods of work which were to play a great role in the subsequent history of the movement. We are building on those foundations.

They learned to take program seriously. They learned to do away forever with the idea that a revolutionary movement, aiming at power, can be led by people who practice socialism as an avocation. The leader typical of the old Socialist Party was a lawyer practicing law, or a preacher practicing preaching, or a writer, or a professional man of one kind or another, who condescended to come around and make a speech once in a while. The fulltime functionaries were merely hacks who did the dirty work and had no real influence in the party. The gap between the rank and file workers, with their revolutionary impulses and desires, and the petty-bourgeois dabblers at the top was tremendous. The early Communist Party broke away from all that, and was able to do it easily because not one of the old type leaders came over wholeheartedly to the support of the Russian revolution. The party had to throw up new leaders out of the ranks, and from the very beginning the principle was laid down that these leaders must be professional workers for the party, must put their whole time and their whole lives at the disposal of the party. If one is thinking of a party that aims to lead the workers in a real struggle for power, then no other type of leadership is worth considering.

In the underground the work of education, of assimilating the writings of the Russian leaders, went on. Lenin, Trotsky, Zinoviev, Radek, Bukharin—these were our teachers. We began to be educated in an entirely different spirit from the old lackadaisical Socialist Party—in the spirit of revolutionists who take ideas and program very seriously. The movement had an intensive internal life, all the more so because it was isolated and driven back upon itself. Faction struggles were fierce and long drawn out.

The movement began to stagnate in the underground blind alley. A few of us in the leadership began to seek a way out, a way to approach the American workers by legal means. These efforts were resisted fiercely. We formed a new faction. Lovestone was closely associated with me in the leadership of this faction. Later we were joined by Ruthenberg upon his release from prison in the spring of 1922.

For a year and a half, two years, this struggle continued unabated, the fight for the legalization of the movement. Resolute positive struggle on our side; equally determined resistance on the other by people convinced in their bones that this signified some kind of betrayal. Finally in December 1921, having a slender majority in the Central Committee, we began to move, taking one careful step at a time, towards legality.

We couldn't legalize the party as such, the resistance in the ranks was still too strong, but we did organize some legal groups for holding lectures. We next called a convention to federate these groups into a central body called the American Labor Alliance, which we converted into a propaganda organization. Then in December 1921, we resorted to the device of organizing the Workers Party as an open, legal organization in addition to the underground Communist Party. We could not dispense with the latter. It was not possible to get a majority to agree to that, but a compromise was effected whereby while retaining the underground party, we set up the Workers Party as a legal extension. Two or three thousand die-hard undergrounders revolted against even this makeshift move toward legality, split away, and formed their own organization.

We continued with two parties—a legal and an illegal one. The Workers Party had a very limited program, but it became the medium through which all our legal public activity was carried on. Control rested in the underground Communist Party. The Workers Party encountered no persecution. The reactionary wave had passed, a liberalistic political mood prevailed in Washington and in the rest of the country. We were able to hold public meetings and lectures, publish newspapers, participate in election campaigns, etc. Then the question arose, did we need this encumbrance of two parties? We wanted to liquidate the underground organization, concentrate all our activity in the legal party, and take a chance on further persecution. We met renewed opposition.

The fight went on uninterruptedly until we finally appealed the matter to the Communist International at the Fourth Congress in 1922. At that Congress I was the representative of the "liquidators" faction, as we were called. This name comes from the history of Bolshevism. At one time following the defeat of the 1905 revolution, a section of the Mensheviks came forward with a proposal to liquidate the underground party in Russia and confine all activity to tsarist "legality." Lenin fought this proposal and its proponents savagely, because it signified a renunciation of revolutionary work and organization. He denounced them as "liquidators." So naturally, when we came forward with a proposal to liquidate the underground party in this country, the leftists with their minds in Russia mechanically transferred Lenin's expression and denounced us as "liquidators."

So we went to Moscow to fight it out before the Communist International. That was the first time I met Comrade Trotsky. In the course of our struggle we tried to get support from individual members of the Russian leadership. In the summer and fall of 1922 I spent many months in Russia. For a long time I was somewhat of a pariah because this campaign about "liquidators" had reached ahead of us, and the Russians didn't want to have anything to do with liquidators. Unacquainted with the situation in America, they tended to be prejudiced against us. They assumed that the party had really been outlawed; and when the question was put to them they were inclined to say offhand: "If you cannot do your work legally do it illegally, but you must do your work."

But that wasn't really how matters stood. The political situation in the United States made a legal Communist Party possible. That was our contention, and all further experience has proved it. Finally, I and some other comrades met with Comrade Trotsky and expounded our ideas for about an hour. After asking a few questions when we had finished, he said, "That is enough. I will support the 'liquidators' and I will talk to Lenin. I am sure he will support you. All the Russians will support you. It is just a question of understanding the political situation. It is absurd to bind ourselves in an underground straitjacket when it is not necessary. There is no question about that."

We asked if he would arrange for us to see Lenin. He told us that Lenin was ill but, if necessary, if Lenin did not agree with him, he'd arrange for us to see him. In a few days the knot began to unravel. A Congress Commission was set up on the American question and we went before the Commission to debate. Already the word had passed down that Trotsky and Lenin favored the "liquidators" and the tide was turning in our favor.

In the discussion at the Commission hearing Zinoviev made a brilliant speech on legal and illegal work, drawing on the vast experience of the Russian Bolsheviks. I have never forgotten that speech. The memory of it serves our party in good stead to this day and will do so in the future, I am sure. Radek and Bukharin spoke along the same lines. These three were in those days the representatives of the Russian Communist Party in the Comintern. The delegates of the other parties, after full and thorough debate, gave complete support to the idea of legalizing the American Communist Party.

With the authority of the Comintern World Congress behind the decision, the opposition in the United States soon subsided. The Workers Party, which had been formed in 1921 as a legal extension of the Communist Party, held another convention, adopted a clearer program, and completely replaced the underground organization. All experience since 1923 has demonstrated the wisdom of that decision. The political situation here justified legal organization. It would have been a terrible calamity and waste and crippling of revolutionary activity to remain underground when it was not necessary. It is very important that revolutionists have the courage to take those risks which can't be avoided. But it is equally important, I think, that they have enough prudence to avoid unnecessary sacrifices. The main thing is to get the work done in the most economical and expeditious manner possible.

A final remark on this question: One little group remained unreconciled to the legalization of the party. They were going to remain underground in spite of us. They were not going to betray Communism. They had their headquarters in Boston and a branch in Cleveland. Every once in a while through the years we would hear of this underground group issuing a pronouncement of some kind.

Seven years later, after we had been expelled from the Communist Party and were organizing the Trotskyist movement, we heard that this group in Boston was somewhat sympathetic to Trotskyist ideas. This interested us, as we were badly in need of any support we could get.

On one of my visits to Boston the local comrades arranged a conference with them. They were very conspiratorial and took us in the old underground manner to the meeting place. A formal committee met us. After exchanging greetings, the leader said, "Now, Comrade Cook, you tell us what your proposition is." Comrade "Cook" was the pseudonym he knew me by in the underground party. He was not going to trifle with my legal name in an underground meeting. I explained why we had been expelled, our program, etc. They said they were willing to discuss the Trotskyist program as the basis for unity in a new party. But they wanted agreement first on one point: The party we were going to organize would have to be an underground organization. So I passed a few jokes with them and went back to New York. I suppose they are still underground.

Now, Comrades, all this is a sort of background, an introduction to the history of our Trotskyist movement. Next week I will deal with the further development of the Communist Party in the early years prior to our expulsion and the reconstitution of the movement under the banner of Trotskyism.

2

Factional Struggles in the Old Communist Party

Last week I sketched the early pioneer days of American Communism. Even though I omitted much, touched only a few high spots, we weren't able to pass the year 1922, the Fourth Congress of the Communist International, the legalization of the underground Communist movement, and the beginning of open work. I spoke about the negative aspects of the early movement and the infantile sicknesses that plagued it, as is almost always the case with young movements, particularly the virulent infantile sickness of ultraleftism.

But these negative aspects, the unrealism of much of the work, were far overshadowed by the positive side—the creation for the first time in America of a revolutionary political party founded on Bolshevik doctrines. That was the great contribution of pioneer Communism. A body of people organized a new political party. They assimilated some of the basic teachings of Communism. They habituated themselves to disciplined procedure, which is one of the prerequisites for the building of a serious workers political party. This had never happened before in the United States. They created the instrument of a professional leadership, likewise one of the most elementary requirements of a serious revolutionary party.

The early movement of Communism demonstrated very powerfully the predominant influence of ideas over everything else. This was strikingly shown in the struggle for supremacy between the IWW (Industrial Workers of the World) and the young Communist Party. In the prewar days the IWW was a rather large militant labor movement. It entered the war as unquestionably the organization embracing within its ranks the largest group of proletarian militants. Yet the nucleus of the Communist Party came out of the Socialist Party. A considerable number of them were petty-bourgeois in origin, a large percentage young people without any experience in the class struggle. Thousands of them were foreign-born workers who had never been really assimilated in the class struggle in America.

Insofar as the human material was concerned, the advantages were all on the side of the IWW. Their militants had been tested in many fights. They had hundreds and hundreds of members in jail, and they used to look with something like contempt on this upstart movement talking so confidently in revolutionary terms. The IWW's imagined that their actions and their sacrifices so far outweighed the mere doctrinal pretensions of this new revolutionary movement that they had nothing to fear from it in the way of rivalry. They were badly mistaken.

Within a few years—by 1922—it became pretty clear that the Communist Party had displaced the IWW as the leading organization of the vanguard. The IWW, with its wonderful composition of proletarian militants, with all their heroic struggles behind them, could not keep pace. They had not adjusted their ideology to the lessons of the war and the Russian revolution. They had not acquired a sufficient respect for doctrine, for theory. That is why their organization degenerated, while this new organization with its poorer material, its inexperienced youth who had seized hold of the living ideas of Bolshevism, completely surpassed the IWW and left it far behind in the space of a few years.

The great lesson of this experience is the folly of taking lightly the power of ideas or imagining that some substitute can be found for correct ideas in the building of a revolutionary movement.

After we settled the basic fight with the ultraleftists about legalization, the party came out into the open. It had already acquired complete hegemony, as I said, over the vanguard of the proletariat in this country. It was regarded on all sides, and properly, as the most advanced and revolutionary grouping in this country. The party began to attract some native trade unionists into its ranks. William Z. Foster, wearing then the glory of his work in the steel strike, and other trade unionists, a fairly large group, came into this foreign-born, somewhat exotic but dynamic Communist Party. The whole orientation of the party began to change. From underground squabbling, unrealistic disputes, and overrefinements of doctrine, the party turned to mass work. The Communists began to occupy themselves with practical problems of the class struggle. The party gradually became "trade unionized" and took its first faltering steps in the American Federation of Labor, the dominant, practically the sole, labor organization at that time.

While we were fighting out the battle for the legalization of the party, we also fought to correct the party's trade union policy. This struggle, too, was successful; the original sectarian position was rejected. The pioneer Communists revised their earlier sectarian pronouncements which had favored independent unionism. They now directed the whole dynamic force of the Communist Party into the reactionary trade unions. The chief credit for this transformation also belongs to Moscow, to Lenin, to the Comintern. Lenin's great pamphlet, *The Infantile Sickness of Left Communism,* cleared up this question quite decisively. By 1922–23 the party was well on the road towards penetrating the trade union movement and began rapidly to acquire a serious influence in some unions in some parts of the country. This was particularly the case in the coal miners union and in the needle trades unions, and elsewhere, too, the party made its influence felt.

But simultaneously with this practical and wholly progressive work, the party plunged into some opportunist adventures. Apparently no party can ever correct a deviation; it must overcorrect it. The stick is bent backward. Thus the young party which a short time before had been concerned with the refinement of doctrine in underground isolation, having nothing to do with the trade union movement—let alone the political movement, the petty-bourgeoisie, and the labor fakers—this same party now plunged into a number of wild ad-

ventures in the field of labor and farmer politics. The attempt
of the party leadership through a series of maneuvers and combinations to form a large farmer-labor party overnight without
sufficient backing in the mass movement of the workers, without sufficient strength of the Communists themselves, threw
the party into turmoil. A new internal struggle was precipitated.

The series of new faction fights which began in the year
1923, six months or so following the liquidation of the old
fight over legalization, continued thereafter almost uninterruptedly up to the time that we Trotskyists were thrown out
of the party in 1928. The fight raged until the spring of 1929
when the Lovestoneite leadership, who had expelled us,
were themselves expelled. Thereafter, the Stalinized Comintern stopped the faction fights by expelling everybody of any
independence of character, and by selecting a new leadership
that jumped whenever the bell rang. They achieved a peaceful monolithism in the party by bureaucratic measures. They
achieved the peace of ideological stagnation and decay.

The faction fights which convulsed the party through all
this time did not prevent the organization from doing a great
deal of work in the class struggle, developing its activities in
many fields. It established for the first time in this country a
revolutionary daily paper. That was quite an achievement for a
party of no more than ten or fifteen thousand members. Propagandistic work was developed on a wide scale. Labor defense
work was organized on a scope and basis never known before.
Many innovations of a progressive nature were introduced into
the labor movement by the Communist Party in that period.
Virtually every serious strike that broke out came under the

leadership of the party. Notably, the great Passaic strike of 1926, which attracted the attention of the entire country, was completely under the leadership of the Communists, who became more and more the unrivaled leaders of every progressive and militant tendency in the American working-class movement.

A great many commentators and sideline experts, supplemented every now and then by a few disillusioned renegades, try to picture this early historical period, the early days of American Communism, as nothing but a mess of stupidity and error and fraud and corruption. This is a thoroughly false and utterly absurd appraisal of that period. The explanation of factional struggles in the early Communist Party lies in causes more serious than the bad will of individuals. I think that if one studies the development carefully, with some knowledge of the facts, he can deduce certain laws of factional struggle which will help him understand the outbreaks of factionalism in other workers political organizations, especially new ones. And of course it is worthwhile mentioning—although the wiseacres never do—that faction fights were not the monopoly of the Communist Party. Since the beginning of politics every political organization has been wracked with faction fights. The factional troubles of the early Communists have attracted attention; and some of the negative features of them, the skullduggery practised in them, are written and talked about as though such things never happened anywhere else. Perversions of history are the specialty of sideline kibitzers like Eugene Lyons and Max Eastman and other triflers who never had one toe in the real struggle of the working class. Recently they have been joined by repentant renegades like Benjamin Gitlow, who got so thoroughly defeated and disillusioned that he rushed into the arms of the very American democracy which he started out as a young rebel to fight. What a pitiful picture a man makes embracing the doctrines of the masters who have broken his spirit.

They represent these faction fights as something utterly monstrous. They wax especially enthusiastic when they find something not exactly commendable from a moralistic point of view. They do not even stop to consider, let alone mention, the ethics and morals of Tammany Hall, or the Republican Party, or the utterly dishonest, corrupt, hypocritical, and disgusting factional clique struggles that we saw in the Socialist Party. Only when they find something off-color in the early record of the Communist Party do they raise their hands in holy horror.

They do not realize that thereby they pay unconscious tribute to the Communist movement, as though to say: One has a right to expect something better from the Communist Party, even in its young days of juvenility and rickets, than from the stable political organizations of the bourgeoisie and petty bourgeoisie. And in that there is more than a kernel of truth. Means must serve ends. Anything that violates truth or honorable dealing in the revolutionary proletarian movement contradicts the great aims of Communism; it is out of place; it sticks out like a sore thumb. These qualities in bourgeois and petty-bourgeois political organizations—all their systematic lying, cheating, stealing, and double-dealing—are native to these organizations, to the environment as a whole.

The factional struggles which marked the whole course of

the Communist movement for its first ten years had numerous causes. It was not as though a gang of bandits combined together and then began to fight over spoils. That was not the case at all. There were no spoils. The overwhelming majority of people came to pioneer Communism with serious purposes and sincere motives to organize a movement for the emancipation of the workers of the whole world. They were prepared to make sacrifices and take risks for their ideal, and they did so. This is true of those who rallied to the banner of the Russian revolution in 1917 and built up the great movement which, by the time of the convention in Chicago in 1919, had between fifty and sixty thousand members. It is especially true of those who, after tremendous persecutions began, stayed with the party in spite of the arrests and deportations, the underground privations and hardships, the financial difficulties. All those snivelers, who remained on the sidelines because they were unable to make such sacrifices or take such risks, try to picture the pioneer Communists as morally corrupt elements. They simply turn the whole picture upside down. The very best elements were attracted to the party in the early days. They were further sifted out by the persecutions and hardships of the underground time. No, the faction fights had something more behind them than the bad will of some individuals. There were, in my opinion, a few rascals, but that doesn't prove anything. You are apt to find a rotten apple or two in any barrel. The causes of the prolonged factional struggles were more fundamental.

In my first lecture I explained the tremendous contradiction implicit in the composition of the party. On one side stood the predominantly foreign-language membership with their unrealistic approach to the problem of building a movement in a country where they were not yet assimilated; with their fanatical conception that they had to control the movement, not for personal gain, but in order to preserve the doctrine which they thought they alone understood. On the other side stood the numerically smaller group of Americans who, even if they did not understand the doctrine of Communism as well as the foreigners—and that was also the case—were convinced that the movement must have an American orientation and an indigenous leadership. This very contradiction fed the factional struggle.

Then there was another factor: the lack of experienced, authoritative leaders. The movement mushroomed almost overnight after the 1917 victory in Russia. All the old authoritative leaders of the Socialist Party rejected Bolshevism and stuck to the safe channels of reformism. Hillquit and Berger, all the big names of the party, turned their backs on the Russian revolution and the aspirations of the young revolutionists in the movement. Even Debs, who expressed sympathy, remained with the party of Hillquit and Berger when the showdown came. The new movement had to find new leaders; those who came to the fore were mostly unknown men, without great experience and without personal authority. It required a whole series of prolonged faction fights for the party to be able to see who were the more qualified leaders and who the accidental figures. Administrations changed rapidly from one convention to another. Temporary, casual people were thrust aside, shouldered aside in these fierce factional fights where if you couldn't stand up and take it, you were shoved aside and knocked down. Many who appeared to have leadership ability one year, and were elected accordingly, would be swept aside the second year and replaced by previously unknown men. All this was a process of selecting leaders in the course of struggle. Is there some other way to do it? I don't know where it has ever been done. An authoritative body of leaders, able to maintain their continuity with the firm support of the party—I don't know how or where any such leadership was ever consolidated except through internal struggles. Engels once wrote that internal conflict is the law of development of every political party. It certainly was the law of development of the early American Communist movement. And not only the early Communist Party; but also the early days of its authentic successor, the Trotskyist movement.

Once a movement has evolved through experience and through struggle and internal conflict to the point where it consolidates a body of leaders who enjoy wide authority, who are capable of working together, and who are more or less homogeneous in their political conceptions, then faction struggles tend to diminish. They become rarer and are less destructive. They take different forms, have more clearly evident ideological content, and are more instructive to the membership. The consolidation of such a leadership becomes a powerful factor in mitigating and sometimes preventing further faction fights. We in the early Communist movement did eventually consolidate a fairly stable leadership, but of a peculiar structure which again reflected the contradiction in the composition of the party. After four or five years of this knocking around, it became quite clear to everybody just who the leaders of the American Communist movement were. And they weren't the people who had been the leaders in 1919–20. Very few of the early leading staff of the movement survived these fights.

The leadership which finally came to the fore in the early Communist movement—and this is a very interesting aspect of its history—didn't consolidate as a single homogeneous group. That was because the party itself was not homogeneous. Instead of a unified leadership with authority and influence over the party as a whole, the outstanding leaders were leaders of factions which reflected the contradictions in the party. The new faction fight that began in 1923, primarily over the question of adventurism in the farmer-labor political movement, and then extended to all the problems of our practical work, our approach to the American workers, methods of trade union work—this protracted struggle was clearly a reflection of the contradictions in the social composition of the party and the different origins and background of the groups.

The fight was organized by Foster and me against what was then the majority, Ruthenberg, Lovestone, Pepper, etc. It soon became apparent that the composition of our grouping was that of a trade union, proletarian faction. Supporting us was the great bulk—practically all—of the trade unionists, experienced American workers, militants, and the more Americanized foreigners.

Pepper-Ruthenberg-Lovestone had most of the intellectuals and the less-assimilated foreign-born workers. The typical leaders of their faction, including the typical secondline leaders, were City College boys, young intellectuals without experience in the class struggle. Lovestone was the outstanding example. They were very clever fellows. On the whole they undoubtedly had more book knowledge than the leaders of the other faction and they knew how to make full use of their advantages. They were tough customers to deal with. But we also knew a thing or two, including things never learned in books, and we gave them plenty of trouble. This fight for control of the party was ferocious, with no holds barred on either side, carried on from year to year regardless of who had the majority at the moment. Sometimes the immediate fight became focalized in what appeared to be unimportant issues. For example, where should the national headquarters of the party be located? Our faction said Chicago; the other faction said New York. We fought over that. But not because we were such stupid fellows, as the kibitzers represent. We thought that if we could move the headquarters to Chicago it would tend to give the party a more American orientation, bring it closer to the mine fields, closer to the center of the American labor movement. We wanted to proletarianize and Americanize the party. Their insistence upon New York had political motivation too. New York had a strong petty-bourgeois element in the party; intellectuals played a bigger role here. They were more comfortable here—in a political sense, I mean. So the struggle over the location of the party headquarters is really quite comprehensible if you go to the bottom of it.

This long, drawn-out fight can be properly—and I think it will be—described on the whole by the honest and objective historians of the future as a struggle between the petty-bourgeois and proletarian tendencies in the party, with the proletarian tendency lacking sufficient clarity of program to develop the fight to its full implications. Now, don't forget, we were all practically greenhorns. We had just become acquainted—and not too well acquainted—with the doctrines of Bolshevism. We had no background of experience in politics; we had no one to teach us; we had to learn everything in struggle through blows on the head. The stumbling proletarian faction made a lot of mistakes and did many contradictory things in the heat of struggle. But the essence of its drive was, in my opinion, historically correct and progressive.

As this fight unfolded, the two main factions—Foster-Cannon on the one side, Ruthenberg-Lovestone-Pepper on the other—produced further division. Indeed, division was implicit from the very beginning because there likewise were stratifications within the Foster-Cannon faction. The group most closely associated with me were pioneer Communists, party men from the beginning, who had adopted the principles of Communism earlier than the Foster wing. The Foster wing was more trade unionist in experience, more limited in its conceptions, less attentive to theoretical and political questions. In the course of the ever-continuing factional struggles, this implicit division became a formal one. The party was then confronted with three factions: the Foster faction, the Lovestone faction (Ruthenberg died in 1927), and the Cannon faction. That division continued until they threw us out of the party in 1928.

All these factions fought endlessly for ideas that were not completely clear to them. As I said before, we had intimations, we knew by and large what we wanted, but we lacked the political experience, the doctrinal education, the theoretical knowledge to formulate our program with sufficient precision to bring things to a proper solution. You recall the big battle we had with the petty-bourgeois opposition in the Socialist Workers Party a couple of years ago. If you study that battle to see how it developed, you can gather how we profited from the experience of the more primitive fight between the petty-bourgeois and proletarian factions in the old Communist Party. Since then we had gained more experience, had studied some books and acquired further knowledge of theory and politics. This enabled us to put the issues clearly and to prevent the fight against Burnham, Shachtman, and Company from bogging down into an unprincipled scramble with no daylight ahead, as had been the case in the old days.

Now, these leaders whom I have mentioned—Ruthenberg, Lovestone, Cannon, Foster—these four people were always in the Political Committee of the party. These four people were always the recognized, authoritative leaders of party; that is, they were leaders of factions which made them part of the leadership of the party. And each faction was so strong, the weight was so evenly distributed among the factions, that no faction could be crushed or eliminated. Too many people were tied up with each of them, too many of the able functionaries of the party. So that, for example, when the Lovestoneites got the majority of the party with the help and bludgeoning of the Comintern, they were not able to do as they wanted, to brush us aside, particularly since the trade union and mass work was virtually monopolized by the other factions. Many of the party organizers, writers, and functionaries were connected intimately with me and could not be replaced. The Foster faction was even stronger, especially in the trade union field. They could not get rid of us; that is, without disrupting the party.

So the party virtually became divided into three provinces, so to speak. Each faction gained enough elbow room to work in certain fields with practically unlimited authority and under a minimum of control. The Foster faction occupied the whole territory of trade union work. We organized the International Labor Defense and ran it virtually as we pleased. This was when the Lovestoneites had a tenuous majority. The Lovestoneites were in control of the party apparatus but didn't hold it strongly enough to dispense with us, so that this peculiar balance of power continued for several years. Naturally, it was not a really centralized party in the Bolshevik sense of the word. It was a coalition of three factions. In the essence of the matter, that's what the party really was.

We couldn't solve the problem ourselves. No faction could decisively defeat the others; no faction would leave the party; no faction was capable enough of formulating its program so as to win a real majority in the party. We had a stalemate, a drawn-out, demoralizing factional struggle with no end, no daylight ahead. Those were discouraging days. To any normal-minded revolutionist it is extremely distasteful to go through not merely weeks and months, but years and years of factional struggle. There are some people who like faction fights; we had people in all the factions who were really never awake until the factional fight started bubbling. Then they became alive. When it came to doing some constructive work—demonstrations, picket lines, building up a wider circulation for the press, helping class-war prisoners—they had no interest in that prosaic routine. But merely announce the holding of a factional caucus meeting, and they would be there every time—in the front seats.

There are certain abnormal types in all movements. We had plenty of them. I could deliver several biographical lectures on the single subject, "professional faction fighters I have known." Such people can never lead a political movement. After the movement finally catches its breath, gets its road clear, professional faction fighters are out of place in its leadership. In the last analysis, leaders must build. These leaders of our old factions were not angels, that I must admit. Not at all. They were very rough fighters in a political sense. They fought with everything they had. But were they self-seeking scoundrels, as they are represented by dilettantes such as Eugene Lyons and Max Eastman, and all these namby-pamby people who stood aside from the movement and measured it by the standards of abstract morality? Not at all. Not even Gitlow, who now belatedly supports this thesis, was a scoundrel to begin with. I think some of them were bad eggs from birth, but the great majority of the leading cadres of all the factions were men who came into the movement for idealistic reasons and purposes. That includes even those who later became degenerate Stalinists and chauvinists. Their degeneration was a long process of evolution, pressure, disappointment, deception, disillusionment, and so forth. Those who came to the movement in the hard days of 1919, or rather, who rallied around the Russian revolution in the war days, founded the party in 1919, stood the gaff during the persecution and the raids in the underground days—they were far superior from a moral standpoint to the politicians of Tammany Hall or the Republican Party or any other bourgeois or petty-bourgeois political movement you can name.

We could have solved our problem had we been able to get the help we needed. That is, the help of more experienced and authoritative people. The problem was too big for us. It can and does happen in the most advanced political movement that local groups removed from the center fall into squabbles which develop into factional struggles and clique formations, until the situation becomes, because of their inexperience, insoluble by their own forces. If they have a wise national leadership, an honest and mature leadership able to intervene intelligently and fairly, nine times out of ten these local stalemates can eventually be resolved and the comrades can find the basis for unification in joint work. Now if we, in those years, could have had the help of the Communist International, the help of the Russian leaders, which we counted on, which we looked for, we unquestionably could have solved our problems. All the factions had good in them. All had talented people. Given normal conditions, correct leadership and help from the Comintern, the great majority of the leaders of all these factions could have been brought together eventually and consolidated into a single leadership. The leadership of these three factions, united and working together under the supervision and direction of more experienced, international leaders, would have been a powerful force for Communism. The Communist Party could have taken a great leap forward. We went to the Comintern, seeking help, but the real source of the trouble was there, although we didn't know it then. The Comintern, unbeknown to us, was beginning to go through its process of degeneration. The honest and capable help we got from Lenin, Trotsky, and the whole Comintern in 1921 and 1922 on the trade union question, and on the underground and legal questions, enabled us to solve the problems and liquidate the old factional fights. Instead of getting such help in later years, we ran into the degeneration of the Comintern, the beginning of its Stalinization. The Comintern leadership looked at our party, as at every other party, not with the aim of clearing up trouble, but of keeping the pot boiling. They were already scheming to get rid of all the independent people, the kickers, the stiff necks, so that they could create out of the mess a docile Stalinist party. They were already trying to create such a party here and everywhere and didn't have much use for any of these fighting leaders. We used to go to Moscow every year. The "American Question" was always on the agenda. There was always an "American Commission" in the Comintern. They saw us battling it out before the Commissions and soon convinced themselves that it would be rather hard to harness those lads to the scheme they had in mind. In all likelihood they were already laying plans to get rid of the most outstanding leaders of all factions and cook up a new faction which would be an instrument of Stalin.

Each time we went to Moscow full of confidence that this time we were going to get some help, some support, because we were on the right line, because our proposals were correct. And each time we were disappointed, cruelly disappointed. The Comintern invariably supported the petty-bourgeois faction against us. At every opportunity they dealt a blow to the proletarian faction which in the early days was in the majority. We first fought it out in the convention of 1923, and we won a two-to-one majority. It was very clear that the mass of the party membership wanted the leadership of the proletarian faction. Later on, after the formal division in the Foster-Cannon faction, we still worked most of the time in a bloc against the Lovestoneites. Each time the party members were given a chance to express themselves, they showed that they wanted this bloc to have the dominant leadership in the party. But the Comintern said, no. They wanted to break up this bloc. And they were especially anxious, for some reason or other, to break up our group—the Cannon group. They must have suspected something. They went far out of their way to take cracks at me. As far back as the Fifth Congress of the Comintern in 1924, out of a clear sky—I was not present at that time—they condemned by resolution some little mistake I had made. Everybody else in the party leadership had made such mistakes or worse, but the Comintern went out of its way to cite my dereliction in order to weaken my prestige.

Then, as the years went by, the campaign against Trotskyism developed. The qualification for leadership in all the parties, the criterion by which leaders were judged in Moscow, was: *who shouted loudest against Trotskyism and Trotsky.* We weren't given any real information about the issues of the struggle in the Russian Party. We were overwhelmed with official documents and all kinds of accusations and slanders; nothing, or next to nothing, on the other side of the question. They abused the confidence of the rank and file of the party. Likewise the leaders of the party, who trusted the Comintern, had that confidence abused time and time again. Every time we went to Moscow, instead of returning with a solution, we came back with a resolution, ostensibly designed for "peace" in the party, but rigged in such a way as to make the faction fight hotter than ever.

There was no such thing as a settlement of the fight. The moment any kind of unity declaration was signed, factional war broke out afresh. Cynicism began to pervade the ranks. It became a maxim that the signing of a "peace agreement" signified that "now the faction fight is going to get really hot." Things came to such a pass that you had to be reserved, you had to watch every step, because you were working in a hostile atmosphere. It became necessary to make reservations every time you agreed to anything. A very bad moral atmosphere began to envelop the party like a fog.

The fact that the degeneration of the Comintern exerted a determining influence in our party is cited by many superficial people as proof of the unrealism of the American movement, of its inability to solve its own problems, etc. Such snivelers only show that they don't have the slightest idea of what an international revolutionary organization is and must be. The influence of Moscow was a perfectly natural thing. The confidence and expectations which the young party of America put in the Russian leadership were completely justified because the Russians had made a revolution. Naturally, the influence and authority of the Russian party was greater in the international movement than any other. The wiser, the more experienced lead the neophytes. So it will be and so it must be in any international organization.

There is no such thing as an even development of all the parties in an International. We have seen this in the Fourth International during the lifetime of Comrade Trotsky, who embodied all the experience of the Russian revolution and the fight against Stalin. Trotsky's authority and prestige were absolutely outstanding in the Fourth International. His word did not have the force of bureaucratic command, but it had a tremendous moral power. And not only that. As was demonstrated time after time in every difficulty and dispute, his patience, his wisdom, and his knowledge were brought to bear constructively and honestly, and always aided every party and every group that asked for his intervention.

Our experience in the Communist Party has been of priceless value in all our daily work; and in all our communications and relations with the less experienced groups of the Fourth International. It is natural that our party, precisely because it has assimilated a wider political experience, wields perhaps a greater influence in the international movement than any other party, now that Comrade Trotsky is not with us any more. If a section of the Fourth International confronts a revolutionary situation in the approximate future and demonstrates that it has a leadership of sufficient caliber to carry through a successful revolution, then the predominant authority and influence would naturally shift to that party. By common consent it would become the leading party of the Fourth International. Those are simply natural and inevitable consequences of the uneven development of the international political movement.

Our misfortune, our tragedy throughout the Comintern, was that the great leaders of the Russian revolution, who really embodied the doctrine of Marxism and who really carried through the revolution, were thrust aside in the course of the reaction against the October revolution and the bureaucratic degeneration of the Russian Communist Party.

The Communist Party in the United States, like the parties in other countries, failed to understand the complicated issues of the great struggle. We fought in the dark, thinking only of our national troubles. That is what poisoned the faction struggles here. That is what caused them to degenerate in the end to unprincipled squabbles and contests for control. Only an international program, comprehended in time, could have saved the young Communist Party of America from degeneration. We did not grasp this until 1928. Then it was too late to save more than a small fragment of the party for its original revolutionary aims.

Each of the three factions which existed in the party from 1923 to 1928 went through its own evolution. The foundation cadres of the American Trotskyist movement came entirely from the Cannon faction. The whole leadership and practically all the original members of the Left Opposition came from our faction. The Lovestone faction was thrown out, as you know, by a brutal ukase of Stalin in 1929. The Lovestoneites developed independently from 1929 to 1939 and then disbanded, going over to the bourgeoisie as supporters of the "democratic" war. The Foster faction and the secondary leaders of some of the other factions were gathered together in a hodgepodge on the basis of unquestioned loyalty to Stalin and the complete surrender of all independence. They were second and third line men. They had to wait in the shadows until the real fighters were thrown out and the time came for errand boys to take their place. They became the official leaders, the manufactured leaders, of the American Communist Party. Then they too went through their natural evolution, until today they have become the vanguard of the social-chauvinist movement.

The important thing to remember is that our modern Trotskyist movement originated in the Communist Party—and nowhere else. Despite all the negative aspects of the party in those early years, and I have recounted them unsparingly; despite its weaknesses, its crudities, its infantile sicknesses, its mistakes; whatever may be said in retrospect about the faction struggles and their eventual degeneration; whatever may be said about the degeneration of the Communist Party in this country—it must be recognized that out of the Communist Party came the forces for the regeneration of the revolutionary movement. Out of the Communist Party in the United States came the nucleus of the Fourth International in this country. Therefore, we should say that the early period of the Communist movement in this country belongs to us; that we are tied to it by indissoluble bonds; that there is an uninterrupted continuity from the early days of the Communist movement, its brave struggles against persecution, its sacrifices, mistakes, faction fights, and degeneration to the eventual resurgence of the movement under the banner of Trotskyism.

We must not surrender, we cannot in justice and truth surrender, the tradition of the first years of American Communism. That belongs to us and upon that we have built.

3

The Beginning of the
Left Opposition

The last lecture brought us up to about the year 1927 in the Communist Party of the United States. The fundamental struggle between Marxism and Stalinism had been going on inside the Russian Communist Party already for four years. It had been going on in the other sections of the Comintern too, including our own, but we didn't really know it.

The issues of the great struggle in the Russian Party were confined at the beginning to extremely complex Russian questions. Many of them were new and unfamiliar to us Americans who knew very little about the internal problems of Russia. They were very difficult for us to understand because of their profound theoretical nature—after all, up to that time we had had no really serious theoretical education—and the difficulty was increased by the fact that we were not presented with full information. We were not supplied with the documents of the Russian Left Opposition. Their arguments were concealed from us. We were not told the truth. On the contrary, we were systematically fed with misrepresentation, distortion, and one-sided documentation.

I make this explanation for the benefit of those who are inclined to ask: "Why didn't you at the very beginning take up the banner of Trotskyism? If things are so clear now to any serious student of the movement, why couldn't you in the early days understand it?" The explanation I have made is one never considered by people who view these great disputes separate and apart from the mechanism of party life. One who bears no responsibilities, who is a mere student or commentator or sideline observer, does not need to exercise any caution or restraint. If he has doubts or uncertainties, he feels perfectly free to express them. That is not the case with a party revolutionist. One who takes upon himself the responsibility of calling workers to join a party on the basis of a program to which they are to devote their time, their energy, their means, and even their lives, has to take a very serious attitude toward the party. He cannot, in good conscience, call for the overthrow of one program until he has elaborated a new one. Dissatisfaction, doubts, are not a program. You cannot organize people on such a basis. One of the strongest condemnations Trotsky leveled at Shachtman in the early days of our dispute on the Russian question in 1939 was this, that Shachtman, who began nursing doubts as to the correctness of our old program without having in his mind any clear idea of a new one, went through the party irresponsibly expressing his doubts. Trotsky said, a party cannot stand still. You cannot make a program out of doubts. A serious and responsible revolutionist cannot disturb a party merely because he has become dissatisfied with this, that, or the other thing. He must wait until he is prepared to propose concretely a different program, or another party.

That was my attitude in the Communist Party in those early years. For my part, I felt great dissatisfaction. I was never enthusiastic about the fight in the Russian party. I could not understand it. And as the fight grew more intense, and the persecutions increased against the Russian Left Opposition, represented by such great leaders of the revolution as Trotsky, Zinoviev, Radek, and Rakovsky—doubt and dissatisfaction accumulated in my mind. This militated against my position, and against the position of our faction in the endless conflicts within the Communist Party. We were still trying to solve things on an American scale: a common error. I think one of the most important lessons that the Fourth International has taught us is that in the modern epoch you cannot build a revolutionary political party solely on a national basis. You must begin with an international program, and on that basis you build national sections of an international movement.

This, by way of digression, was one of the big disputes between the Trotskyists and the Brandlerites, the London Bureau people, Pivert, etc., who advanced the idea that you can't talk about a new international until you first build up strong national parties. According to them, only after having created formidable mass parties in the various countries, could you federate them into an international organization. Trotsky proceeded in just the opposite way. When he was deported from Russia in 1929, and was able to undertake his international work with free hands, he propounded the idea that you *begin* with an international program. You organize people, no matter how few there may be in each country, on the basis of the international program; you gradually build up your national sections. History has given its verdict on this dispute. Those parties which began with a national approach and wanted to push aside this problem of international organization, all suffered shipwreck. National parties could not take root because in this international epoch there is no longer any room for narrow national programs. Only the Fourth International, starting in each country from the international program, has survived.

That principle wasn't understood by us in the early Communist Party. We were engrossed in the national struggle in America. We looked to the Communist International to give us help with our national problems. We did not want to bother with the problems of the other sections or those of the Comintern as a whole. This fatal error, this national narrow-mindedness, is what pushed us into the blind alley of faction struggles.

Things began to grow very critical for us. None of the factions wanted to split or leave the party. They were all loyal, fanatically loyal, to the Comintern and had no thought of breaking with it. But the discouraging internal situation grew worse, appeared hopeless. It became obvious that we must either find a way to unite the factions or permit one faction to become predominant. Some of the wiser ones, or rather, some of the more cunning ones, and those who had the best sources of information in Moscow, began to realize that the way to gain the favor of the Comintern and thereby place the great weight of its authority on the side of their faction, was to become energetic and aggressive in the fight against Trotskyism. Campaigns against "Trotskyism" were ordained from Moscow in all the parties of the world. The expulsions of Trotsky and Zinoviev in the fall of 1927 were followed by demands that all the parties immediately take a position, with the implied threat of reprisals from Moscow against any individual or group failing to take a "correct" position—that is, in favor of the expulsions. Campaigns of "enlightenment" were carried on. The Lovestoneites were in the vanguard of the fight against Trotskyism. Thereby they purchased for themselves the support of the Comintern and enjoyed it throughout that period. They organized "enlightenment" campaigns. Membership meetings, branch meetings, section meetings were held all over the party to which representatives of the Central Committee were sent in order to enlighten the membership on the necessity for the expulsions of the organizer of the Red Army and the Chairman of the Comintern.

The Fosterites, who weren't as quick and cunning as the Lovestoneites, but who had a good deal the same will, followed suit. They really ran races with the Lovestoneites to show who were the greatest anti-Trotskyists. They vied in making speeches on the subject.

Looking back on it now, it is an interesting circumstance, which rather foreshadows what was to follow, that I never took part in any of these campaigns. I voted for the stereotyped resolutions, I regret to say, but I never made a single speech or wrote a single article against Trotskyism. That was not because I was a Trotskyist. I didn't want to get out of line with the majority of the Russian party and the Comintern. I refused to take part in the campaigns only because I didn't understand the issues. Bertram D. Wolfe, Lovestone's chief lieutenant, was one of the greatest Trotsky-baiters. At the slightest provocation he would make a speech two hours long, explaining how the Trotskyists were wrong on the agrarian question in Russia. I could not do that because I didn't understand the question. He didn't understand it either, but, in his case, that wasn't so much of an obstacle. The real objective of the Lovestoneites and Fosterites in making these speeches and carrying on these campaigns was to ingratiate themselves with the powers in Moscow.

Someone may ask, "Why didn't you make speeches in favor of Trotsky?" I couldn't do that either because I didn't understand the program. My state of mind then was that of doubt and dissatisfaction. Of course, if one had no responsibility to the party, if he were a mere commentator or observer, he could merely speak his doubts and have it over with. You can't do that in a serious political party. If you don't know what to say, you don't have to say anything. The best thing is to remain silent.

The Central Committee of the Communist Party held a plenum in February, the famous February plenum of 1928, which followed a few months after the expulsion of Trotsky and Zinoviev and all the leaders of the Russian Opposition. A big campaign was already on to mobilize the parties of the world to support Stalin's bureaucracy. At this plenum we fought and disputed over the factional issues in the party, the estimate of the political situation, the trade union question, the organization question—we fought furiously over all these questions. That was our real interest. Then we came to the last point on the agenda, the Russian question. Bertram D.

Wolfe, as the reporter for the Lovestoneite majority, "explained" it at great length, for about two hours. Then the question was thrown open for discussion. One by one, each member of the Lovestone and Foster factions took the floor to express agreement with the report and add a few touches to show that he understood the necessity for the expulsions and was in favor of them.

I didn't speak. Naturally, because of my silence, the other members of the Cannon faction felt somewhat constrained from speaking. They didn't like the situation and organized a sort of pressure campaign. I remember to this day, how I sat at the back of the hall, disgruntled, bitter, and confused, sure that there was something phony about the question but not knowing what it was. Bill Dunne, the black sheep of the Dunne family, who was at that time a member of the Political Committee, and my closest associate, came back with a couple of the others. "Jim, you have got to speak on this question. It is the Russian question. They will cut our faction to pieces if you don't say something on this report. Get up and say a few words for the record."

I refused to do it. They persisted, but I was adamant. "I am not going to do it. I am not going to speak on this question." That was not "wise politics" on my part, although in retrospect it may appear so. It was not an anticipation of the future at all. It was simply a mood, a stubborn personal feeling that I had on the question. We didn't have any real information. We didn't really know what the truth was. By that time, 1927, the disputes in the Russian party had begun to embrace international questions—the question of the Chinese revolution and the Anglo-Russian Committee. Almost any member of our party can tell you now what the problems of the Chinese revolution were because, since that time, extensive material has been published. We have educated our young comrades on the lessons of the Chinese revolution. But in 1927 we provincial Americans didn't know anything about it. China was far away. We never saw any of the theses of the Russian Opposition. We didn't understand the colonial question too well. We didn't understand the profound theoretical issues involved in the Chinese question and the dispute which followed, so we couldn't take a position honestly. The Anglo-Russian question seemed a little clearer to me. That was the question of the great struggle between the Russian Opposition and the Stalinists over the formation of the Anglo-Russian Committee, a committee of Russian and English trade unionists which became a substitute for independent Communist work in England. This policy throttled the independent activity of the English Communist Party at the crucial moment of the general strike of 1926 in that country. Quite by accident, in the spring of that same year, I had come across one of the documents of the Russian Opposition on that dispute and it had a profound influence on me. I felt that at least on this question of the Anglo-Russian Committee, the Oppositionists had the right line. At any rate, I was convinced that they were not the counterrevolutionists they were pictured to be.

In 1928, after the February plenum, I made one of my more or less regular national tours. I had the habit of making at least one tour of the country from coast to coast every year, or every two years, so as to get a breath of the real America, to get the feel of what was going on in America. Looking back at it now you can trace many of the unrealistic ideas and mistakes, and much of the narrow-mindedness of some of the party leaders in New York, to the fact that they had lived all their lives on the island of Manhattan and didn't have the real feel of this great, diversified country. I made my 1928 tour under the auspices of the International Labor Defense and prolonged it four months. I wanted to get a bath in the mass movement away from the stifling atmosphere of the everlasting faction fights. I wanted an opportunity to think out a few things on the Russian question, which troubled me more than anything else. Vincent Dunne has reminded me more than once that on my way back from the Pacific Coast, when I stopped in Minneapolis, he and Comrade Skoglund asked me among other things what I thought of the expulsion of Trotsky and Zinoviev, and that I answered them, "Who am I to condemn the leaders of the Russian revolution," thereby indicating to them that I was not very sympathetic to the expulsion of Trotsky and Zinoviev. They remembered that when the fight broke out in the open a few months later.

In the late spring and early summer of 1928, the Sixth World Congress of the Comintern was called in Moscow. We departed for Moscow as usual on such occasions in a big delegation representing all the factions; going there, I am sorry to say, not preoccupied with the problems of the international movement which we as representatives of one section might help to solve, but all of us more or less preoccupied primarily with our own little fight in the American party; going to the World Congress to see what help we could get to fry our own fish here at home. Unfortunately, that was the attitude of prac-

tically everybody. On departing for the Congress I didn't have
any hope of getting a real clarification of the Russian question,
the dispute with the Opposition. By that time it appeared that
the Opposition had been completely wiped out. The leaders
were expelled. Trotsky was in exile in Alma Ata. All over the
world what sympathizers they may have had were thrown out
of the party. There seemed to be no prospect of reviving the
question. But it continued to bother me nevertheless. And it
bothered me so much that I couldn't take a very effective part
in our faction fight in Moscow.

Naturally, we continued the faction fight when we got there.
We immediately lined up our delegations in caucuses and
began to see what we could do to cut each other down,
drawing up mutual accusations and endlessly debating the
thing before the commission there. I was a more or less sullen
participant in the business. Just about that time they began to
apportion the commissions. That is, the leading members of
each delegation were appointed to various commissions of
the Congress, some on the trade union commission, some on
the political commission, some on the organization commission. In addition there was the program commission. The
Sixth Congress undertook to adopt for the first time a program, a finished program of the Comintern. The Comintern
was organized in 1919, and up to 1928, nine years later it still
had no finished program. That doesn't mean that in the early
years there was a lack of attention and interest in the question
of the program. It simply is an indication of how seriously the
greatest Marxists took the question of the program and how
carefully they elaborated it. They began with some basic
resolutions in 1919. They adopted others in 1920, 1921, 1922.

At the Fourth Congress they had the beginning of a discussion on the program. The Fifth Congress didn't pursue the question. Thus we came to the Sixth Congress in 1928, and we had before us the draft of a program which bore the authorship of Bukharin and Stalin.

I was put on the program commission, partly because the other faction leaders weren't much interested in the program. "Leave that to Bukharin. We don't want to bother with that. We want to get on the political commission which is going to decide about our faction fight; on the trade union commission; or some other practical commission which is going to decide something about some little two-by-four trade union question worrying us." Such was the general sentiment of the American delegation. I was shoved onto the program commission as a sort of honor without substance. And to tell you the truth, I was not much interested in it either.

But that turned out to be a bad mistake—putting me on the program commission. It cost Stalin more than one headache, to say nothing of Foster, Lovestone, and the others. Because Trotsky, exiled in Alma Ata, expelled from the Russian party and the Communist International, was appealing to the Congress. You see, Trotsky didn't just get up and walk away from the party. He came right back after his expulsion, at the first opportunity with the convening of the Sixth Congress of the Comintern, not only with a document appealing his case, but with a tremendous theoretical contribution in the form of a criticism of the draft program of Bukharin and Stalin. Trotsky's document was entitled, "The Draft Program of the Communist International: A Criticism of Fundamentals." Through some slipup in the apparatus in Moscow, which was supposed to be bureaucratically airtight, this document of Trotsky came into the translating room of the Comintern. It fell into the hopper, where they had a dozen or more translators and stenographers with nothing else to do. They picked up Trotsky's document, translated it, and distributed it to the heads of the delegations and the members of the program commission. So, lo and behold, it was laid in my lap, translated into English! Maurice Spector, a delegate from the Canadian Party, and in somewhat the same frame of mind as myself, was also on the program commission and he got a copy. We let the caucus meetings and the Congress sessions go to the devil while we read and studied this document. Then I knew what I had to do, and so did he. Our doubts had been resolved. It was as clear as daylight that Marxist truth was on the side of Trotsky. We made a compact there and then—Spector and I—that we would come back home and begin a struggle under the banner of Trotskyism.

We didn't begin the fight in Moscow at the Congress, although we were already thoroughly convinced. From the day I read that document I considered myself, without a single wavering doubt thereafter, a disciple of Trotsky. Because we didn't raise the fight in Moscow, some purists on the sidelines might again demand: "Why didn't you take the floor at the Sixth Congress and speak up for Trotsky?" The answer is, we couldn't have best served our political ends by doing so. And that is what you are in politics for—to serve ends. The Comintern was already pretty well Stalinized. The Congress was rigged. For us to have disclosed our complete position at the Congress would probably have resulted in our detention in Moscow until we were cut to pieces and isolated at home. Lovestone, when his time came, was later caught in this Moscow trap. My duty, and my political task as I saw it, was to organize a base of support for the Russian Opposition in my own party. In order to do that I had first to get home. Therefore I kept quiet at the Stalinized Congress. Frankness among friends is a virtue; in dealing with unscrupulous enemies it is the attribute of a fool.

At that we weren't too cautious in keeping our sentiments hidden. I, especially, was considered more and more as "monkeying" with Trotskyism. Gitlow has related in his pathetic ghostwritten book of repentance that the GPU had checked on my activities in Moscow and had reported to the Comintern that "Cannon in talks with Russians had disclosed that he had strong Trotskyist leanings." They had me under suspicion but hesitated to proceed against me too brusquely. They thought that maybe they could straighten me out and that this would be much better than to have an open scandal. They had good reason to assume that I would make a scandal if it came to an open fight.

So eventually we came back home—I think in September—with nothing solved so far as the faction fight in the American party was concerned. The Lovestoneites had gained a few inches in the fight in Moscow, but at the same time Stalin had included some qualifications in the resolution which laid the basis for getting rid later of the Lovestoneites. I had smuggled Trotsky's criticism of the draft program out of Russia, bringing it home with me. We came back home and I proceeded immediately with my determined task to recruit a faction for Trotsky.

You may think that was a simple thing to do. But here was

the state of affairs. Trotsky had been condemned in every party of the Communist International, and once again condemned by the Sixth Congress, as counterrevolutionary. Not a single member in the party was known as an outspoken supporter of Trotskyism. The whole party was regimented against it. By that time the party was no longer one of those democratic organizations where you can raise a question and get a fair discussion. To declare for Trotsky and the Russian Opposition meant to subject yourself to the accusation of being a counterrevolutionary traitor; and being expelled forthwith without any discussion. Under such circumstances the task was to recruit a new faction in secret before the inevitable explosion came, with the certain prospect that this faction, no matter how big or small it might be, would suffer expulsion and have to fight against the Stalinists, against the whole world, to create a new movement.

From the very beginning I had not the slightest doubt about the magnitude of the task. If we had permitted ourselves any illusions we would have been so disappointed at the results that it might have broken us up. I began quietly to seek out individuals and to talk to them conspiratively. Rose Karsner was my first firm adherent. She never faltered from that day to this. Shachtman and Abern, who worked with me in the International Labor Defense, and were both members of the National Committee, though not of the Political Committee, joined me in the great new endeavor. A few others came along. We were doing quite well, making a little headway here and there, working cautiously all the time. A rumor was going around about Cannon being a Trotskyist, but I never said so openly; and nobody knew what to do about the rumor. Moreover, there was a little complication in the party situation which also worked in our favor. As I have related, the party was divided into three factions, but the Foster faction and the Cannon faction were working in a bloc and had at that time a joint caucus. This put the Fosterites between the devil and the deep sea. If they didn't expose hidden Trotskyism and fight it energetically, they would lose the sympathy and support of Stalin. But, on the other hand, if they got tough with us and lost our support they couldn't hope to win the majority in the coming convention. They were torn by indecision, and we exploited their contradiction mercilessly.

Our task was difficult. We had one copy of Trotsky's document, but didn't have any way of duplicating it; we didn't have a stenographer; we didn't have a typewriter; we didn't have a mimeograph machine; and we didn't have any money. The only way we could operate was to get hold of carefully selected individuals, arouse enough interest, and then persuade them to come to the house and read the document. A long and toilsome process. We got a few people together and they helped us spread the gospel to wider circles.

Finally, after a month or so, we were exposed by a little indiscretion on the part of one of the comrades, and we had to face the issue prematurely in the joint Foster-Cannon caucus. The Fosterites raised it in the form of an inquiry. They had heard so and so and they wanted an explanation. It was clear that they were greatly worried and still undecided. We took the offensive. I said: "I consider it an insult for anybody to cross-examine me. My position in the party has been pretty clearly established now for ten years and I resent anybody questioning it." So we bluffed them for another week, and in that week we made a few new converts here and there. Then they called another meeting of the caucus to consider the question again. By this time Hathaway had returned from Moscow. He had been to the so-called Lenin School in Moscow; in reality it was a school of Stalinism. He had been all smartened up in the Stalin school and knew better how to proceed against "Trotskyism" than the local shoemakers. He said the way to proceed is to make a motion: "This caucus condemns Trotskyism as counterrevolutionary," and see where everybody stands on the motion. We objected to this on the ground—dissimulatingly formalistic, but a necessary tactic in dealing with a police-minded graduate of the Stalin School— that the question of "Trotskyism" had been decided long ago, and that there was absolutely no point in raising this issue again. We said, we refused to be a party to any of this folderol.

We debated it four or five hours and they still didn't know what to do with us. They faced this dilemma: if they became tarnished with "Trotskyism" they would lose sympathy in Moscow; if, on the other hand, they split with us, their case would be hopeless so far as getting a majority was concerned. They wanted the majority very badly and they nourished the hope—oh, how they hoped!—that a smart fellow like Cannon would eventually come to his senses and not just go and start a futile fight for Trotsky at this late day. Without saying so directly, we gave them a little ground to think that this might be so. Decision was postponed again.

We gained about two weeks with this business. Finally the Fosterites decided among themselves that the issue was getting too hot. They were hearing more and more rumors of Cannon, Shachtman, and Abern proselyting party members for Trotskyism. The Fosterites were scared to death that the Lovestoneites would get wind of this and accuse them of being accomplices. In a panic they expelled us from the joint caucus and brought us up on charges before the Political Committee. We were given a trial before a joint meeting of the PC and the Central Control Commission. We reported that trial in the early issues of the *Militant*. Naturally, it was a kangaroo court, but we had full scope to make a lot of speeches and to cross-examine the Fosterite witnesses. That was not because of party democracy. We were given our "rights" because the Lovestoneites, who were in the majority in the Political Committee, were anxious to compromise the Fosterites. In order to serve their purposes they gave us a little leeway, and we made the most of it. The trial dragged on day after day—more and more party leaders and functionaries were invited to attend—until we finally had an audience of about 100. Up till then we hadn't admitted anything. We had confined ourselves to cross-examining their witnesses and tarnishing and compromising the Fosterites, and one thing and another. Finally, when we tired of this, and since the report was spreading throughout the party of what was going on, we decided to strike. I read to a hushed and somewhat terrified audience of party functionaries a statement wherein we declared ourselves 100 percent in support of Trotsky and the Russian Opposition on all the principled questions, and announced our determination to fight along that line to the end. We were expelled by the joint meeting of the Central Control Commission and the Political Committee.

The very next day we had a mimeographed statement circulating through the party. We had anticipated the expulsion. We were ready for it and struck back. About a week later, to their great consternation, we hit them with the first issue of the *Militant*. The copy had been prepared and a deal made with the printer while we were dragging on the trial. We were expelled on October 27, 1928. The *Militant* came out the next week as a November issue, celebrating the anniversary of the Russian revolution, giving our program, and so forth. Thus began the open fight for American Trotskyism.

We certainly didn't have too bright a prospect to begin with. But we gained steadily in the first weeks and built firmly from the outset because we started right. We broke the logjam of unprincipled factionalism in the party with a charge of dynamite. With just one blast we rid ourselves of all the old errors and mistakes of the American party factions when we put ourselves on the ground of a principled program of internationalism. We were sure of what we were fighting about. All the little organizational machinations, that had loomed up so big in the old squabbles, were just thrown off like an old coat. We began the real movement of Bolshevism in this country, the regeneration of American Communism.

It was not too promising a struggle from the point of view of numbers. The three of us who signed the declaration—Abern, Shachtman, and myself—felt pretty lonely as we walked down to my house to lay plans to build a new party that was to take power in the United States. All three of us had been working for the ILD. We were immediately thrown out of there, with back wages coming to us and not paid. We didn't have any money at all, and didn't know where we could get any. We planned the first issue of the *Militant* before we knew how we were going to pay for it. But we made a deal with the printer to give us credit for one issue. We wrote to some friends in Chicago who sent us some money and we got out the paper. We announced proudly that it was going to be published twice a month. So it was.

Very shortly after we were thrown out of the party, we discovered a group of Hungarian comrades who had been expelled from the party for various reasons in the factional struggles a year or two before. Independently of us, unknown to us, they had come into contact with some Russian Oppositionists working in Amtorg—the Soviet commercial agency in New York—and had become convinced Trotskyists. They certainly looked like an army of a million people to us. We found a little group of Italian Oppositionists in New York, followers of Bordiga, not really Trotskyists, but they worked with us for a while. We conducted a quite energetic fight. We answered accusations militantly. We began to circulate new material of the Russian Opposition through the *Militant*—Trotsky's criticism of the draft program, and so on. Soon one could see the beginning of the crystallization of a faction that had a future before it because it had a clear principled program.

While it was a small faction for a long time, it was a very convinced and fanatical and determined faction. We began to gain recruits throughout the country. Our most important big acquisition was from Minneapolis. Minneapolis has played a role not only in teamsters' strikes struggles, but also in building American Trotskyism. We gained supporters in Chicago.

We were badly handicapped in many respects. We hadn't had time prior to our expulsion to communicate with the party members outside New York very much. The first that most comrades in the Communist Party knew about our position was the news that we had been expelled. The crude tactics of the party leadership helped us a great deal. Their method was to go up and down the country, putting a motion in every committee and branch to approve the expulsion of Cannon, Shachtman, and Abern. And everybody who wanted to ask a question or to get more information was accused of being a Trotskyist and expelled forthwith. That helped us a whole lot; they pushed such comrades right into a position where we could at least talk to them. In Minnesota, where we had good friends of long association, the commissar of the Lovestone gang summoned them to a meeting and demanded an immediate vote on a motion to approve our expulsion. They refused. "We want to know what this is; we want to hear what these comrades have to say." They were immediately expelled. They communicated with us. We supplied them with the documentary material, the *Militant*, etc. Eventually, practically all those who had been expelled for hesitancy in voting to confirm our expulsion became sympathetic to us and most of them joined us.

We emphasized from the very beginning that it is not simply a question of democracy. The question is the program of Marxism. If we had been content to organize people on the basis of discontent with the bureaucracy we could have gained more members. That is not a sufficient basis. But we utilized the issue of democracy to get a sympathetic hearing and then immediately began pounding away on the rightness of Trotskyism on all the political questions.

You can easily imagine what a tremendous shock our

stand and expulsion were to all the party members. For years it had been drilled into them that Trotsky was a Menshevik. He had been expelled as a "counterrevolutionist." Everything had been turned upside down. The minds of the helpless members had been filled with prejudices against Trotsky and the Russian Opposition. Then, out of a clear sky, three party leaders declare themselves Trotskyists. They are expelled and immediately go to the party members wherever they can find them and say: "Trotsky is right on all the principled questions, and we can prove it to you." That was the situation with which a good many comrades were confronted. Many of those expelled for hesitating to vote against us didn't want to leave the party. They didn't know anything about Trotskyism at that time, and were more or less convinced that it was counterrevolutionary. But the stupidity of the bureaucracy in throwing them out gave us a chance to talk with them, to confer with them, supply them with literature, etc. This created the basis for the first consolidation of the faction.

In those days every individual loomed up as enormously important. If you have only four people to start a faction with, when you can find a fifth one—that's a 25 percent increase. According to legend, the Socialist Labor Party, 'way back in the old days, once made a jubilant announcement that in the election they had doubled their vote in the state of Texas. It turned out that instead of their usual vote of one they had obtained two.

I will never forget the day we got our first recruit in Philadelphia. Soon after we were expelled, while the hue and cry was raging against us in the party, there came a knock on my door one day and there was Morgenstern of Philadelphia, a young man but an old "Cannonite" in the factional fights. He said, "We heard about your expulsion for Trotskyism, but we didn't believe it. What is the real lowdown?" In those days you didn't take anything for good coin unless it came from your own faction. I can remember to this day going into the back room, getting out the precious Trotsky document from its hiding place and handing it to Morgie. He sat down on the bed and read the long "criticism"—it is a whole book—from beginning to end without stopping once, without looking up. When he finished, he had made up his mind and we began to work out plans to build a nucleus in Philadelphia.

We recruited other individuals the same way. Trotsky's ideas were our weapons. We ran the "criticism" serially in the *Militant*. We had only the one copy, and it was a long time before we were able to publish it in pamphlet form. Because of its size we could not get it mimeographed. We had no mimeograph of our own, no typist, no money. Money was a serious problem. We had all been deprived of our positions in the party and had no incomes of any kind. We were too busy with our political fight to seek other jobs in order to make a living. On top of that we had the problem of financing a political movement. We could not afford an office. Only when we were a year old did we finally manage to rent a ramshackle office on Third Avenue, with the old "El" roaring in the window. When we were two years old we obtained our first mimeograph machine, and then we began to sail forward.

4

The Left Opposition
Under Fire

Last week we finally got out of the Stalinized Communist Party, found ourselves expelled, formed the faction of Trotskyism, and began our great historic struggle for the regeneration of American Communism. Our action brought about a fundamental change in the whole situation in the American movement, the transformation, virtually at one blow, of a demoralizing, degenerating national faction fight into a great historical principled struggle with international aims. In this abrupt transformation one can see illustrated once again the tremendous power of ideas, in this case the ideas of unfalsified Marxism.

These ideas made their way through a double set of obstacles. The long, drawn-out national faction fight, which I have briefly described in the preceding lectures, had brought us into a blind alley. We were lost in petty organizational considerations and demoralized by our nationalistic outlook.

The situation seemed insoluble. On the other side, in distant Russia, the Bolshevik-Leninist Opposition was completely smashed in an organizational sense. The leaders were expelled from the party, proscribed, outlawed, and subjected to criminal prosecution. Trotsky was in exile in faraway Alma Ata. Units of his supporters throughout the world were scattered, disorganized. Then, through a conjuncture of events, the situation was righted, and everything began to fall into its proper place. A single document of Marxism was sent by Trotsky from Alma Ata to the Sixth Congress of the Comintern. It found its way through a fissure in the secretarial apparatus, reaching the hands of a few delegates—in particular, a single delegate of the American party and a single delegate of the Canadian party. This document, expressing these all-conquering ideas of Marxism, falling into the right hands at the right time, sufficed to bring about the rapid and profound transformation which we reviewed last week.

The movement which then began in America brought repercussions throughout the entire world; overnight the whole picture, the whole perspective of the struggle changed. Trotskyism, officially pronounced dead, was resurrected on the international arena and inspired with new hope, new enthusiasm, new energy. Denunciations against us were carried in the American press of the party and reprinted throughout the whole world, including the Moscow *Pravda*. Russian Oppositionists in prison and exile, where sooner or later copies of *Pravda* reached them, were thus notified of our action, our revolt in America. In the darkest hour of the Opposition's struggle, they learned that fresh reinforcements had taken the field across the ocean in the United States, which by virtue of the power and weight of the country itself, gave importance and weight to the things done by the American Communists.

Leon Trotsky, as I remarked, was isolated in the little Asiatic village of Alma Ata. The world movement was in decline, leaderless, suppressed, isolated, practically nonexistent. With this inspiring news of a new detachment in faraway America, the little papers and bulletins of the Opposition groups flared into life again. Most inspiring of all to us was the assurance that our hard-pressed Russian comrades had heard our voice. I have always thought of this as one of the most gratifying aspects of the historic fight we undertook in 1928—that the news of our fight reached the Russian comrades in all corners of the prisons and exile camps inspiring them with new hope and new energy to persevere in the struggle.

As I have said, we began our fight with a rather clear vision of what we were up against. We didn't take the step lightly or without due thought and preparation. We anticipated a long, drawn-out struggle against heavy odds. That is why, from the very beginning, we held out no optimistic hopes of quick victory. In every issue of our paper, in every pronouncement, we emphasized the fundamental nature of the fight. We stressed the necessity of aiming far ahead, of having endurance and patience, of awaiting the further development of events to prove the rightness of our program.

First in order, of course, was the launching of our paper, the *Militant*. The *Militant* was not a surreptitiously distributed mimeographed bulletin, such as satisfies many little cliques, but a full-sized printed paper. Then we set to work, the three of us—Abern, Shachtman, and Cannon—whom they disdainfully called the "Three Generals Without an Army." That became a popular designation and we had to admit there was some truth in it. We couldn't help admitting that we had no army, but that did not shake our confidence. We had a program, and we were sure that the program would enable us to recruit the army.

We began an energetic correspondence; wherever we knew anybody, or whenever we heard of somebody who was interested, we would write him a long letter. The nature of our agitational and propagandistic work was necessarily transformed. In the past we, and especially I, had been accustomed to speaking to fairly large audiences—not long before our expulsion I had made my national tour, speaking to hundreds and sometimes thousands of people. Now we had to speak to individuals. Our propagandistic work consisted mainly of finding out names of isolated individuals in the Communist Party, or close to the party, who might be interested, arranging an interview, spending hours and hours talking to a single individual, writing long letters explaining all our principled positions in an attempt to win over one person. And in this way we recruited people—not by tens, not by hundreds, but one by one.

No sooner had the explosion taken place in the American movement, that is, the United States, than Spector carried through his part of the compact in Canada; the same thing took place there; a substantial Canadian group was formed, and began cooperating with us. Comrades with whom we had been in contact came to our banner in Chicago, Minneapolis, Kansas City, Philadelphia—not big groups as a rule. Chicago began with a couple of dozen, I think. The same number in Minneapolis. Three or four in Kansas City; two in

Philadelphia, the redoubtable Morgenstern and Goodman. In some places single individuals took up our fight alone. In New York we picked up a few here and there—individuals. Cleveland, St. Louis, and the minefields of southern Illinois. This was about the range of our organizational contact in the first period.

While we were busy with our singlejack agitation, as we used to call it in the IWW—that is, proselytizing one person to another—the *Daily Worker,* with its comparatively big circulation, blazed away at us in full-page and sometimes double-page articles day after day. These articles explained at great length that we had sold out to American imperialism; that we were counterrevolutionists in league with the enemies of labor and the imperialist powers scheming to overthrow the Soviet Union; that we had become the "advance guard of the counterrevolutionary bourgeoisie." This was printed day after day in a campaign of political terrorization and slander against us, calculated to make it impossible for us to retain any contact with individual members of the party. It was made a crime punishable by expulsion to speak with us on the street, to visit us, to have any communication with us. People were brought up on trial in the Communist Party charged with having attended a meeting at which we spoke; with having bought a paper which we sold on the streets in front of the headquarters on Union Square; or with having had some connections with us in the past—they were compelled to prove that they had not maintained this contact afterwards. A wall of ostracism separated us from the party members. People whom we had known and worked with for years became strangers to us overnight. Our whole lives, you must remember, had been in the Communist movement and its periphery. We were professional party workers. We had no interests, no associations of a social nature outside the party and its periphery. All our friends, all our associates, all our collaborators in daily work for years had been in this milieu. Then, overnight, this was closed to us. We were completely isolated from it. That sort of thing usually happens when you change your allegiance from one organization to another. As a rule, it isn't so serious because when you leave one set of associations, political, personal, and social, you are immediately propelled into a new milieu. You find new friends, new people, new associates. But we experienced only one side of that process. We were cut off from our old associations without having new ones to go to. There was no organization we might join, where new friends and co-workers could be found. With nothing but the program and our bare hands we had to create a new organization.

We lived in those first days under a form of pressure which is in many respects the most terrific that can be brought to bear against a human being—social ostracism from people of one's own kind. In a large measure, I personally had been prepared for that ordeal by an experience of the past. During the first World War, I lived as a pariah in my own hometown among the people I had known all my life. Consequently the second experience was, perhaps, not as hard on me as on some of the others. Many comrades who sympathized with us personally, who had been our friends, and many who sympathized at least in part with our ideas were terrorized against coming with us or associating with us because of that terrible penalty of ostracism. That was no easy experience for our tiny band of Trotskyists, but it was a good school just the same. Ideas that are worth having are worth fighting for. The slander, ostracism, and persecution which our young movement throughout the country stood up against in the first days of the Left Opposition in America was excellent training in preparation for withstanding the social pressure and isolation that is to come in connection with the second World War, when the real weight of capitalist society begins to bear down upon the stiff-necked dissenters and oppositionists.

The first weapon of the Stalinists was slander. The second weapon employed against us was ostracism. The third was gangsterism.

Just imagine, here was a party with a membership and periphery of tens of thousands of people, with not one daily but no less than ten daily papers in their arsenal, with innumerable weeklies and monthlies, with money and a huge apparatus of professional workers. This relatively formidable power was arrayed against a mere handful of people without means, without connections—without anything but their program and their will to fight for it. They slandered us, they ostracized us, and when that failed to break us, they tried to beat us down physically. They sought to avoid having to answer any arguments by making it impossible for us to speak, to write, to exist.

Our paper was aimed directly at the members of the Communist Party. We didn't try to convert the whole world. We took our message first to those whom we considered the vanguard, those most likely to be interested in our ideas. We knew that we had to recruit at least the first detachments of the movement from their ranks.

After our little paper was printed, then the editors, as well as the members, had to go out to sell it. We would write the paper. We would next go to the print shop, hovering over the printer's forms until the last error was corrected, waiting anxiously to see the first copy come off the press. That was always a thrill—a new issue of the *Militant,* a new weapon. Then with bundles packed under our arms we would go out to sell them on street corners in Union Square. Of course it wasn't the most efficient thing in the world for three editors to transform themselves into three newsboys. But we were short of help and had to do it; not always, but sometimes. Nor was this all. In order to sell our papers on Union Square we had to defend ourselves against physical attacks.

As I thumbed through Volume I of the *Militant* today, re- freshing my mind about some of the events of those days, I read the first story about the physical attacks against us which began a few weeks after we were expelled. The Stalin- ists had been taken by surprise at first. Before they knew what had hit them we had a paper off the press and our com- rades were in front of the Communist Party headquarters selling the *Militant* at a nickel a copy. It created a tremen- dous sensation. For a few weeks they did not know what to do about it. Then they decided to try the Stalin method of physical force.

The first report in the *Militant* tells of two women com- rades of the Hungarian group who went there with bundles of the paper one evening and attempted to sell them. They were set upon by hoodlums, pushed and kicked and driven away from the public streets, their papers torn up. This was reported in the *Militant* as the first gangster attack against us.

Then it became a more or less regular thing. We stood our

ground. We raised a big hullabaloo and scandalized them all over town. We mobilized all our forces to go there Saturday afternoons, forming a guard around the editors and defying the Stalinist hoodlums to drive us away. One fight after another took place.

This consumed the first few weeks. By December 17 the Plenum of the Central Committee of the Communist Party was held in New York City. And here again I want to point out one of the important lessons of our tactics in this fight. That is, we didn't turn our backs on the party, but went right back to it. Having been expelled on October 27, we came to the Plenum on December 17, knocked on the door and said: "We have come to appeal against our expulsion." They set a time and permitted us to make our appeal before approximately 100 to 150 of the party leaders. Now the Lovestoneites didn't do this from considerations of democracy or faithful adherence to the constitution. They did it for factional reasons. You see, our expulsion didn't end the faction fight between the Fosterites and the Lovestoneites. The Lovestoneites, who were in the majority, conceived the cunning idea that if we were given the floor it would help them to compromise the Fosterites as "Trotskyist conciliators." Through that crack we entered the Plenum. We had no illusions. We weren't even thinking of convincing them. We weren't concerned with their little petty-larceny strategy against the Fosterites. We were thinking of making our formal appeal and printing the speech in the *Militant* as propaganda for distribution.

The "Three Generals Without an Army" appeared at the December Plenum as the representatives of all the expelled. I made a speech of about two hours. Then we were ushered out. The next day the speech was set up on the linotype for the next number of the *Militant* under the heading "Our Appeal to the Party."

I mentioned the weapons of slander, ostracism, and gangsterism employed by the Stalinists against us. The fourth weapon in the arsenal of the leaders of American Stalinism was burglary. They were so afraid of this little group, armed with the great ideas of Trotsky's program, that they wanted by all means to crush it before it could get a hearing. One Sunday afternoon, returning from a meeting of our first New York branch—12 or 13 people gathered solemnly to form the organization and lay the groundwork for the overthrow of American capitalism—I found the apartment ransacked from top to bottom. In our absence they had jimmied the lock on the door of my home and broken in. Everything was in disorder; all my private papers, documents, records, correspondence—anything they could lay their hands on—were strewn over the floor. Evidently we had surprised them before they could cart the plunder away. While I was on tour a few weeks later they came back and finished the job. This time they took everything.

We continued to fight along our lines. We scandalized them mercilessly, cried to high heaven, publicized their burglary and gangsterism, and made them wince with our exposures. They could not snuff us out nor silence us. Here, of course, we had the tremendous advantage of our past experiences. We had been through the mill. We had taken part in a good many fights and they couldn't bluff us with a few burglaries and slanders. We knew how to exploit all these things against them to good effect. We fought with political weapons, which are stronger than the gangster's blackjack or the burglar's jimmy. We appealed to the good will and communist conscience of the members of the party and began recruiting the people who came to us at first as a protest against this Stalinist procedure.

Within a few weeks, on January 8, 1929, we organized the first Trotskyist public meeting in America. I looked over the first bound volume of the *Militant* today and saw the advertisement of that meeting on the front page of the issue of January 1, 1929. I admit I felt a little emotion as I recalled the time we threw that bombshell into the radical circles of New York. In front of this Labor Temple a big sign announced that I was going to speak on "The Truth About Trotsky and the Russian Opposition." We came to this meeting prepared to protect it. We had the assistance of the Italian group of Bordigists, our Hungarian comrades, a few individual sympathizers of Communism who didn't believe in stopping free speech, and our own valiant newly-recruited forces. They were deployed around the platform in the Labor Temple and near the door to see to it that the meeting wasn't interrupted. And that meeting did go through without interruption.

The hall was filled, not only with sympathizers and converts, but also with all kinds of people who came there from all kinds of motives, interest, curiosity, etc. The lecture was very successful, consolidated our supporters, and gained some recruits. It also threw greater alarm into the camp of the Stalinists, and pushed them further along the road of violence against us.

We next planned a national tour on the same subject. I tried to speak in New Haven, but there we were completely outnumbered. The Stalinists surrounded us and the meeting was entirely broken up. I spoke in Boston; there we made better preparations. I arrived a few days early, went around to a few old IWW friends of mine to see if they could not get some boys from the waterfront to help us uphold free speech. We had about ten of these lads around the platform. A gang of Stalinist hoodlums was also there, bent on breaking up the meeting, but evidently they became convinced that they would get their own heads broken if they tried it. The Boston meeting was a success. Needless to say, my chairman on this historic occasion was Antoinette Konikow. A group of eight to ten comrades was consolidated in Boston around the program of Trotsky.

In Cleveland we had a fight. The well-known Amter was District Organizer in Cleveland and he brought a squad to our meeting to break it up. We also had a few boys who had come over to us, and they lined up a number of sympathizers, radicals, and others who wanted fair play and free speech. Instructed by our experience in New Haven, our forces were organized in a squadron around the speaker. I began my lecture and after a few sentences, as I recall, I used the expression, "I want to explain to you the revolutionary significance of this fight."

Amter stood up and said, "You mean, counterrevolutionary significance."

This apparently was the signal. The Stalinist gang began to howl and whistle. "Sit down, counterrevolutionist," "traitor," "agent of American imperialism," and so on and so forth. That went on for about fifteen minutes, pandemonium. Their idea was to make it impossible for me to be heard above the tumult. This was the way they were going to clarify the question, by simply stopping me from speaking. We had other ideas. It became clear that the Amterites intended to howl all night if necessary. Our squadron was ready, waiting for me to give the signal. I finally said, "O.K., go ahead." Thereupon they went after Amter and his gang, took them one by one and threw them down the stairs, and cleared the hall and the atmosphere of Stalinists. Then everything was fine; the meeting proceeded without further disturbance. We had the most wonderful peace and quiet.

In Chicago, a few nights later, the Stalinists had a little gang, but couldn't make up their minds whether they wanted to start a fight or not. I went through with the lecture.

As I travelled along the road, various Stalinist functionaries came to see me in the night like the Biblical figure Nicodemus. One of them was B. K. Gebert, who in later years became a big figure in the Communist Party and District Organizer in Detroit. He came to see me in the hotel at Chicago, a heartbroken man. He despised all these methods used against us. Gebert was a conscientious Communist, sympathized with our fight, but couldn't leave the party. He couldn't bring himself to the idea of breaking with the whole life he had known and of starting out anew. This was the case with many. Various forms of compulsion affect various people. Some are afraid of a physical blow; some shrink from slander; others fear ostracism. The Stalinists employed all these methods. The cumulative effect of it was to terrorize hundreds and even thousands of people who, in a free atmosphere, would have sympathized with us and supported us to one degree or another.

At my meeting in Minneapolis, as I testified years later in the Northern Minnesota District Federal Court, we were taken off guard. Our forces were rather strong in Minneapolis. The recognized leaders of the Minneapolis Communist movement, V. R. Dunne, Carl Skoglund, and others, had all come out in our support. They were pretty strong physically too, and they became careless. In organizing the meeting on the theory that the hoodlums wouldn't try any monkey business there, no special plans were made for defense. That was an error. Our people were late in coming. The Stalinist gang arrived first, assaulted Oscar Coover at the door with blackjacks, forced their way in, and occupied the front seats in a rather small hall. When I arose to speak they began howling in the manner of Amter and his gang at Cleveland. After a few minutes we tied into them, and a free-for-all fight ensued. Then the cops came in and broke up the meeting. That was a rather scandalous and demoralizing thing for Minnesota. It was decided that I should stay over and try another meeting. We went down to the IWW hall with a proposal for a united front to protect free speech. Together with them, a few sympathizers, and isolated individuals we formed a Workers Defense Guard. A meeting was scheduled in the IWW hall; the handbill advertised that this meeting would be held under the protection of the Workers Defense Guard. The Guard came there equipped with clubs, oversized hatchet handles purchased at a hardware store, nice and handy. The guards lined up along the walls and in front of the speaker. Others were posted at the door. The chairman calmly announced that questions and discussion would be permitted, but that no one should interfere while the speaker had the floor. The meeting went off smoothly, without any sign of disturbance. The organization of our group in Minneapolis was completed in good shape.

In New York, as we began holding more regular meetings, the Stalinists intensified their attempts to stop us. One meeting here in the Labor Temple was broken up. Their standing plan was to come in such force as to rush the speaker off the platform, take over the meeting, and turn it into an anti-Trotskyist demonstration. They never succeeded in doing that because we always had our guard on the platform equipped with the necessary implements. The Stalinists never reached the platform, but they did start such a free-for-all fight that the cops came in force and the meeting was broken up in disorder. The Stalinists tried the same thing a second time but were routed and driven out. Things really came to a climax when the Stalinists made their last attempts to break up our meetings at a hall on the Upper East Side where our Hungarian group used to meet. We held a May Day celebration there May 1, 1929—the spring after our expulsion. Looking through the *Militant* today I saw the announcement of the May Day meeting at the Hungarian Hall and the appended statement that it would be under the protection of the Workers Defense Guard. It was well guarded; our strategy was not to let the disturbers in. Our own comrades, sympathizers, and all those who were obviously coming to celebrate May Day were admitted. When the Stalinists tried to force their way in, they met our Guard at the head of the stairs, and got blows over the head until they decided they could not storm that stairway. We held the meeting in peace.

The following Friday, I think it was, the Stalinists decided to take revenge on the Hungarian group for their inability to break up the May Day meeting as instructed. The Hungarian comrades were holding a closed meeting—eight or ten people quietly transacting the ordinary business of a branch. Among those present were the Communist veteran, Louis Basky, a man of about 50, and his aged father, a man about 80, who was a militant partisan of his son and of the Trotskyist movement. Several women comrades were there. Suddenly the hall was raided by a gang of Stalinist hoodlums. They rushed right in and began beating both the women and men, including old man Basky. Our comrades grabbed chairs or chair legs and defended themselves as best they could. At a stage in the bloody fight, one of those present, a woodworker by profession, who had one of the tools of his trade in his pocket, saw a couple of these hoodlums beating the old man. He went berserk when he saw that and went to work on one of the pair. They carried the Stalinist thug to the hospital. He stayed there three weeks, the doctors uncertain whether he was going to pull out of it or not.

That put a stop to the attacks on our meetings. The Stalinists had brought things near a terrible tragedy and scandalization of the whole Communist movement. They became convinced that we would not surrender our right to meet and speak, that we would stand up and fight, that they could not break us up. Thereafter, there were only isolated instances of violence against us. We did not win our free speech from the Stalinist gangsters by a change of heart on their part but by our determined and militant defense of our rights.

Meanwhile we gained new members and sympathizers because of the fight we were putting up. We were only a handful of people, and all the weapons of slander and ostracism and violence were brought to bear against us. But we stood our ground. By one means or another we brought out our paper regularly. We came back stronger after every fight, and this attracted sympathy and support. Many of the radical people in New York, sympathizers of the Communist Party, and even some members, would come to our meetings to help protect them in the interests of free speech. They were attracted by our fight, by our courage, and revolted by the methods of the Stalinists. They would then start reading our material and studying our program. We began to win them over, one by one, and to make political converts to Trotsky-ism out of them. So we can say that the very first nucleus of American Trotskyism was recruited in the fire of a real strug-gle. Week by week, month by month, we built these little groups in various cities, and soon we had the skeleton of a national organization.

The *Militant* was coming out every two weeks; how, I couldn't tell you now, and I wouldn't want to have the finan-cial assignment of doing it over again. We did it with the help of loyal friends. By one means and another we did it, at the cost of rather heavy sacrifices. But these sacrifices were nothing compared to the intellectual and spiritual compensa-tion we derived from getting out our paper, spreading our message, and feeling that we were worthily carrying out the great mission that had been thrust upon us.

In all this time we had no contact with Comrade Trotsky. We didn't know whether he was dead or alive. There were re-ports of his being sick. We never dared to hope that we would ever see him or have any direct contact with him. Our only connection with him was that document I brought back from Moscow, and other documents we later received from the European groups. In issue after issue of the *Militant* we began to publish, one after another, the various documents and theses of the Russian Left Opposition covering the whole period, from 1924 to 1929. We broke the blockade against the ideas of Trotsky and his co-workers in Russia.

Then in the early spring of 1929, a few months after our expulsion, the press of the world was rocked by the announcement that Trotsky was being deported from Russia. This announcement didn't say where he would be sent. Day after day the press was full of all kinds of speculative stories, but no information as to his whereabouts. This continued for a week or more. We hung in suspense not knowing whether Trotsky was dead or alive, until finally the news came through that he had landed in Turkey. We established our first contact with him there in the spring of 1929, four or five months after we started the movement in his name and on the basis of his ideas. I wrote him a letter; we soon received an answer. Thereafter, except for the time he was interned in Norway, until the day of his death, we were never without the most intimate contact with the founder and inspirer of our movement.

On February 15, 1929, not quite four months after our expulsion, as the Communist Party was preparing its national convention, we published the "Platform" of our faction—a complete statement of our principles and our position on the questions of the day, national and international. To compare this platform with the resolutions and theses that we, as well as other factions, used to write in the internal national faction fights, is to see what an abyss separates people who have acquired an international theoretical outlook from national-minded factionalists fighting in a restricted area. Our platform began with our declaration of principles on an international scale, our view of the Russian question, our position on the great theoretical questions at the bottom of the fight in the Russian party—the question of socialism in one country. From there our platform proceeded to national questions, to the trade union question in the United States, to the detailed problems of party organization, etc. For the first time in the long, drawn-out faction fight in the American Communist movement a really rounded international Marxist document was thrown into the arena. That was the result of adherence to the Russian Left Opposition and its program.

We printed this platform in the *Militant,* first as our proposal to the convention of the Communist Party, because although expelled we maintained our position as a faction. We didn't run away from the party. We didn't start another one. We turned back to the party membership and said: "We belong to this party, and this is our program for the party convention, our platform." Naturally, we didn't expect the bureaucrats to permit us to defend it in the convention. We didn't expect them to adopt it. We were aiming at the Communist rank and file. It was this line, this technique, which gave us our approach to the rank-and-file members of the Communist Party. When Lovestone, Foster, and Company said to them: "These fellows, these Trotskyists, are enemies of the Communist International; they want to break up the party;" we could show them it wasn't so. Our answer was: "No, we are still members of the party, and we are submitting a platform for the party that will give it a clearer principled position and a better orientation." In this way we kept our contact with the best elements in the party. We refuted the slander that we were enemies of Communism and convinced them that we, ourselves, were its loyal defenders. By this means we first gained their attention and eventually recruited many of them, one by one, into our group.

On March 19, I see by my notes, we held a meeting in the Labor Temple to protest the deportation of Trotsky from the Soviet Union. At the height of the world sensation created by this news we called a mass meeting here in this Labor Temple with Cannon, Abern, and Shachtman advertised as speakers. We protested against this infamy and again declared in public our solidarity with Trotsky.

Under the date of May 17, 1929, the *Militant* carried the call for the first National Conference of the Left Opposition in the United States. The main task of this conference, as announced in the call and subsequent preconference articles, was to adopt the platform. This platform, which Cannon, Abern, and Shachtman had drawn up and submitted to the Communist Party as a draft, became the draft of a platform for our organization, submitted to our first conference.

Another task of the conference was further to clarify our ranks as to our position on the Russian question. If you study the history of American Bolshevism from 1917 to the present day, you will find that at every juncture, at every critical occasion, at every turn of events, it was the Russian question that dominated the dispute. It was the Russian question that determined the allegiance of people, whether revolutionary or reformist, from 1917 up to the split in the Socialist Party in 1919. At the time of the expulsion of the Trotskyists in 1928;

in the innumerable fights we had with the various factions and groups in the course of our own development; up to our fight with the petty-bourgeois opposition in the Socialist Workers Party in 1939 and 1940—the overriding issue was always the Russian question. It was dominant every time because the Russian question is the question of the proletarian revolution. It is not the abstract problem of a prospective revolution; it is the question of the revolution itself, one that actually took place and still lives. The attitude toward that revolution today, as yesterday, and as in the beginning, is the decisive criterion in determining the character of a political group.

We had to clarify that question at our first conference, because no sooner had we been expelled and begun to fight the Stalinist bureaucracy, then all kinds of people wanted to join us on one little condition: that we turn our backs on the Soviet Union and on the Communist Party and build an anti-Communist organization. We could have recruited hundreds of members in the first days had we accepted that condition.

There were others who wanted to abandon the idea of functioning as a faction of the Communist Party and proclaim a completely independent Communist movement. The task of our conference was also to clarify that issue. Shall we start a new independent party and renounce any future work in the CP, or shall we continue to declare ourselves a faction? That question had to be answered decisively.

Another problem referred to the first National Conference was the nature and form of our national organization, and the election of our national leaders. Up to that time "The Three Generals" had functioned as the leadership simply by virtue of the fact that they had started the fight. That was a good enough certificate to begin with: those who take the initiative become leaders of an action by a higher law than any referendum. But this could not continue indefinitely. We recognized that it was necessary to have a conference and to elect a leading committee. We were fortunate enough to receive Comrade Trotsky's answer to our communication in time for this conference. His answer, as all of his letters, as all of his articles, was permeated with political wisdom. His friendly advice helped us in solving our problems.

The *Militant* reports that 31 delegates and 17 alternates from 12 cities attended the first conference of the American Trotskyists, representing a total of about 100 members throughout the country. The conference was held in Chicago in May 1929. You can see from the figures I have cited that nearly half of the members of our young organization came as delegates or alternates to form this historic conference. It met in a spirit of unanimity, enthusiasm, and unbounded confidence in our great future. The very first preparation we made was the practical one of protecting the conference against Stalinist hoodlums. The whole delegation, a total of 48, were all enlisted in the army of self-defense. If the Stalinists had attempted to interfere with that conference they would have been given a good answer for their pains. But they decided to leave us alone and we convened for days in peace.

Let me repeat. There were 31 delegates and 17 alternates from 12 cities, representing approximately 100 members in our national organization. We called ourselves *The Communist League of America, Left Opposition of the Communist Party.* We were sure we were right. We were sure that our program was correct. We went from that conference with the confident assurance that the whole future development of the regenerated Communist movement in America, up to the time the proletariat takes power and begins organizing the socialist society, would trace its origin to that first National Conference of the American Trotskyists at Chicago in May 1929.

5

The Dog Days of the
Left Opposition

Our last lecture brought us up to the first National Conference of the Left Opposition in May 1929. We had survived the difficult first six months of our struggle, kept our forces intact, and gained some new recruits. At the first conference we consolidated our forces into a national organization, set up an elected leadership, and defined our program more precisely. Our ranks were firm, determined. We were poor in resources and very few in numbers, but we were sure that we had laid hold of the truth and that with the truth we would conquer in the end. We came back to New York to begin the second stage of the struggle for the regeneration of American Communism.

The fate of every political group—whether it is to live and grow or degenerate and die—is decided in its first experiences by the way in which it answers two decisive questions.

The first is the adoption of a correct political program. But that alone does not guarantee victory. The second is that the group decide correctly what shall be the nature of its activities, and what tasks it shall set itself, given the size and capacity of the group, the period of the development of the class struggle, the relation of forces in the political movement, and so on.

If the program of a political group, especially a small political group, is false, nothing can save it in the end. It is just as impossible to bluff in the political movement as in war. The only difference is that in wartime things are brought to such a pitch that every weakness becomes exposed almost immediately, as is shown in one stage after another in the current imperialist war. The law operates just as ruthlessly in the political struggle. Bluffs do not work. At most they deceive people for a time, but the main victims of the deception, in the end, are the bluffers themselves. You must have the goods. That is, you must have a correct program in order to survive and serve the cause of the workers.

An example of the fatal result of a light-minded bluffing attitude toward program is the notorious Lovestone group. Some of you who are new to the revolutionary movement may never have heard of this faction which once played such a prominent role, inasmuch as it has disappeared completely from the scene. But in those days the people who constituted the Lovestone group were the leaders of the American Communist Party. It was they who carried through our expulsion, and when about six months later, they themselves were expelled, they began with far more numerous forces and resources than we did. They made a much more imposing appearance in the first days. But they didn't have a correct program and didn't try to develop one. They thought they could cheat history a little bit; that they could cut corners with principle and keep larger forces together by compromises on the program question. And they did for a time. But in the end this group, rich in energies and abilities, and containing some very talented people, was utterly destroyed in the political fight, ignominiously dissolved. Today, most of its leaders, all of them as far as I know, are on the bandwagon of the imperialist war, serving ends absolutely opposite to those which they set out to serve at the beginning of their political work. The program is decisive.

On the other hand, if the group misunderstands the tasks set for it by the conditions of the day, if it does not know how to answer the most important of all questions in politics—that is, the question of what to do next—then the group, no matter what its merits may otherwise be, can wear itself out in misdirected efforts and futile activities and come to grief.

So, as I said in my opening remarks, our fate was determined in those early days by the answer we gave to the question of the program and by the way we analyzed the tasks of the day. Our merit, as a newly created political force in the American labor movement—the merit which assured the progress, stability, and further development of our group— consisted in this, that we gave correct answers to both those questions.

The conference didn't take up every question posed by the political conditions of the time. It took up only the most important questions, that is, those which had to be answered first. And the first of these was the Russian question, the question of the revolution in existence. As I remarked in the previous lecture, ever since 1917 it has been demonstrated over and over again that the Russian question is the touchstone for every political current in the labor movement. Those who take an incorrect position on the Russian question leave the revolutionary path sooner or later.

The Russian question has been elucidated innumerable times in articles, pamphlets, and books. But at every important turn of events it arises again. As late as 1939 and 1940 we had to fight the Russian question over again with a petty-bourgeois current in our own movement. Those who want to study the Russian question in all its profundity, all its acuteness, and all its urgency can find abundant material in the literature of the Fourth International. Therefore I do not need to elucidate it in detail tonight. I simply reduce it to its barest essentials and say that the question confronting us at our first convention was whether we should continue to support the Soviet state, the Soviet Union, despite the fact that the direction of it had fallen into the hands of a conservative, bureaucratic caste. There were people in those days, calling themselves and considering themselves revolutionary, who had broken with the Communist Party, or had been expelled from it, and who wanted to turn their backs entirely on the Soviet Union and what remained of the Russian revolution and start over, with a "clean slate" as an anti-Soviet party. We rejected that program and all those who urged it on us. We could have had many members in those days if we had compromised on that issue. We took a firm stand in favor of supporting the Soviet Union; of not overturning it, but of trying to reform it through the instrumentality of the party and the Comintern.

In the course of development it was proved that all those who, whether from impatience, ignorance, or subjectivity—whatever the cause might be—prematurely announced the death of the Russian revolution, were in reality announcing their own demise as revolutionists. Each and every one of these groups and tendencies degenerated, fell apart at the very base, withdrew to the sidelines, and in many cases went over into the camp of the bourgeoisie. Our political health, our revolutionary vitality, were safeguarded, first of all, by the correct attitude we took toward the Soviet Union despite the crimes that had been committed, including those against us, by the individuals in control of the administration of the Soviet Union.

The trade union question had an extraordinary importance then as always. At that time it was particularly acute. The Communist International, and the Communist parties under its direction and control, after a long experiment with right-wing opportunist politics, had taken a big swing to the left, to ultraleftism—a characteristic manifestation of the bureaucratic centrism of the faction of Stalin. Having lost the Marxist compass, they were distinguished by a tendency to jump from the extreme right to the left, and vice versa. They had gone through a long experience with right-wing politics in the Soviet Union, conciliating the kulaks and Nepmen, until the Soviet Union, and the bureaucracy with it, came to the brink of disaster. On the international arena, similar policies brought similar results. In reacting to this, and under the relentless criticisms of the Left Opposition, they introduced an ultraleftist overcorrection in all fields. On the trade union question they swung around to the position of leaving the established unions, including the American Federation of Labor, and starting a new made-to-order trade union movement under the control of the Communist Party. The insane policy of building "Red Unions" became the order of the day.

Our first National Conference took a firm stand against that policy, and declared in favor of operating within the existing labor movement, confining independent unionism to the unorganized field. We mercilessly attacked the revived sectarianism contained in this theory of a new "Communist" trade union movement created by artificial means. By that stand, by the correctness of our trade union policy, we assured that when the time arrived for us to have some access to the mass movement we would know the shortest route to it. Later events confirmed the correctness of the trade union policy adopted at our first conference and consistently maintained thereafter.

The third big important question we had to answer was whether we should create a new independent party, or still consider ourselves a faction of the existing Communist Party and the Comintern. Here again we were besieged by people who thought they were radicals: ex-members of the Communist Party who had become completely soured and wanted to throw out the baby with the dirty bath water; syndicalists and ultraleftist elements who, in their antagonism to the Communist Party, were willing to combine with anybody ready to create a party in opposition to it. Moreover, in our own ranks there were a few people who reacted subjectively to the bureaucratic expulsions, the slander and violence and ostracism employed against us. They also wanted to renounce the Communist Party and start a new party. This approach had a superficial attraction. But we resisted, we rejected that idea. People who oversimplified the question used to say to us: "How can you be a faction of a party when you are expelled from it?"

We explained: It is a question of correctly appraising the membership of the Communist Party, and finding the right tactical approach to it. If the Communist Party and its members have degenerated beyond reclamation, and if a more progressive group of workers exists (either actually or potentially by reason of the direction in which such a group is moving) out of which we can create a new and better party—then the argument for a new party is correct. But, we said, we don't see such a group anywhere. We don't see any real progressiveness, any militancy, any real political intelligence in all these diverse oppositions, individuals, and tendencies. They are nearly all sideline critics and sectarians. The real vanguard of the proletariat consists of those tens of thousands of workers who have been awakened by the Russian revolution. They are still loyal to the Comintern and to the Communist Party. They haven't attentively followed the progess of gradual degeneration. They haven't unraveled the theoretical questions which are at the bottom of this degeneration. It is impossible even to get a hearing from these people unless you place yourself on the ground of the party, and strive not to destroy but to reform it, demanding readmission to the party with democratic rights.

We solved that problem correctly by declaring ourselves a faction of the party and the Comintern. We named our organization *The Communist League of America (Opposition)*, in order to indicate that we were not a new party but simply an opposition faction to the old one. Experience has richly demonstrated the correctness of this decision. By remaining partisans of the Communist Party and the Communist International, by opposing the bureaucratic leaders at the top, but appraising correctly the rank and file as they were at that time, and seeking contact with them, we continued to gain new recruits from the ranks of the Communist workers. The overwhelming majority of our members in the first five years of our existence came from the CP. Thus we built the foundations of a regenerated Communist movement. As for the anti-Soviet and antiparty people, they never produced anything but confusion.

Out of this decision to form, at that time, a faction and not a new party, flowed another important and troublesome question which was debated and fought out at great length in our movement for five years—from 1928 until 1933. That question was: What concrete task shall we set for this group of 100 people scattered over the broad expanse of this vast country? If we constitute ourselves as an independent party, then we must appeal directly to the working class, turn our backs on the degenerated Communist Party, and embark on a series of efforts and activities in the mass movement. On the other hand, if we are to be not an independent party but a faction, then it follows that we must direct our main efforts, appeals, and activities, not to the mass of 40 million American workers, but to the vanguard of the class organized in and around the Communist Party. You can see how these two questions dovetailed. In politics—and not only in politics— once you say "A" you must say "B." We had to either turn our face towards the Communist Party, or away from the

Communist Party in the direction of the undeveloped, unorganized, and uneducated masses. You cannot eat your cake and have it too.

The problem was to understand the actual situation, the stage of development at the moment. Of course, you have to find a road to the masses in order to create a party that can lead a revolution. But the road to the masses leads through the vanguard and not over its head. That was not understood by some people. They thought they could bypass the Communistic workers, jump right into the midst of the mass movement, and find there the best candidates for the most advanced, the most theoretically developed group in the world, that is, the Left Opposition which was the vanguard of the vanguard. This conception was erroneous, the product of impatience and the failure to think things out. Instead of that, we set as our main task *propaganda,* not *agitation.*

We said: Our first task is to make the principles of the Left Opposition known to the vanguard. Let us not delude ourselves with the idea we can go to the great unschooled mass now. We must first get what is obtainable from this vanguard group, consisting of some tens of thousands of Communist Party members and sympathizers, and crystallize out of them a sufficient cadre either to reform the party, or, if after a serious effort that fails in the end—and only when the failure is conclusively demonstrated—to build a new one with the forces recruited in the endeavor. Only in this way is it possible for us to reconstitute the party in the real sense of the word.

At that time there appeared on the horizon a figure who is also perhaps strange to many of you, but who in those days made an awful lot of noise. Albert Weisbord had been a member of the CP and got himself expelled along about 1929 for criticism, or for one reason or another—it was never quite clear. After his expulsion Weisbord decided to do some studying. It frequently happens, you know, that after people get a bad blow they begin to wonder about the cause of it. Weisbord soon emerged from his studies to announce himself as a Trotskyist; not 50 percent Trotskyist as we were, but a real genuine 100 percent Trotskyist whose mission in life was to set us straight.

His revelation was: The Trotskyists must not be a propaganda circle, but go directly into "mass work." That conception had to lead him logically to the proposal of forming a new party, but he couldn't do that very conveniently because he didn't have any members. He had to apply the tactic of going first to the vanguard—on us. With a few of his personal friends and others he began an energetic campaign of "boring from within" and hammering from without this little group of 25 or 30 people whom we had by that time organized in New York City. While we were proclaiming the necessity of propagandizing the members and sympathizers of the Communist Party as a link to the mass movement, Weisbord, proclaiming a program of mass activity, directed 99 percent of his mass activity not at the masses, and not even at the Communist Party, but at our little Trotskyist group. He disagreed with us on everything and denounced us as false representatives of Trotskyism. When we said, yes, he said, yes positively. When we said 75, he raised the bid. When we said, "Communist League of America," he called his group the "Communist League of Struggle" to make it stronger. The heart and core of the fight with Weisbord was this question of the nature of our activities. He was impatient to jump into mass work over the head of the Communist Party. We rejected his program and he denounced us in one thick mimeographed bulletin after another.

Some of you may perhaps have the ambition to become historians of the movement, or at least students of the history of the movement. If so, these informal lectures of mine can serve as guideposts for a further study of the most important questions and turning points. There is no lack of literature. If you dig for it, you will find literally bales of mimeographed bulletins devoted to criticism and denunciation of our movement—and especially of me, for some reason. That sort of thing has happened so often that I long ago learned to accept it as matter of course. Whenever anybody goes crazy in our movement he begins to denounce me at the top of his voice, entirely aside from provocation of any sort on my part. So Weisbord denounced us, particularly me, but we fought it out. We stuck to our course.

There were impatient people in our ranks who thought that Weisbord's prescription might be worth trying, a way for a poor little group to get rich quick. It is very easy for isolated people, gathered together in a small room, to talk themselves into the most radical proposals unless they retain a sense of proportion, of sanity and realism. Some of our comrades, disappointed at our slow growth, were lured by this idea that we needed only a program of mass work in order to go out and get the masses. This sentiment grew to such an extent that Weisbord created a little faction inside our organization. We were obliged to declare an open meeting for discussion. We admitted Weisbord, who wasn't a formal member, and gave him the right to the floor. We debated the question hammer and tongs. Eventually we isolated Weisbord. He never enrolled more than 13 members in his group in New York. This little group went through a series of expulsions and splits and eventually disappeared from the scene.

We consumed an enormous amount of time and energy debating and fighting out this question. And not only with Weisbord. In those days we were continually pestered by impatient people in our ranks. The difficulties of the time pressed heavily upon us. Week after week and month after month we appeared to be gaining hardly an inch. Discouragement set in, and with it the demand for some scheme to grow faster, some magic formula. We fought it down, talked it down, and held our group on the right line, kept its face turned to the one possible source of healthy growth: the ranks of the Communist workers who still remained under the influence of the Communist Party.

The Stalinist "left turn" piled up new difficulties for us. This turn was in part designed by Stalin to cut the ground from under the feet of the Left Opposition; it made the Stalinists appear more radical even than the Left Opposition of Trotsky. They threw the Lovestoneites out of the party as "right wingers," turned the party leadership over to Foster and Company, and proclaimed a left policy. By this maneuver they dealt us a devastating blow. Those disgruntled elements in the party, who had been inclined toward us and who had opposed the opportunism of the Lovestone group, became reconciled to the party. They used to say to us: "You see, you were wrong. Stalin is correcting everything. He is taking a radical position all along the line in Russia, America, and everywhere else." In Russia the Stalin bureaucracy declared war on the kulaks. All over the world the ground was being cut from under the feet of the Left Opposition. A whole series of capitulations took place in Russia. Radek and others gave up the fight on the excuse that Stalin had adopted the policy of the Opposition. There were, I would say, perhaps hundreds of Communist Party members, who had been leaning towards us, who gained the same impression and returned to Stalinism in the period of the ultraleft swing.

Those were the real dog days of the Left Opposition. We had gone through the first six months with rather steady progress and formed our national organization at the conference with high hopes. Then recruitment from the party membership suddenly stopped. After the expulsion of the Lovestoneites, a wave of illusion swept through the Communist Party. Reconciliation with Stalinism became the order of the day. We were stymied. And then began the big noise of the first Five Year Plan. The Communist Party members were fired with enthusiasm by the Five Year Plan which the Left Opposition had originated and demanded. The panic in the United States, the "depression," caused a great wave of disillusionment with capitalism. The Communist Party in that situation appeared to be the most radical and revolutionary force in the country. The party began to grow and swell its ranks and to attract sympathizers in droves.

We, with our criticisms and theoretical explanations, appeared in the eyes of all as a group of impossibilists, hairsplitters, naggers. We were going around trying to make people understand that the theory of socialism in one country is fatal for a revolutionary movement in the end; that we must clear up this question of theory at all costs. Enamored with the first successes of the Five Year Plan, they used to look at us and say, "These people are crazy, they don't live in this world." At a time when tens and hundreds of thousands of new elements were beginning to look toward the Soviet Union, going forward with the Five Year Plan, while capitalism appeared to be going up the spout; here were these Trotskyists, with their documents under their arms, demanding that you read books, study, discuss, and so on. Nobody wanted to listen to us.

In those dog days of the movement we were shut off from all contact. We had no friends, no sympathizers, no periphery around our movement. We had no chance whatever to participate in the mass movement. Whenever we tried to get into a workers organization we would be expelled as counterrevolutionary Trotskyists. We tried to send delegations to the unemployed meetings. Our credentials would be rejected on the ground that we were enemies of the working class. We were utterly isolated, forced in upon ourselves. Our recruitment dropped to almost nothing. The Communist Party and its vast periphery seemed to be hermetically sealed against us.

Then, as is always the case with new political movements, we began to recruit from sources none too healthy. If you are ever reduced again to a small handful, as well the Marxists may be in the mutations of the class struggle; if things go badly once more and you have to begin over again, then I can tell you in advance some of the headaches you are going to have. Every new movement attracts certain elements which might properly be called the lunatic fringe. Freaks always looking for the most extreme expression of radicalism, misfits, windbags, chronic oppositionists who had been thrown out of half a dozen organizations—such people began to come to us in our isolation, shouting, "Hello, Comrades." I was always against admitting such people, but the tide was too strong. I waged a bitter fight in the New York branch of the Communist League against admitting a man to membership on the sole ground of his appearance and dress.

They asked, "What have you against him?"

I said, "He wears a corduroy suit up and down Greenwich Village, with a trick mustache and long hair. There is something wrong with this guy."

I wasn't making a joke, either. I said, people of this type are not going to be suitable for approaching the ordinary American worker. They are going to mark our organization as something freakish, abnormal, exotic; something that has nothing to do with the normal life of the American worker. I was dead right in general, and in this mentioned case in particular. Our corduroy-suit lad, after making all kinds of trouble in the organization, eventually became an Oehlerite.

Many people came to us who had revolted against the Communist Party not for its bad sides but for its good sides; that is, the discipline of the party, the subordination of the individual to the decisions of the party in current work. A lot of dilettantish petty-bourgeois-minded people who couldn't stand any kind of discipline, who had either left the CP or been expelled from it, wanted, or rather thought they wanted to become Trotskyists. Some of them joined the New York branch and brought with them that same prejudice against discipline in our organization. Many of the newcomers made a fetish of democracy. They were repelled so much by the bureaucratism of the Communist Party that they desired an organization without any authority or discipline or centralization whatever.

All the people of this type have one common characteristic: they like to discuss things without limit or end. The New York branch of the Trotskyist movement in those days was just one continuous stew of discussion. I have never seen one of these elements who isn't articulate. I have looked for one but I have never found him. They can all talk; and not only can, but *will;* and everlastingly, on every question. They were iconoclasts who would accept nothing as authoritative, nothing as decided in the history of the movement. Everything and everybody had to be proved over again from scratch.

Walled off from the vanguard represented by the Communist movement and without contact with the living mass movement of the workers, we were thrown in upon ourselves and subjected to this invasion. There was no way out of it. We had to go through the long, drawn-out period of stewing and discussing. I had to listen, and that is one reason my gray hairs are so numerous. I was never a sectarian or screwball. I never had patience with people who mistake mere garrulousness for the qualities of political leadership. But one could not walk away from this sorely beset group. This little fragile nucleus of the future revolutionary party had to be held together. It had to go through this experience. It had to survive somehow. One had to be patient for the sake of the future; that is why we listened to the windbags. It was not easy. I have thought many times that, if despite my unbelief, there is anything in what they say about the hereafter, I am going to be well rewarded—not for what I have done, but for what I have had to listen to.

That was the hardest time. And then, naturally, the movement slid into its inevitable period of internal difficulties, frictions, and conflicts. We had fierce quarrels and squabbles, very often over little things. There were reasons for it. No small isolated movement has ever been able to escape it. A small isolated group thrown in upon itself, with the weight of the whole world pressing down upon it, having no contact with the workers mass movement and getting no sobering corrective from it, is bound in the best case to have a hard time. Our difficulties were increased by the fact that many recruits were not first class material. Many of the people who joined the New York branch weren't really there by justice. They weren't the type who, in the long run, could build a revolutionary movement—dilettantes, petty-bourgeois undisciplined elements.

And then, the everlasting poverty of the movement. We were trying to publish a newspaper, we were trying to publish a whole list of pamphlets, without the necessary resources. Every penny we obtained was immediately devoured by the expenses of the newspaper. We didn't have a nickel to turn around with. Those were the days of real pressure, the hard days of isolation, of poverty, of disheartening internal difficulties. This lasted not for weeks or months, but for years. And under those harsh conditions, which persisted for years, everything weak in any individual was squeezed to the surface; everything petty, selfish, and disloyal. I had been acquainted with some of the individuals before, in the days when the weather was fairer. Now I came to know them in their blood and bones. And then in those terrible days I learned also to know Ben Webster and the men of Minneapolis. They always supported me, they never failed me, they held up my hands.

The greatest movement, with its magnificent program of the liberation of all humanity, with the most grandiose historic perspectives, was inundated in those days by a sea of petty troubles, jealousies, clique formations, and internal fights. Worst of all, these faction fights weren't fully comprehensible to the membership because the great political issues which were implicit in them had not yet broken through. However, they were not mere personal quarrels, as they so often appeared to be, but, as is now quite clear to all, the premature rehearsal of the great, definitive struggle of 1939–40 between the proletarian and petty-bourgeois tendencies within our movement.

Those were the hardest days of all in the thirty years that I have been active in the movement—those days from the conference of 1929 in Chicago until 1933, the years of the terrible hermetically sealed isolation, with all the attendant difficulties. Isolation is the natural habitat of the sectarian, but for one who has an instinct for the mass movement it is the most cruel punishment.

Those were the hard days, but in spite of everything we carried out our propaganda tasks, and on the whole we did it very well. At the conference in Chicago we had decided that at all costs we were going to publish the whole message of the Russian Opposition. All the accumulated documents, which had been suppressed, and the current writings of Trotsky were then available to us. We decided that the most revolutionary thing we could do was not to go out to proclaim the revolution in Union Square, not try to put ourselves at the head of tens of thousands of workers who did not yet know us, not to jump over our own heads.

Our task, our revolutionary duty, was to print the word, to carry on *propaganda* in the narrowest and most concentrated sense, that is, the publication and distribution of theoretical literature. To that end we drained our members for money to buy a secondhand linotype machine and set up our own print shop. Of all the business enterprises that have ever been contrived in the history of capitalism, I think this was the best, considering the means available. If we weren't interested in the revolution, I think that we could easily qualify, just on the basis of this enterprise, as very good business experts. We certainly did a lot of corner cutting to keep that business going. We assigned a young comrade, who had just finished linotype school, to operate the machine. He wasn't a first-class mechanic then; now he is not only a good mechanic but also a party leader and a lecturer on the staff of the New York School of Social Science. In those days the whole weight of the propaganda of the party rested on this single comrade who ran the linotype machine. There was a story about him—I don't know whether it is true or not—that he didn't know much about the machine. It was an old broken-down, secondhand job that had been palmed off on us. Every once in a while it would stop working, like a tired mule. Charlie would adjust a few gadgets and, if that didn't help, take a hammer and give the linotype a crack or two and knock some sense into it. Then it would begin to work properly again and another issue of the *Militant* would come out.

Later on, we had amateur printers. About half of the New York branch used to work in the print shop at one time or another—painters, bricklayers, garment workers, bookkeepers—all of them served a term as amateur typesetters. With a very inefficient and overstaffed shop we ground out certain results through unpaid labor. That was the whole secret of the Trotskyist printing plant. It wasn't efficient from any other standpoint, but it was kept going by the secret that all slave masters since Pharaoh have known: If you have slaves you don't need much money. We didn't have slaves but we did have ardent and devoted comrades who worked night and day for next to nothing on the mechanical as well as the editorial side of the paper. We were short of funds. All bills were always overdue, with the creditors pressing for immediate payment. No sooner would the paper bill be met than we had to pay rent on the building under threat of eviction. The gas bill then had to be paid in a hurry because without the gas the linotype wouldn't work. The electric bill had to be paid because the shop could not operate without power and light. All the bills had to be paid whether we had the money or not. The most we could ever hope to do was to cover the rent, the paper cost, installment payments, and repairs on the linotype and the gas and light bills. There was seldom anything left over for the "hired help"—not only for the comrades who worked in the shop, but also those in the office, the leaders of our movement.

Great sacrifices were made by the rank and file of our comrades all the time, but they were never greater than the sacrifices made by the leaders. That is why the leaders of the movement always had strong moral authority. The leaders of our party were always in a position to demand sacrifices of the rank and file—because they set the example and everybody knew it.

Somehow or other the paper came out. Pamphlets were printed one after another. Different groups of comrades would each sponsor a new pamphlet by Trotsky, putting up the money to pay for the paper. In that antiquated printshop of ours a whole book was printed on the problems of the Chinese revolution. Every comrade who wants to know the problems of the Orient has to read the book which was published under those adverse conditions—at 84 East 10 Street, New York City.

And in spite of everything—I have cited many of the negative sides and difficulties—in spite of everything, we gained a few inches. We instructed the movement in the great principles of Bolshevism on a plane never known in this country before. We educated a cadre that is destined to play a great role in the American labor movement. We sifted out some of the misfits and recruited some good people one by one; we gained a member here and there; we began to establish new contacts.

We tried to hold public meetings. It was very difficult because in those days nobody wanted to listen to us. I remember the grand efforts we made one time to mobilize the whole organization to distribute leaflets, to have a mass meeting in this very room. We got 59 people, including our own members, and the whole organization was uplifted with enthusiasm. We went around saying to each other: "We had 59 people present at the lecture the other night. We are beginning to grow."

We received help from outside New York. From Minneapolis, for example. Our comrades who later gained great fame as labor leaders weren't always famous labor leaders. In those days they were coal heavers, working ten and twelve hours a day in the coal yards, heaving coal, the hardest kind of physical labor. Out of their wages they used to dig up as high as five or ten dollars a week and shoot it in to New York to make sure the *Militant* came out. Many times we had no money for the paper. We would send a wire to Minneapolis and get back a telegraphic money order for $25 or something like that. Comrades in Chicago and other places did the same things. It was by a combination of all these efforts and all those sacrifices throughout the country that we survived and kept the paper going.

There was an occasional windfall. Once or twice a sympathizer would give us $25. Those were real holidays in our office. We had a "revolving rent fund" which was the last resource of our desperate financial finagling. A comrade with rent to pay, say $30 or $40 due on the fifteenth of the month, would lend it to us on the tenth to pay some pressing bill or other. Then in five days we would get another comrade to lend his rent money to enable us to pay the other comrade back in time to satisfy his landlord. The second comrade would then stall off his landlord while we swung another deal, borrowed somebody else's rent to repay him. That went on all the time. It gave us some floating capital to cut the corner.

Those were cruel and heavy times. We survived them because we had faith in our program and because we had the help of Comrade Trotsky and our international organization.

Comrade Trotsky began his great work in exile for the third time. His writings and his correspondence inspired us and opened up for us a window on a whole new world of theory and political understanding. The intervention of the International Secretariat was of decisive help to us in the solution of our difficulties. We sought their advice and were sensible enough to heed it when it was given. Without international collaboration—that is what the word "internationalism" means—it is not possible for a political group to survive and develop on a revolutionary path in this epoch. This gave us the strength to persevere and to survive, to hold the organization together, and to be ready when our opportunity came.

In my next lecture I will show you that we were ready when the opportunity did come. When the first crack in this wall of isolation and stagnation appeared, we were able to leap through it, out of our sectarian circle. We began to play a role in the political and labor movement. The condition for that was to keep our program clear and our courage strong in those days when capitulations were taking place in Russia and discouragement was overcoming the workers everywhere. One defeat after another descended upon the heads of the vanguard of the vanguard. Many began to question. What to do? Is it possible to do anything? Isn't it better to let things slide a little? Trotsky wrote an article, "Tenacity! Tenacity! Tenacity!" That was his answer to the wave of discouragement that followed the capitulation of Radek and others. Hold on and fight it out—that is what the revolutionists must learn, no matter how small their numbers, no matter how isolated they may be. Hold on and fight it out until the break comes, then take advantage of every opportunity. We held out until 1933, and then we began to see daylight. Then the Trotskyists started to get on the political map of this country. In the next lecture I shall tell you about that.

6

The Break with
the Comintern

We have now had five lectures in this course. With the fifth one last week, as you will remember, we covered the first four years of the Left Opposition, the Communist League of America—1928 to 1932. These were the times, as I remarked last week, of the severest isolation and the greatest hardship for the new movement.

Last week I emphasized, perhaps overemphasized, the negative sides of the movement in that period: the stagnation, the poverty of forces and material means, the inevitable internal difficulties accruing from such a set of circumstances, and the lunatic fringe which plagued us as it plagues every new radical movement. This isolation together with its attendant evils was imposed upon us by objective factors beyond our control. We could not prevent it, not with the best efforts, the best will. It was the condition of the times. The most important of these factors making our isolation so almost absolute was the upsurge of the Stalinist movement which resulted from the crisis in all the bourgeois countries at the same time that the Soviet Union was bounding forward under the first Five Year Plan of industrialization. The enhanced prestige of the USSR, and of Stalinism which appeared to be its legitimate representative in the eyes of uncritical people—and the great masses are uncritical—made our oppositionist movement appear somewhat bizarre, unrealistic. Besides that, there was great stagnation in the general labor movement. There were no strikes. The workers were quiescent. They were not interested in any theoretical questions. They were not even interested in any actions at that time. All this acted against our small group and pushed it into a corner.

Our task in that difficult time was to hold on, to clarify the great questions, to educate our cadres in preparation for the future when objective conditions would open up possibilities for an expansion of the movement. Our task also was to test out to the very end the possibilities of reforming the Communist parties and the Communist International, which up to that time had embraced practically the whole workers vanguard in this country and throughout the world. The events which began to break over the world in the early part of 1933 showed that we had succeeded magnificently in our main task. When things began to move, when the opportunity came to break out of our isolation, we were ready. We lost no time in grasping the opportunities presented to us, beginning in 1933, and especially in 1934.

Our movement had been educated in a great school under the direction and inspiration of Comrade Trotsky, the school of internationalism. Our cadres had been forged together in the heat of study and dispute over the greatest world questions.

The great weakness of the American Communist movement in the past, as I have mentioned in previous lectures, was its national-mindedness, not in theory but in practice; its ignorance of international events and unconcern about them; its lack of real instruction and of serious interest in theory. These faults were corrected in our young movement. We educated a group of people who proceeded in all questions from fundamental considerations of theory, from international experience, and learned how to analyze international events. The mysteries of the Russian problem were solved by our movement. In article after article, pamphlet after pamphlet, and book after book, Comrade Trotsky opened up for us a world view on all questions. He gave us a clear understanding of the complexities of a workers state in a capitalist encirclement, a workers state degenerating and throwing up a retrograde bureaucracy but still retaining its basic foundations.

Germany was already then becoming the center of the world problem. Trotsky as far back as 1931 wrote a pamphlet which he called *Germany, the Key to the International Situation.* Before all others he perceived the menacing growth of fascism and the inevitability of a fundamental showdown between fascism and Communism. Before anyone else, and clearer than anyone else, he analyzed what was coming in Germany. He educated us to an understanding of it and tried to prepare the German Communist Party and the German workers for that fatal test.

The Spanish revolution, which broke out in December 1930, was also studied and comprehended by our young movement, first of all with the assistance of the theoretical writings and interpretations of Comrade Trotsky.

We took time in those days of isolation to study the Chinese question. I mentioned last week that during this difficult period our movement, despite all its poverty and weakness, managed to publish a full-sized book, *Problems of the Chinese Revolution*. This book contained suppressed theses, articles, and expositions of the Russian Opposition, written in the decisive days of the Chinese revolution, 1925, 1926, and 1927. That great world historical battle had unfolded, you may say, behind the backs of the blindfolded members of the Comintern, who had never been permitted to learn what the great masters of Marxism in the Russian Left Opposition had to say about these events. We published the suppressed documents. Our comrades were educated on the problems of the Chinese revolution. That is one of the important reasons—in fact, it is *the* important reason—why our party has such a clear and firm stand on the colonial question today; why we do not lose our heads over the defense of China and the struggle of India for independence. The significance that this great uprising of the Asiatic peoples can have for the international proletarian revolution is clearly understood by our party. That is part of its heritage from those days of isolation and study.

In the early part of 1933 we began to intervene more actively in the general labor movement. After long propagandistic preparation, we started our turn towards mass work. I have already told you about the fight we had in our organization with some impatient people who wanted to begin with mass work, jump over our own heads so to speak, leaving for the future the education of our cadre, the definition of our program and our propagandistic work. That was turning things upside down. We worked out our program, formed our cadre, did our preliminary propagandistic work first. Then, when opportunities arose for activity in the labor movement, we were ready to put our activity to some purpose. We did not engage in activity merely for the sake of activity, which some wit once described as all motion and no direction. We were prepared to enter the mass movement with a clearly defined program and with methods calculated to bring the maximum results to the revolutionary movement from the minimum amount of required activity.

In reading the bound volumes of the *Militant,* which contain a chronological record of our activities and plans and hopes, it is reported that on January 22, 1933, there was an unemployment conference in New York. It had been called, of course, on the initiative of the Stalinist organization but it was a little different from some of their previous conferences from which we had been excluded. This time, in their waverings and wanderings from right to left, they started dabbling with the united front, trying to interest some non-Stalinist organizations in a general unemployment movement. To that end, they issued a call inviting all organizations to the conference. We commented in our paper that this was a turn in the right direction toward the united front, at least a half turn. I wrote an article which pointed out that by inviting "all organizations" they had finally opened up a small crack through which the Left Opposition might enter that movement; we would make our way through that crack and open it wider. We showed up at that conference—Shachtman and Cannon, big as life—prepared to tell the entire proletariat how the struggle against unemployment should be carried out. And it was no joke either. Our program was the correct one, and we explained it at length. The *Militant* carried a full report of our speeches advocating a united front of the political parties and the trade unions for unemployment relief.

On January 29, 1933, there was held at Gillespie, Illinois, a conference of the Progressive Miners Union and other independent labor organizations to consider the question of a new labor federation. I attended the conference by invitation from a group of the Progressive Miners, and spoke there. This was the first time in nearly five years that I had been able to get out of New York. It was also the first time that any representative of the American Left Opposition had a chance to speak to workers as such outside the small circle of intellectual radicals. We seized the opportunity. I was sent out there by our League, spent a few days with the miners, and made some important contacts. It felt very good to be once again in touch with the living movement of the workers, the mass movement.

Coming back on the bus from Gillespie to Chicago—I recall it very distinctly—I read newspaper accounts of the appointment of Hitler as Chancellor by President Hindenburg. I had the feeling then, at that moment, that things were beginning to break. The stagnation, the stalemate in the world labor movement was breaking wide open. Things were moving to a showdown. We were fully ready to take our part in the new situation. As I checked the reports the other day, preparing my notes for this lecture, it seemed to me that this action of our League, our reaching out for the first time to participate in a workers mass meeting in Gillespie, Illinois, was symbolic of our attunement to the new period. Our action was unconsciously synchronized with the breakup of the stalemate in Germany. We reacted very energetically to this new development, to the beginnings of new stirrings in the labor movement here, and especially the situation in Germany. We were like athletes, trained and poised for action, but restrained by external difficulties and unable to move forward. Then suddenly a new situation opened up and we leaped into it.

Our first reaction to the German events was to call a mass meeting in New York. For a long time we had abandoned the idea of mass meetings because the masses wouldn't come. The best we could do was to hold small open forums, lectures, circle gatherings, etc. This time we essayed a mass meeting: Stuyvesant Casino, February 5, 1933. "The Meaning of the German Events" with Shachtman and Cannon as speakers. The report in the *Militant* said that 500 people turned out to our mass meeting.

We sounded the alarm on the impending showdown between fascism and Communism in Germany. Then, while the issues were so acute, every day in Germany witnessing new developments, we did an absolutely unprecedented thing for a group so small as ours. We transformed our weekly *Militant*— by that time it had become a weekly—and brought it out three times a week, each issue blazing away with the message of Trotskyism on the events in Germany. If you should ask me how we did it I wouldn't be able to explain. But we did it. It wasn't possible, but there is a saying among Trotskyists that in times of crisis you do not do what is possible, but what is necessary. And we thought it necessary to break out of our routine discussions and criticisms of the Stalinists, to do something to shock the whole workers movement into realizing how fateful for the whole world were the happenings in Germany. We wanted to call all workers, and especially the Communist workers, to attention. We speeded up the tempo. We began to shout, to sound the alarm. Our comrades ran to every meeting they could find, to every slightest gathering of workers, with bundles of the *Militant* under their arms, shouting at the top of their voices: "Read the *Militant!*" "Read the truth about Germany!" "Read what Trotsky says!"

Our slogan during the German events was: *The United Front of the Workers' Organizations and Battle to the Death!* The united fighting front of all workers' organizations against fascism! The Stalinists and the Social Democrats rejected the united front in Germany. They both pretend otherwise after the events, seeking to blame each other, but they are both liars, both guilty of betrayal. They divided the workers, and neither of them had any will to fight. Through that division the monstrous plague of fascism came to power in Germany, and threw its dark shadow over the whole world.

We did everything we could to awaken, arouse, and educate the American Communist workers in those fateful weeks. We held a series of mass meetings—not only the one I have mentioned. We had a series in Manhattan and, for the first time, we branched out into the Boroughs. They had so surrounded and so isolated us that we had never been able to get out of Fourteenth Street in the early days. We had only one branch because we didn't have enough people to divide up; everything was concentrated around this little area of Fourteenth Street and Union Square where radical workers congregate.

But in this crisis of Germany we branched out and held meetings in Brooklyn and in the Bronx. All over the country, the *Militant* reports, mass meetings were held by the local branches of the Communist League of America. Hugo Oehler—at that time a member of our organization—was sent on tour to speak about Germany. We were extremely aggressive in our approach to the Stalinists. We were determined at all costs to get our message to those willing to listen. We even invaded a Stalinist mass meeting in the Bronx, turning the tables on them. Shachtman and I, flanked by a few of our comrades, just walked into this Stalinist mass meeting and asked for the floor. The audacity of the demand seemed to nonplus the fakers in charge and there were demands from the floor "let 'em speak!" We spoke and gave our message to the Stalinist meeting.

With new life beginning to stir in the general labor movement, we neglected no opportunity to take part in the new activities. In March 1933 a statewide unemployment conference was sponsored by the Stalinists in Albany, with about 500 delegates. The same regulations which enabled us to appear at the local conference in New York, also enabled us to send delegates to Albany. I appeared at the conference, took the floor and made a speech to the 500 delegates on the Marxist conception of the united front in the unemployed movement. That speech is printed in the *Militant* of March 10, 1933. National and international issues were coordinated. At the same time that we were shouting at the top of our voices about Germany, we took time to participate in a conference on unemployment in the state of New York.

You know that the advice, the explanations, the warnings of Trotsky went unheeded. The German Communist Party, under the direct leadership and control of Stalin and his gang in Moscow, capitulated in Germany without a struggle. Fascism triumphed without even the semblance of a civil war, without even a scuffle in the street. And that, as Trotsky has explained many times, and Engels before him, is the worst and most demoralizing of all defeats—the defeat without battle, because those who are so defeated lose confidence in themselves for a long time. A party which fights may be vanquished by superior forces. Nevertheless it leaves behind a tradition, a moral inspiration, which can be a tremendous factor in galvanizing the proletariat to rise again later at a more favorable juncture. Such a role was played in history by the Paris Commune. The international socialist movement was raised on its glorious memory.

The 1905 revolution in Russia was inspired by the heroic struggle of the Paris Communards of 1871. Similarly, the revolution of 1905 in Russia, which was defeated after a battle, became the great moral capital of the Russian proletariat and was a tremendous influence in unleashing the proletarian revolution which triumphed in 1917. The Bolsheviks always spoke of 1905 as the dress rehearsal for 1917.

But what role in history can play the miserable capitulation of the Social Democrats and Stalinists in Germany? Here was the most powerful proletariat in Western Europe. The Social Democrats and Stalinists combined had polled more than 12 million votes in the last election. Had the German workers been united in action they could have scattered the fascist riffraff to the four winds with one solid blow. This powerful proletariat, disunited and betrayed by the leadership, was conquered without a fight. The most horrible, barbarous regime was imposed upon them by the fascists. Before the event, Trotsky said that a failure to fight would be the worst betrayal in history. So it was. Ten unsuccessful insurrections, said Trotsky, could not demoralize the proletariat one-hundredth part as much as one capitulation without a fight which would deprive them of confidence in themselves. After this capitulation, this tragic culmination of the German situation, many people began to think of everything that Trotsky had said and done in the effort to aid the workers to avoid the catastrophe. What finally happened began to appear to many people as complete verification, if even in a negative sense, of all that he had said and explained. The prestige and authority of Trotsky and the Trotskyist movement began to grow enormously, even among those circles which had been inclined to dismiss us as sectarians and hairsplitters.

In the Communist Party, however, here as in other countries, in the Comintern as a whole, there was no deep reaction. It became clear then that these parties had become so bureaucratized, so corrupted from within, so demoralized, that even the cruellest betrayal in history was not capable of producing a real uprising in the ranks. It became clear that the Communist International was dead to the revolution, had been destroyed by Stalinism.

And then, in the unfolding dialectic of history, a peculiar contradictory development began to manifest itself. In 1914–1918, the international Social Democracy betrayed the prole-

tariat in support of the imperialist war. The Social Democratic parties renounced internationalism and put themselves
at the service of their own bourgeoisie. It was this betrayal
which prompted the revolutionary Marxists to form the new
International, the Communist International, in 1919. The
Communist International arose in struggle against the traitors, with the program of Marxism regenerated as its banner
and Lenin and Trotsky as its leaders. But, in the course of
events from 1919 to 1933—a brief 14 years—that very International had been converted into its polar opposite; it had become the greatest obstacle and greatest retarding factor in the
international labor movement. The Communist International
of Stalin betrayed the proletariat even more shamefully, more
ingloriously, than had the Second International of the Social
Democrats in 1914.

Revolutionary workers of the new generation were repelled
by Stalinism. In the further course of development, under the
terrific pressure of these international events, and particularly
the rise of fascism in Germany, the Social Democratic parties
began to disclose leftist and centrist tendencies of all kinds.
There were many reasons for this phenomenon. The Communist parties were so walled off by the bureaucracy from any
independent thought or revolutionary life that the radical
workers were repelled from them. In search of revolutionary
expression, many of them found their way into the more
loosely constructed parties of Social Democracy. Also, the
younger generation of Social Democrats, who didn't have on
their shoulders the blame for the betrayals of 14 years ago, and
who were not part of this tradition or mentality, were growing
restless under the terrific pressure of events and searching for a

radical solution. Left-wing groupings likewise began to develop inside the Social Democrats, particularly in the youth organizations. And that world trend was also reflected in the United States in an upsurge of the Socialist Party. The split of 1919 and a secondary split of 1921 had left the Socialist Party in America in shambles. Nothing remained but an empty hulk. The rebel youth, everything vital and alive, poured into the young Communist organization. The Socialist Party languished for years with a few thousand members, mainly supported by the traitorous gang of the Jewish daily *Forward* and the labor skates of the garment unions in New York who needed the Socialist Party as a pseudoradical covering and protection against their left-wing workers. The Socialist Party for years was just an ugly caricature of a party. But as the Communist Party became more and more bureaucratized, as it expelled more and more honest workers and closed the door to others, the Socialist Party began to experience a revival. Its loose and democratic structure attracted a whole new stratum of workers who had never before been in a political movement. Thousands of them, awakened to radicalism by the economic crisis, streamed into the Socialist Party. It experienced an upsurge and growth in membership; by 1933 not less than 25,000 members were enrolled in its ranks. Also, as a result of this new blood and the development of the young generation, the party began to show a little vigor, a leftist, centrist tendency took shape in the ranks.

Similarly, here as in other countries, there was also the development outside the Communist Party of independent groupings of workers who had hitherto not been connected with radical parties but were awakened to radicalism as a result of their own experiences. Such a unique movement in this country was the Conference for Progressive Labor Action. It was led by A. J. Muste. The CPLA started as a progressive movement in the trade unions. Under the impact of the crisis it turned more and more in a radical direction. By the end of 1933 the Muste movement was busily discussing the problem of transforming itself from a loose grouping of activists in the trade unions into a political party.

Upon the capitulation of the Comintern in Germany, Trotsky gave the signal to the revolutionary Marxists of the world. "The Comintern is bankrupt. We must have new parties and a new International." The long experiment, the long years of effort as a faction to influence the Communist Party, even though expelled from it, had run their course. It was not any decree of ours that made the Communist Party beyond reform. It was the demonstration of history itself. We simply recognized reality. On that basis we changed our strategy and tactics completely.

From a faction of the Communist International we announced ourselves as the heralds of a new party and a new International. We began to appeal directly to the workers awakening to radicalism and without political affiliation or experience. Through long years of effort—by maintaining our position as a faction of the Comintern—we had recruited from the ranks of the Communist vanguard the precious cadres of the new movement. Now, we began to turn our attention to the Socialist Parties and independent groups and to the left and centrist groups within them. In that period the *Militant* printed numerous reports and analyses of the development of the Left Wing in the Socialist Party. There were articles about the Conference for Progressive Labor Action and its plan to transform itself into a political party. There were sympathetic approaches to the Young Peoples Socialist League. And, as we did it here, following the line of Trotsky, it was done on an international scale. Groups of Trotskyists everywhere began to establish contact with the newly developed and apparently viable Left Wing in the Social Democracy.

The time had come to transform our whole activity, to make the turn to mass work. Just as in our first days we had rejected the premature demand that we—with our little handful of people—drop everything and jump into the mass movement, so now, toward the end of 1933, having completed our preliminary work and prepared ourselves, we adopted the slogan: "Turn from a propaganda circle to mass work."

That proposal precipitated a new internal crisis. The "turn" brought the issue of sectarianism into the open. It had to be fought out to the end. Politics is the art of making the right move at the right time. The impatience of some people to escape isolation imposed by objective circumstances had caused a crisis and internal conflict in the early days of our organization. Now the situation was reversed. The objective conditions had radically changed. The opportunity presented itself for us to enter into the mass movement, to establish contact with workers, to penetrate deeply into the fermenting left socialist and independent movements. It was necessary to seize the opportunity without delay. Our decision to do so met determined resistance from comrades who had adapted themselves to isolation and grown comfortable in it. In that atmosphere some people had developed a sectarian mentality. The attempt to propel the Trotskyist movement out of its isolation into the cold and turbulent waters of the mass movement caused shivers to run up and down their spines. These shivers were rationalized into "principles." That marked the beginning of the fight against sectarianism in our organization, a fight which was carried through to the end in classic form.

We began to recruit faster. We attracted greater attention with our propaganda on the German events. People began to come to us unexpectedly, unknown people, to obtain our literature. "What does Trotsky say?" "What did he write about Germany?"

We passed a great milestone: Toward the end of our first five years of struggle we had built up the New York branch to a total of fifty people. I remember this because a rule in the constitution of our organization limited the size of branches to fifty members. A branch reaching that size was required to be divided into two branches. We wrote this into the constitution at our first conference in 1929. We could have put the whole national membership into two branches in those days, but we were looking forward to the day when our ship would come in. I remember the question arose in 1933 for the first time of complying with the constitution on this point, and we had a dispute as to how the branch should be divided.

On May 1 and 2, 1933, the great national Mooney Congress was held in Chicago, initiated by the Stalinists, but with many trade unions participating. We sent a delegation to this Congress and I had the opportunity to speak to several thousand people. It was a refreshing experience after the long confinement in the restricted circle of internal debate. There I entered into the beginnings of political collaboration with Albert Goldman who was still in the Communist Party but on the way to breaking with their line. Both his speech at the Mooney Congress and mine on the united front were direct attacks on Stalinist policy. This prepared the ground for Goldman's expulsion and his later affiliation with us. That was the start of an extremely fruitful collaboration.

From Chicago, the *Militant* reports, I went on tour, speaking on two subjects: "The Tragedy of the German Proletariat" and "America's Road to Revolution." A group of Stalinist intellectuals in New York, who had either belonged to the party or worked in its periphery, began chafing under the manifest falsity of the Stalinist line as revealed by the German events. Eventually they broke with the CP and came over to us. This was our first acquisition in bulk. Up to then, people had been joining us one by one. Now a group joined us, a group of intellectuals. That was significant. The movements of the intellectuals must be studied very attentively as symptoms. They move a little faster in the realm of ideas than the workers. Like the leaves at the top of a tree, they shake first. When we saw a group of rather serious intellectuals in New York breaking with Stalinism, we had to realize that this was the beginning of a movement that would soon be manifested in the ranks, and that more Stalinist workers would be coming to us.

An important development in the last months of 1933 was the action taken by the Conference for Progressive Labor Action. Under the impulse of growing radicalization in the ranks of the workers whom they had recruited, and sensing no doubt that the Communist Party was becoming less attractive to the radical workers, the CPLA held a conference in Pittsburgh and tentatively announced the formation of a new political party. Tentatively, that is, it elected a provisional committee charged with the task of organizing the "American Workers Party."

The split of Benjamin Gitlow and his little group from the Lovestoneites occurred at that time. That period also saw a big upsurge of the centrist Left Wing in the Socialist Party, and a more and more radical position taken by the Young Peoples Socialist League. In all workers organizations there was ferment and change. One who had a political eye could see that things were really happening now, and that this was not the time to be sitting in the library mulling over principles. This was the time for action on these principles; this was the time to be right on top of things, to take advantage of every opportunity presented by the new developments in the other organizations and movements.

I must say that not a single one of them got away from us. We didn't wait for any invitation. We approached them. We issued a manifesto on the front page of the *Militant* calling for the formation of a new party and a new International. We invited all groupings, whoever they might be, who were interested in forming a new revolutionary party and a new International, to discuss with us the basis of the program. We said, we have a program, but it is not presented to you as an ultimatum. It is our contribution to the discussion. If you have other ideas for the program, let's put them all on the table and discuss them in peaceful and comradely fashion. Let's try to resolve the differences on the program and join forces to build a new united party.

We campaigned for the new party. Our great advantage over the other groups—the advantage which assured our hegemony—was that we knew what we wanted. We had a clearly defined program and that gave us a certain aggressiveness. The other left elements were not sure enough of themselves to take the initiative. That fell to us. We were beating the drums every week, in fact all the time, for a new party, writing letters to these people, writing critical but sympathetic reviews of their press and all their resolutions. Our rank-and-file comrades were instructed and drilled to establish connections with the rank-and-file members of these other groups, to interest them in the discussion from all sides and top and bottom, and thus prepare the way for the coming fusion of the serious and honest revolutionary elements in a single party. Meantime our own organization was growing, attracting more attention and gaining more sympathy and respect. In all these radical circles there was respect for Trotskyists as the honest Communists, and for Trotsky as the great Marxist thinker who had understood the German events when no one else did. We were admired for the way we had stuck to our guns and stood our ground despite persecution and adversity. Our organization was respected throughout the labor movement. This was important capital for us when the time came to promote the fusion of the various left groupings into one party.

After five years of struggle our ranks had become consolidated on a firm programmatic foundation. They had been educated in the great principled questions, had acquired facility in explaining them, and in applying them to the events of the day. We were ready, prepared by our past experience. In many respects that experience had been somewhat dismal and negative to be sure. But it was precisely that period of isolation, hardship, discussion, study, and assimilation of theoretical ideas that prepared our young movement for this new time of bloom when the movement was opening up in all directions. Then we were ready for a very sharp tactical turn. Our ranks were infused in those days with new hopes and with great, high ambitions. By the end of 1933 we felt confident that we were on the way to the reconstitution of a genuine Communist Party in this country. We were sure that the future belonged to us. A lot of struggles were yet ahead of us but we felt that we were over the hill, that we were on our way. History has proved that we were right in those assumptions. Thereafter things moved very rapidly and continually in our favor. Our progress from that time on has been practically uninterrupted.

7

The Turn to
Mass Work

I have remarked that the most important of all questions for a political group or party, once it has elaborated its program, is to give the correct answer to the question: *What to do next?* The answer to this question is not and cannot be determined simply by the desire or the whim of the party or the party leadership. It is determined by the objective circumstances and the possibilities inherent in the circumstances.

We have discussed the first five years of our existence as a Trotskyist organization in the United States. During that time our small numbers, the general stagnation in the labor movement, and the complete domination of all radical movements by the Communist Party, imposed upon us the position of a faction of the Communist Party. Likewise these circumstances made obligatory that our primary work be propaganda rather than mass agitation. As has already been pointed out, in the terminology of Marxism quite a sharp distinction is drawn between propaganda and agitation, a distinction which is slurred over in popular language. People commonly describe as propaganda any kind of publicity, agitation, teaching, propagation of principles, etc. In the terminology of the Marxist movement, as it was defined most precisely by Plekhanov, agitation and propaganda are two distinct forms of activity. Propaganda he defined as the dissemination of many fundamental ideas to a few people; what we perhaps in America are accustomed to call education. Agitation he defined as the dissemination of a few ideas, or only one idea, to many people. Propaganda is directed toward the vanguard; agitation toward the masses.

At the end of our last lecture we came to a break in the objective situation in which our party had been working. The Comintern had been shattered by the debacle in Germany; and at the fringes of the Communist movement it was losing its authority. Many people, previously deaf to anything we said, were awakening to an interest in our ideas and criticisms. On the other hand, the masses who had remained dormant and stagnant during the first four years of the cataclysmic economic crisis, began to stir again. The Roosevelt administration was in office. There had been a slight revival of industry. The workers were streaming back into factories, regaining the self-confidence which they had lost to a large extent during the terrible mass unemployment. There was a great movement toward trade union organization, and strikes were beginning to develop. This sweeping change in the objective situation posed wholly new tasks for the Trotskyist movement, the Communist League of America, the Left Opposition, as we called ourselves up to then. The German debacle had con-

firmed the bankruptcy of the Comintern and started a movement away from it on the part of the most advanced and criti-
cal-thinking workers. Conversely, the moribund Social Democracy was beginning to show new life within its Left Wing
because of the revolutionary trend in the youth and proletarian
sections. Independent movements with a radical inclination
were growing up, consisting of workers and some intellectuals
who had been shut off from the Communist Party by its bureaucratic life and not yet attracted to the Social Democracy.
The American labor movement was awakening from its long
sleep, stagnation was giving way to new life and a new movement. The Trotskyist organization in this country was confronted with an opportunity and a demand, inherent in the
objective situation, to make a radical change in orientation and
in tactics. This opportunity, as I said, found us fully prepared
and ready.

We lost no time in adapting ourselves to the new situation.
We transformed the whole nature of our work and our outlook. We shook our membership to the bottom with discussions of the proposals of the leadership to change our course
and break out of our five years' isolation. With our limited
forces and resources we took advantage of every opportunity
to work in the wider environment. All our activity from then
on was governed by one general concept concretized in the
slogan: "Turn from a propaganda circle to mass work"—and
to do this in both fields, the political as well as the economic.

It was one of the great proofs of the viability of our movement, and of its firm principled foundation, that we carried
out a uniform and symmetrical transformation of our work in
both fields. We leaped into the mass movement at every op-

portunity without getting bogged down in trade union fetishism. We concerned ourselves with every sign and every tendency of a leftward development in the other political movements without neglecting trade union work. On the political
field our leading slogan was the call for a new party and a
new International. We approached other groups which previously had confronted us solely as rivals and with which we
had previously had no close contact. We began to study
these other groups most attentively, to read their press, to
have our members establish contacts of a personal nature
with rank-and-file members to learn what they were thinking.
We tried to familiarize ourselves with every nuance of
thought and feeling in these other political movements.

We sought closer contact and cooperation with them in
joint actions of one kind or another, and talked of amalga-
mations and fusions leading toward the consolidation of a
new revolutionary workers party. On the economic field we
reaped the first fruits of our correct trade union policy, at
which we had hammered away for five years. We had coun-
terposed this policy to the sectarian, dual unionist trade
union policy espoused by the Communist Party during its
ill-fated "Third Period," the period of its ultraleft swing.
Likewise, in counterposition to the opportunist policy of the
Social Democracy, the policy of subordinating principles to
seeking offices and acquiring fictitious, not real, influence,
we had given a clear line to all the militant elements in the
trade union movement who followed our press. We had
considerable influence in directing them into the main current of the trade unions which was at that time represented
by the American Federation of Labor.

Despite the great conservatism, the craft-mindedness, and the corruption of the AFL leadership, we insisted at all times that the militants must not separate themselves from this main current of American unionism and must not set up artificial and ideal unions of their own which would be isolated from the mass. The task of the revolutionary militants, as we defined it, was to plunge into the labor movement as it existed and try to influence it from within. The American Federation of Labor held a convention in October 1933. This convention, for the first time in many years, recorded a sweeping increase in membership as a result of the awakening of the workers, the strikes and organization campaigns which, nine times out of ten, were initiated from below. The workers were streaming into the various AFL unions without much encouragement or direction from the ossified bureaucracy.

In preparing the notes for this lecture, I looked over some of the articles and editorials we wrote at that time. We were not merely critical. We did not merely stand aside explaining what fakers and betrayers the leaders of the American Federation of Labor were, although they were that without doubt. In an editorial written in connection with the American Federation of Labor convention of October 1933 we said that the great movement of the masses into the trade unions can be seriously influenced only from within. "From this it follows: Get into the unions, stay there, work within." This key thought permeated all our comments.

We expanded our activities on the political field. The *Militant* of that period, October–November 1933, records a tour of Comrade Webster who was at that time the National Secretary of our organization. He had returned from Europe where he had visited Comrade Trotsky and had attended an International Conference of the Left Opposition following the German collapse. His tour carried him as far west as Kansas City and Minneapolis, reporting on the International Conference, proclaiming the message of the new party and the new International, addressing larger audiences than we had known before, acquiring new contacts, giving wider advertisement to the revivified Trotskyist movement.

In November, according to the *Militant*, we held a banquet in Stuyvesant Casino to celebrate the Fifth Anniversary of American Trotskyism. To this banquet came as a guest speaker one of the former leaders of the Communist Party who had been instrumental in expelling us from the party five years before. This was the well-known Ben Gitlow, who, having made the practice of expulsion somewhat popular, had himself become a victim of it. He had been expelled along with the other Lovestoneites. Four and one-half years later, he came to a break with the Lovestoneites and was circulating around as an independent Communist. As such he attended this banquet of ours at Stuyvesant Casino, November 4, 1933.

In October of that same year, while these developments were being recorded on the political front, the Paterson silk workers engaged in a general strike. Our small organization plunged into this strike, tried to influence it, made some new contacts in the process. We devoted an entire edition of the *Militant*, a special edition, to the Paterson strike. I mention this as one of the symptomatic illustrations of our orientation in that period. We were seeking openings and grasping at every opportunity to take the doctrine of Trotskyism out of the closed propaganda circle of the vanguard and bring it, in an agitational form, to the mass of the American workers.

On the political front, in November the *Militant* carried an editorial addressed to the Conference for Progressive Labor Action. The Muste organization was about to hold a convention where, it was projected, the CPLA would be transformed from a network of trade union committees into a political organization. We were right on top of that new development. We wrote an editorial in a very friendly tone, recommending to them that at their convention they take note of our invitation to all independent radical political groups to discuss the question of forming a united party, and especially suggesting that they interest themselves in the question of internationalism. The CPLA had been not only a strictly trade union group, but also a strictly national group without international contacts and without much interest in international affairs. In this editorial we pointed out to them that any group aspiring to organize an independent political party must interest itself as a fundamental requirement in internationalism and take a position on the decisive international questions.

I note that in November we had an editorial entitled, "United Front Against Hooliganism." This was written in connection with a meeting that had been held in Chicago where Comrade Webster spoke on his tour. The Communist Party had revived its hooligan tactics of earlier years; a gang of Stalinists attempted to disrupt the meeting. Fortunately our party was prepared and gave them more than they brought. The most they succeeded in doing was to interrupt the meeting until the comrades of the guard disposed of them.

In connection with this event we carried an editorial calling on all workers organizations to cooperate with us in organizing a united front workers guard in order, as the editorial said, "to defend free speech in the labor movement and teach a lesson to those who interfere with it." Sporadically, over the entire 13, nearly 14, years of our existence, the Stalinists have resorted to their hooligan attempts to silence us. Each time we not only fought back, but sought the assistance of other groups for cooperative defense. While we never succeeded in forming any permanent united front defense movement, we had partial success on each occasion. It was sufficient to secure our rights, and so far we have managed to maintain them. This is very important to remember in connection with a new attempt of the Stalinists in one part of the country to silence us. At the present time, out in California, the *Militant* reports such an attempt and you see our party right back in the groove, forming united fronts, running in all directions for support, and scandalizing them all over town, forcing the Stalin gang to back down. Our people are still distributing the paper at the forbidden places in California.

I read in the December 16, 1933, issue of the *Militant* a statement to the Communist Party by a group of Brooklyn comrades announcing their break with the Communist Party, denouncing the hooligan tactics of the Stalinists and their false policies, and declaring their adherence to the Communist League of America. Especially significant about this particular statement was the fact that the leader of this group had been the captain of the hooligan squad of the Communist Party in Brooklyn. He had been sent out with others to break up the street meetings of the Left Opposition. In the course of the fight he saw our comrades not only stand their ground and give back blow for blow, but also give the ignorant, misguided young hoodlums a propaganda speech and a tract for the good of their souls. He was converted right on the firing line. That happened continually.

Many of the people who were the most active militants in the early days had been ignorant young Stalinists to begin with. They started out to fight us and then, like Saul on the road to Damascus, they were struck by a blinding light, converted and made into good Communists, that is, Trotskyists. That is an important thing to remember now if you are attacked by Stalinists in front of union halls: Many of these ignorant young Stalinists sent out to attack us don't know what they are doing. In time we will convert some of them if we combine the two forms of education. You know, in every well-regulated trade union they have educational committees and "educational" committees, and they both serve very good purposes. The one arranges lectures for the education of the membership and the other provides for the education of scabs who won't listen to lectures.

There is a legendary story of a debate on educational activity in the Barbers Union of Chicago years ago. This union had an "educational" committee and part of the duty of its members was to take care of the plate glass windows of the scab shops. They rode around in automobiles. A wave of economy and radicalism combined had been sweeping through the union, and one impractical radical made a motion that they take the automobiles away from the "educational" committee in order to save money. He said: "Let them ride bicycles." An old timer asked indignantly: "Where the devil will they carry their stones on bicycles?" So they let the "educational" committee keep their automobiles, the educational committee arranged a good program of lectures at the union meetings, and everything was fine.

At the turn of that eventful year of 1933, an organization movement began among the hard-pressed hotel workers in New York City, who had been without union protection for years. After a series of unsuccessful strikes and the disruptive work of the Stalinists, union organization had dwindled down. It had become reduced primarily to a small independent union, a relic of old times, with a few shops under its control, and a special "red" union of the Stalinists. This revived organization movement offered us our first big chance in the mass movement since 1928. We had an opportunity to penetrate this movement from the beginning, to shape its development, and eventually to have the leadership of a great general strike of hotel workers in New York. The affair ended in a disgraceful debacle through the incompetence and treachery of some individual members of our movement who were placed in key positions. But the experience and the lessons of that first attempt, which ended so disastrously, paid rich returns and assured later successes for us in the trade union field. We are using the capital of that first experience even to this very day in trade union questions.

The hotel organization campaign began, and as so frequently happens in trade union developments, luck played a part. By chance, a few members of our party belonged to this independent union which became the medium for the organization campaign. As the hotel workers began to turn toward unionism in a big way, this handful of Trotskyists found themselves in the midst of a swirling mass movement. We had a comrade, an old-time militant in the trade, and after years of isolation he suddenly found himself an influential figure. Then we had in the party at that time a man named B. J. Field, an intellectual. He had never been engaged in trade union work before. But he was a man of many intellectual accomplishments, and in our general push toward mass work, in our drive for contact with the mass movement, Field was assigned to go into the hotel situation to help our faction and to give the union the benefit of his knowledge as a statistician, an economist, and a linguist.

It happened that the most strategically important sector in the hotel situation was a group of French chefs. Because of their strategic position in the trade and their prestige as the most skilled craftsmen, they played, as is always the case with the best mechanics everywhere, a predominant role. Many of these French chefs could not speak or discuss things in English. Our intellectual could talk French with them till the cows came home. This gave him extraordinary importance in their eyes. The old secretary was leaving office, and before anybody knew what had happened, the French chefs insisted that Field should be secretary of this promising union, and he was duly elected; naturally that meant not only an opportunity for us, but also a responsibility. The organization campaign then went on with full force. Our League gave the most energetic help from the start. I personally participated quite actively and spoke at several organization mass meetings. After five years of isolation down on Tenth Street and Sixteenth Street, making innumerable speeches at small forums and internal meetings—and not only making the speeches, but listening to other speakers interminably—I was happy to have an opportunity to speak to hundreds and hundreds of workers on elementary trade unionism.

Hugo Oehler, who later became a quite famous sectarian, but who, strangely enough, was an excellent trade unionist—and more than that, a member of this craft—was sent into this union to help. In addition, a number of other comrades were assigned to help in the organizing campaign. We publicized the campaign in the *Militant* and gave whatever help we could, including advice and direction to our comrades, until the movement culminated in a general strike of New York hotel workers on January 24, 1934. At the invitation of the union committee, I made the main speech at the mass meeting of the hotel workers, the night when the general strike was proclaimed. Thereafter the National Committee of our League assigned me to devote my whole time to assisting and collaborating with Field and the fraction in the hotel workers union. Many others—a dozen or more—were assigned to help in every way from picketing to running errands, from writing publicity to distributing handbills and sweeping up the headquarters; any and every kind of task which would be required of them in such a situation.

Our League went all out for the strike, just as we had done in the German crisis in the early part of 1933. When the German situation came to the breaking point, we brought out the *Militant* three times a week in order to dramatize the events and increase our striking power. We did the same thing in the New York hotel strike. The *Militant* was carried by our comrades to all meetings and picket lines. So that every worker in the industry on strike saw the *Militant* every other day popularizing the strike, giving the strikers' side, exposing the bosses' lies, and offering some ideas on ways of making the strike successful. Our whole organization, all over the country, was mobilized to help the New York hotel strike as task number one; to help the union win the strike and to help our comrades establish the influence and prestige of Trotskyism in the fight. That is one of the characteristics of Trotskyism. Trotskyism never does anything halfway. Trotskyism acts according to the old motto: Whatever is worth doing at all is worth doing well. That is the way we acted in the hotel strike. We poured everything we had into that task to make it successful. The whole New York organization was mobilized; they scraped down to the bottom of their pockets, to the last dime, to pay the tremendous expense of the three-times-a-week *Militant*. The comrades all over the country did likewise. We strained the organization almost to the breaking point to help that strike.

But we did not become trade union fetishists. Simultaneously with our concentration in the hotel strike, we made a decisive move on the political front. The *Militant* of January 27, the very issue of the paper which carried the first report of the general strike, published also an open letter addressed to the Provisional Organization Committee of the American Workers Party, which the Conference for Progressive Labor Action had set up at their Pittsburgh conference in the preceding month. In this open letter we took note of their convention decision to move toward the constitution of a political party; we proposed to open discussions with the objective of coming to an agreement on program so that we could form a political party unitedly, putting their forces and ours to-

THE TURN TO MASS WORK **159**

gether in one organization. It is symptomatic, it is significant, that the initiative came from us. In every relationship ever established between the Trotskyists and any other political grouping, the initiative always came from the Trotskyists. That was not because of our personal superiority or because we were less bashful than other people—we have always been modest enough—but because we knew what we wanted all the time. We had a more clearly defined program and were always sure of what we were doing, or at least we thought we were. This gave us confidence, initiative.

The hotel strike had a very promising beginning. A series of great mass meetings were held, culminating in a mass meeting in the annex of Madison Square Garden with not less than 10,000 in attendance. There I had the privilege of speaking as one of the featured speakers of the strike committee, along with Field and others. Our comrades in the union were in a position from the start to influence strike policy most decisively, although we never pursued the policy of monopolizing strike leadership. Our policy always has been to draw into cooperation all the leading militants, and share responsibility with them, in order that the strike leadership may be really representative of the membership and sensitively responsive to it.

Naturally, the strike began to encounter many of the difficulties which scuttled so many strikes of that period, particularly the machinations of the Federal Labor Board. It required political awareness to prevent the ostensible "help" of these governmental agencies from being transformed into a noose for the strike. We had sufficient political experience, we knew enough about the role of government mediators, to have some ideas about how to deal with them—not to turn one's back on them in sectarian fashion, but to utilize every possibility they might afford to bring the bosses into negotiations; and to do this without placing the slightest confidence in these people or giving them the initiative.

All this we tried to impress upon our brilliant young intellectual prodigy, B. J. Field. But he in the meantime had gone through a certain transformation; from nothing he had suddenly become everything. His picture was in all the New York papers. He was the leader of a great mass movement. And strange as it may seem, sometimes these things which are purely external, having absolutely nothing to do with what is inside a man, exert a profound effect on his self-estimation. This, unfortunately, was the case with Field. By nature he was rather conservative, and by no means free from petty-bourgeois sentiment, from being impressed by government representatives, politicians, and labor skates, into whose company he was suddenly thrust. He began to carry out his negotiations with these people, and to conduct himself generally, like a Napoleon, as he thought, but in reality like a schoolboy. He disregarded the fraction of his own party in the union—which is always the sign of a man who has lost his head. But it often happens with party members who are suddenly projected into important strategic positions in unions. They are seized by the utterly irrational idea that they are bigger than the party, that they don't need the party any more. Field began to disregard the militants of his own party fraction who were right there by his side and should have been the machine through which he carried out everything. Not only that. He began to disregard the National

Committee of the League. We could have helped him a lot because our committee embodied the experience not of one strike but of many, to say nothing of the political experience which would have been so useful in dealing with the Labor Board sharks. We wanted to help him because we were bound up in the situation as much as he was. All over town, and all over the country in fact, everybody was talking about the Trotskyist strike. Our movement was on trial before the labor movement of the country. All our enemies were hoping for disaster; nobody wanted to help us. We knew very well that if the strike had a bad outcome the Trotskyist organization would get a black eye. No matter how far Field might depart from party policy, it would not be Field who would be remembered and blamed for the failure, but the Trotskyist movement, the Trotskyist organization.

Each day that went by, our heedless intellectual pulled farther away from us. We tried hard, in the most comradely way, in the most humble way, to convince this swellheaded fool that he was leading not only himself but the strike to destruction, and was threatening to bring discredit upon our movement. We begged him to consult us, to come and talk to the National Committee about the policy of the strike, which was beginning to sag because it was being directed wrongly. Instead of organizing the militancy of the ranks from below, and thus coming to the negotiations with a power behind him—the only thing that really counts in negotiations when the chips are down—he was moderating the militancy of the masses and spending all his time running around from one conference to another with these government sharks, politicians, and labor skates who had no other purpose except to knife the strike.

Field became more and more disdainful. How could he, who had no time, come down and meet with us? All right, we said, we have time; we will meet you at mealtime in a restaurant a block from the union headquarters. He didn't have the time even for that. He began to pass disparaging remarks. There was a little political group down on Sixteenth Street, and all they had was a program and a handful of people; and here he was with 10,000 strikers under his influence. Why should he bother with us? He said, "I could not get in contact with you even if I wanted to; you haven't even got a telephone in your office." That was true, and we really winced under the accusation—we had no telephone. That deficiency was a relic of our isolation, a hangover from the past when we had no need of a telephone because nobody wanted to call us up, and we couldn't call anyone. Besides, up till then, we couldn't afford a telephone.

Eventually the hotel strike bogged down for lack of militant policy because of a crawling reliance on the Labor Board which was aiming to scuttle the strike. Days were wasted in futile negotiations with Mayor LaGuardia, while the strike was dying on its feet for lack of proper leadership. Meanwhile our enemies were waiting to say: "We told you so. The Trotskyists are nothing but sectarian hairsplitters. They can't do mass work. They can't lead strikes." It was a heavy blow to us. We had the name of leading the strike but not the influence to shape its policy, thanks to the treachery of Field. We were in danger of having our movement compromised. If we should condone what was being done by Field and his group we could only spread demoralization in our own ranks. We could convert our young revolutionary group into a caricature model of the Socialist Party, which had people all over the trade union movement but had no serious party influence because the Socialist Party trade unionists never felt any obligation to the party.

We had before us a fundamental problem which is decisive for every revolutionary political party: Shall trade union functionaries determine the party line and lay down the law to the party, or shall the party determine the line and lay down the law to the trade union functionaries? The problem was posed point-blank in the midst of this strike. We did not evade the issue. The decisive action which we took at that time colored all the future developments of our party in the trade union field and did a great deal to shape the character of our party.

We put Mr. Field on trial in the middle of the strike. Big as he was, we brought charges against him for violating party policy and party discipline, before the New York organization. We had a full discussion—as I recall, it lasted two Sunday afternoons—to give everybody in the League a chance to speak. The great man Field disdained to appear. He had no time. So he was tried in his absence. By this time he had organized a little faction of his own of League members whom he had misled, and who had become unbalanced by the magnitude of the mass movement as against the size of our little political grouping on Sixteenth Street. They came down to the League meetings as Field's spokesmen, full of arrogance and impudence and said: "You can't expel us. You are only expelling yourselves from the trade union mass movement."

Like many trade unionists before them, they felt bigger than the party. They thought they could violate party policy and break party discipline with impunity because the party wouldn't dare to discipline them. That is what really happened in the case of the Socialist Party, and that is one important reason why the Socialist Party has wound up in such a pitiful debacle in the trade union field. All its great trade union leaders, lifted into office with the help of the party, are still there but once in office they never paid any attention to the party or its policy. Labor leaders were above discipline in the Socialist Party. The party never summoned up enough courage to expel any of them, because they thought that thereby they would lose their "contact" with the mass movement. We had no such thoughts. We proceeded resolutely to expel Field and all those who solidarized themselves with him in that situation. We threw them out of our organization in the midst of the strike. Those members of the Field faction who didn't want to break with the party, who agreed to accept the discipline of the party, were given an opportunity to do so and are still members of the party. Some of those whom we expelled remained in political isolation for years. Eventually they drew the lessons of that experience and returned to us.

That was a very drastic action, considering the circumstances of the strike in progress; and by that action we startled the radical labor movement. Nobody outside our organization ever dreamed that a little political grouping like ours, confronted with a member at the head of a movement of 10,000 workers, would dare to expel him at the height of his glory, when his picture was all over the newspapers and he seemed to be a thousand times bigger than our party. There were two reactions at first. One reaction was summed up by people who said: "This means the end of the Trotskyists; they have lost their trade union contacts and forces." They were mistaken. The other reaction, the important one, was summed up by those who said: "The Trotskyists mean business." Those who predicted fatal consequences from this disgrace and debacle of the hotel strike were soon refuted by further developments. Many who saw this little political grouping take a stand like that towards an "untouchable" trade union leader at the head of a big strike acquired a healthy respect for the Trotskyists.

Serious people were attracted to the League, and our whole membership was stiffened up with a new sense of discipline and responsibility toward the organization. Then, right on the heels of the hotel disaster, came the Minneapolis coal yard strike. Before the hotel strike grew cold there was a flare-up in Minneapolis and a strike of the coal yard workers. It was led by this group of Minneapolis Trotskyists who are known to all of you, and conducted as a model of organization and militancy. Party discipline of our comrades in this endeavor—100 percent effective—was in no small degree affected and reinforced by the unfortunate experience we had in New York. Whereas the tendency of the trade union leaders in New York had been to pull away from the party, in Minneapolis the leaders came closer to the party and conducted the strike in the most intimate contact with the party, both locally and nationally.

The coal yard strike came to a smashing victory. The Trotskyist trade union policy, carried out by able and loyal men, was brilliantly vindicated in this battle of the coal yards, and did much to counterbalance the bad impressions of the New York hotel strike.

Following these events, we addressed another letter to the American Workers Party proposing that we send a committee to discuss fusion with them. There were elements in their ranks who by no means wanted to talk to us. We were the last people they wanted to unite with, but there were others in the AWP who were seriously interested in uniting with us to form a bigger party. And, since we didn't keep our approaches a secret, but always printed them in the paper where the membership of the American Workers Party could read about them, the leaders found it judicious to agree to meet us. Formal negotiations for the fusion of the American Workers Party and the Communist League began in the spring of 1934.

As you know, and as it will be related in the subsequent lectures, this approach and these negotiations eventually culminated in a fusion of the AWP and the Communist League, and the launching of a united political party. This was done not without political efforts and not without overcoming difficulties and obstructions. When you stop to think that in the leadership of the American Workers Party at that time were such people as Ludwig Lore, who is one of the chief jingoists in the democratic front today, and that another was such a man as J. B. Salutsky-Hardman, you can readily understand that our task was not easy. Salutsky, the literary lackey of Sidney Hillman and editor of the official organ of the Amalgamated Clothing Workers, well knew who the Trotskyists were and wanted no truck with them. His role in the American Workers Party was precisely to prevent it from developing into anything more than a plaything; to prevent its developing in a revolutionary direction; above all, to keep it free from any contact with the Trotskyists who mean business when they talk about a revolutionary program. In spite of them, the negotiations began.

We were active on other sectors of the political front. On March 5, 1934, was held the historic debate between Lovestone and myself in Irving Plaza. After five years, the representatives of the two warring tendencies in the Communist movement met and crossed swords again. The score was evening up. They had begun by expelling us from the Communist Party as Trotskyists, as "counterrevolutionists." Then, after their own expulsion, they deprecated us as a little sect with no membership and influence, while they had a comparatively big movement to begin with. But, in those five years, we had been gradually cutting them down to our size. We were growing, becoming stronger; they were declining. There was quite a wide interest in our proposal for a new party, and the Lovestone organization was not free from it.

As a result the Lovestoneites found it necessary to accept our invitation for a debate on the subject. "Strike out for a new party and a new International"—that was my program in the debate. Lovestone's program was: "Reform and Unify the Communist International." This was nearly a year after the German debacle. Lovestone still wanted to reform the Communist International, and not only to reform it but to unify it. How? By first having the Lovestoneites taken back in. Then we, the Trotskyists, who had been so unceremoniously kicked out, should be readmitted. The same on an international scale. But by that time we had turned our backs on the bankrupt Comintern. Too much water had passed over the mill, too many mistakes had been made, too many crimes and betrayals had been committed, too much blood had been spilled by the Stalinist International. We called for a new International with a clean banner. I debated from that point of view. That debate was a tremendous success for us.

There was widespread interest and we had a large audience. The *Militant* reports that there were 1,500 people, and I think there must have been very close to that many. It was the biggest audience that we had ever spoken to on a political issue since our expulsion. It was something like old times to be fighting once again before a real audience with an old antagonist, although now the struggle took place on a far different, on a higher plane. In the audience, in addition to the members and adherents of the two organizations represented by the debaters, were many left-wing Socialists and Yipsels, some Stalinists, and a good many independent radicals and members of the American Workers Party. It was a critical occasion. Many people, breaking with the Stalinists, were wavering between the Lovestoneites and the Trotskyists at that time. Our slogan of the new party and the new International was more in accord with reality and necessity, and it gained the sympathy of the great majority of those who were turning away from Stalinism. Our program was so much more compelling, so much more realistic, that we swung practically all the wavering elements to our side. The Lovestoneites could not make much progress with their outmoded program of "unifying" the bankrupt Comintern after the German betrayal.

The success of this debate set the stage for a series of lectures on the program of the Fourth International. Illustrative of the upsurge of our movement was the fact that we had to get a bigger hall for the lectures than we had used before. We had to move to Irving Plaza. The audiences at lectures were three or four times bigger than we had been accustomed to in the five years of our worst isolation.

Trotskyism was putting itself on the political map in those days and was striking hard, full of confidence. The *Militant* of March and April 1934 reports a national tour by Shachtman, extending for the first time all the way to the West Coast. His subject was: "The New Party and the New International." On March 31, 1934, the whole front page of the *Militant* was devoted to a Manifesto of the International Communist League (the world Trotskyist organization) addressed to the revolutionary socialist parties and groups of both hemispheres, calling upon them to rally to the call for a new International against the bankrupt Second and Third Internationals.

Trotskyism on a world scale was on the march. We in the United States were in step. In truth, we were at the head of the procession of our international organization, taking advantage of every opportunity and confidently advancing on all fronts. And when our really great opportunity came in the trade union movement, in the great Minneapolis strikes of May and of July–August 1934, we were fully ready to show what we could do, and we did it.

8

The Great
Minneapolis Strikes

The year 1933, the fourth year of the great American crisis, marked the beginning of the greatest awakening of the American workers and their movement towards union organization on a scale never seen before in American history. That was the background of all the developments within the various political parties, groups, and tendencies. This movement of the American workers took the form of a tremendous drive to break out of their atomized state and to confront the employers with the organized force of unionism.

This great movement developed in waves. The first year of the Roosevelt administration saw the first strike wave of considerable magnitude yield but scanty results in the way of organization because it lacked sufficient drive and adequate leadership. In most cases the efforts of the workers were frustrated by governmental "mediation" on one side and brutal suppression on the other.

The second great wave of strikes and organization movements took place in 1934. This was followed by a still more
powerful movement in 1936–37, of which the high points
were the sit-down strikes in the auto and rubber factories and
the tremendous upsurge of the CIO.

Our lecture tonight deals with the strike wave of 1934 as
represented in the Minneapolis strikes. There, for the first
time, the effective participation of a revolutionary Marxist
group in actual strike organization and direction was demonstrated. The basis of these strike waves and organization
movements was a partial industrial revival.

This has been mentioned before and must be repeated
again and again. In the depths of the depression, when unemployment was so vast, the workers had lost their self-
confidence and feared to make any move under the ominous
threat of unemployment. But with the revival of industry, the
workers gained new confidence in themselves and began a
movement to wrest back some of those things which had
been taken away from them in the depths of the depression.
The ground for the mass activity of the Trotskyist movement
in America was, of course, laid by the action of the masses
themselves. In the spring of 1934 the country had been elec-
trified by the Auto-Lite strike in Toledo in which some new
methods and new techniques of militant struggle had been
introduced. A political, or at least semipolitical grouping,
represented by the Conference for Progressive Labor Action,
which had set up the Provisional Committee for the formation of the American Workers Party, had led this tremen-
dously significant strike in Toledo through the medium of
their Unemployed League. There was shown for the first

time what a great role can be played in the struggles of industrial workers by an unemployed organization led by militant elements. The unemployed organization in Toledo, which had been formed and was under the leadership of the Musteite group, practically took over the leadership of this Auto-Lite strike and raised it to a level of mass picketing and militancy far beyond the bounds ever contemplated by the old-line craft union bureaucrats.

The Minneapolis strikes raised the level even higher. If we measure by all standards, including the decisive criterion of political direction and the maximum exploitation of every possibility inherent in a strike, we must say that the high point of the 1934 wave was the strike of the Minneapolis drivers, helpers, and inside workers in May, and its repetition on a still higher scale in July–August 1934. These strikes put American Trotskyism to a crucial test.

For five years we had been a voice crying in the wilderness, confining ourselves to criticism of the Communist Party, to the elucidation of what appeared to be the most abstract theoretical questions. More than once we had been accused of being nothing but sectarians and hairsplitters. Now, with this opportunity presented in Minneapolis to participate in the mass movement, American Trotskyism was put squarely to the test. It had to demonstrate in action whether it was indeed a movement of good-for-nothing sectarian hairsplitters, or a dynamic political force capable of participating effectively in the mass movement of the workers.

Our comrades in Minneapolis began their work first in the coal yards, and later extended their organizing campaign among the general drivers and helpers. That was not a preconceived plan worked out in the general staff of our movement. The drivers of Minneapolis were not by far the most decisive section of the American proletariat. We began our real activity in the labor movement in those places where the opportunity was open to us. It is not possible to select such occasions arbitrarily according to whim or preference. One must enter into the mass movement where a door is open. A chain of circumstances made Minneapolis the focal point of our first great endeavors and successes in the trade union field. We had in Minneapolis a group of old and tested Communists who were at the same time experienced trade unionists. They were well-known men, rooted in the locality. During the depression they worked together in the coal yards. When the opportunity opened up to organize the yards, they seized it and quickly demonstrated their capacities in the successful three-day strike. Then the extension of the organizing work to the trucking industry generally followed as a matter of course.

Minneapolis wasn't the easiest nut to crack. In fact it was one of the hardest in the country; Minneapolis was a notorious open-shop town. For fifteen or twenty years the Citizens Alliance, an organization of hard-boiled employers, had ruled Minneapolis with an iron hand. Not a single strike of any consequence had been successful in those years. Even the building trades, perhaps the most stable and effective of all the craft unions, were kept on the run in Minneapolis and driven off the most important construction jobs. It was a town of lost strikes, open shops, miserably low wages, murderous hours, and a weak and ineffectual craft union movement.

The coal strike, mentioned in our discussion last week,

was a preliminary skirmish before the great battles to come. The smashing victory of that strike, its militancy, its good organization, and its quick success, stimulated the general organization of the truck drivers and helpers, who up to that time and throughout the years of the depression, had been cruelly exploited and without benefit of organization. True, there was a union in the industry, but it was holding on to the ragged edge of nothing. There was only a small handful of members with some poor kind of contract with one or two transfer companies—no real organization of the mass of truck drivers and helpers in the town.

The success of the coal strike uplifted the workers in the trucking industry. They were tinder for the spark; their wages were too low and their hours too long. Freed for so many years from any union restraints, the profit-hungry bosses had gone too far—the bosses always go too far—and the ground-down workers heard the union message gladly.

Our trade union work in Minneapolis, from beginning to end, was a politically directed campaign. The tactics were guided by the general policy, hammered home persistently by the *Militant*, which called on the revolutionists to enter into the mainstream of the labor movement represented by the American Federation of Labor.

It was our deliberate course to go along the organizational line the masses were traveling, not to set up any artificially constructed unions of our own in contradiction to the impulse of the masses to go into the established trade union movement. For five years we had waged a determined battle against the ultraleft dogma of "Red Unions"; such unions set up artificially by the Communist Party were boycotted by the workers, thus isolating the vanguard elements. The mass of the workers, groping for organization, had a sound instinct. They sensed the need of help. They wanted to be in contact with other organized workers, not off on a sideline with some howling radicals. It is an unfailing phenomenon: The helpless, unorganized mass in industry have an exaggerated respect for established unions, no matter how conservative, how reactionary, these unions may be. The workers fear isolation. In that respect they are wiser than all the sectarians and dogmatists who have tried to prescribe for them the exact detailed form of a perfect union. In Minneapolis, as elsewhere, they had a strong impulse to get in with the official movement, hoping for its assistance in the fight against the bosses who had made life pretty tough for them. Following the general trend of the workers, we also realized that if we were to make the best of our opportunities, we should not put unnecessary difficulties in our path. We should not waste time and energy trying to sell the workers a new scheme of organization they did not want. It was far better to adapt ourselves to their trend, and also to exploit the possibilities of getting assistance from the existing official labor movement.

It wasn't so easy for our people to enter the American Federation of Labor in Minneapolis. They were marked men who had been doubly expelled, doubly damned. In the course of their struggles they had been thrown not only out of the Communist Party, but also the American Federation of Labor. During the "Red Purge" of 1926–1927, at the height of the reaction in the American labor movement, practically all of our comrades who had been active in the trade unions in Minneapolis had been expelled. A year later, to make their isolation complete, they were expelled from the Communist Party.

But the pressure of the workers toward organization was stronger than the decrees of trade union bureaucrats. It had been demonstrated that our comrades had the confidence of the workers and had the plans whereby they could be organized. The pitiful weakness of the union movement in Minneapolis, and the feeling of the members of the craft unions that some new life was needed—all this worked in favor of our people making their way back into the American Federation of Labor through the Teamsters Union. In addition, there was the fortuitous circumstance, a lucky accident, that at the head of Local 574 and the Teamsters Joint Council in Minneapolis was a militant unionist named Bill Brown. He had a sound class instinct, and he was strongly attracted by the idea of getting the cooperation of some people who knew how to organize the workers and give the bosses a real fight. That was a fortunate circumstance for us, but such things do happen now and then. Fortune favors the godly. If you live right and conduct yourself properly, you get a lucky break now and then. And when an accident comes your way—a good one—you should grab it and make the most of it.

We certainly made the most of this accident, the circumstance that the President of Teamsters Local 574 was that wonderful character, Bill Brown, who held open the door of the union to the "new men" who knew how to organize the workers and lead them in battle. But our comrades were new members in this union. They weren't in there long enough to be officers; they were just members when the fight began to pop. So not a single one of our people—that is, members of the Trotskyist group—was an official of the union during the three strikes. But they organized and led the strikes just the same. They were constituted as an "Organizing Committee," a sort of extralegal body set up for the purpose of directing the organization campaign and leading the strikes.

The organizing campaign and the strikes were carried on virtually over the head of the official leadership of the union. The only one of the regular officials who really participated in a direct way in the actual leadership of the strikes was Bill Brown, along with the Organizing Committee. This Organizing Committee had one merit which was demonstrated in the beginning—other merits were revealed later—they knew how to organize workers. This is one thing the ossified labor skates in Minneapolis did not know and apparently could not learn. They know how to disorganize them. This breed is the same everywhere. They know how, sometimes, to let the workers into the unions when they break the doors down. But to go out and really organize the workers, stir them up and inspire them with faith and confidence—the traditional craft union bureaucrat cannot do that. That is not his field, his function. It is not even his ambition.

The Trotskyist Organizing Committee organized the workers in the trucking industry and then proceeded to line up the rest of the labor movement to support these workers. They did not lead them into an isolated action. They began working through the Central Labor Union, by conferences with the labor skates as well as by pressure from below, to put the whole labor movement in Minneapolis on record in support of these newly organized truck drivers; worked tirelessly to involve the officials of the Central Labor Union in the campaign, to have resolutions passed endorsing their demands, to make them take official responsibility. When the time came for action, the labor movement of Minneapolis, as represented by the official unions of the American Federation of Labor, found themselves in advance in a position of having endorsed the demands and being logically bound to support the strike.

In May the general strike burst into flames. The bosses, grown complacent from long unchallenged domination, were greatly surprised. The lesson of the coal strike had not yet convinced them that "something new" had been added to the trade union movement in Minneapolis. They still thought they could nip this thing in the bud. They tried stalling and maneuvering, and bogging our people down in the negotiations with the Labor Board where so many new unions had been cut to pieces. Right in the middle of the business, when they thought they had the union tangled in this web of negotiations for indefinite delay, our people just cut through it at one stroke. They hit them on the nose with a general strike. The trucks were tied up and the "negotiations" were taken to the streets.

This May general strike shook Minneapolis as it had never been shaken before. It shook the whole country, because this was no tame strike. This was a strike that began with such a wallop that the whole country heard about it, and about the role of the Trotskyists in its leadership—the bosses advertised that widely, and also hysterically. Then we saw again the same response among the observing radical workers that had followed our resolute action in the case of Field and the New York hotel strike. When they saw the performances in the May strike in Minneapolis, that same sentiment was expressed again: "These Trotskyists mean business. When they undertake anything, they go through with it." The jokes about the Trotskyist "sectarians" began to turn sour.

There was no essential difference, in fact I don't think there was any serious difference at all between the strikers in Minneapolis and the workers involved in a hundred other strikes throughout the land in that period. Nearly all the strikes were fought with the greatest militancy by the workers. The difference was in the leadership and the policy. In practically all the other strikes the militancy of the rank-and-file workers was restrained from the top. The leaders were overawed by the government, the newspapers, the clergy, and one thing or another. They tried to shift the conflict from the streets and the picket lines to the conference chambers. In Minneapolis the militancy of the rank and file was not restrained but organized and directed from the top.

All modern strikes require political direction. The strikes of that period brought the government, its agencies, and its institutions into the very center of every situation. A strike leader without some conception of a political line was very much out of date already by 1934. The old-fashioned trade union movement, which used to deal with the bosses without governmental interference, belongs in the museum. The modern labor movement must be politically directed because it is confronted by the government at every turn. Our people were prepared for that since they were political people, inspired by political conceptions. The policy of the class struggle guided our comrades; they couldn't be deceived and outmaneuvered, as so many strike leaders of that period were, by this mechanism of sabotage and destruction known as the National Labor Board and all its auxiliary setups. They put no reliance whatever in Roosevelt's Labor Board; they weren't fooled by any idea that Roosevelt, the liberal "friend of labor" president, was going to help the truck drivers in Minneapolis win a few cents more an hour. They weren't deluded even by the fact that there was at that time in Minnesota a Farmer-Labor Governor, presumed to be on the side of the workers.

Our people didn't believe in anybody or anything but the policy of the class struggle and the ability of the workers to prevail by their mass strength and solidarity. Consequently, they expected from the start that the union would have to fight for its right to exist; that the bosses would not yield any recognition to the union, would not yield any increase of wages or reduction of the scandalous hours without some pressure being brought to bear. Therefore they prepared everything from the point of view of class war. They knew that power, not diplomacy, would decide the issue. Bluffs don't work in fundamental things, only in incidental ones. In such things as the conflict of class interests one must be prepared to fight.

Proceeding from these general concepts, the Minneapolis Trotskyists, in the course of organizing the workers, planned a battle strategy. Something unique was seen in Minneapolis for the first time. That is, a strike that was thoroughly organized beforehand, a strike prepared with the meticulous detail which they used to attribute to the German army—down to the last button sewn on the uniform of the last individual soldier. When the hour of the deadline came, and the bosses thought they could still maneuver and bluff, our people were setting up a fortress for action. This was noted and reported by the *Minneapolis Tribune,* the mouthpiece of the bosses, only at the last moment, a day before the strike. The paper said: "If the preparations made by their union for handling it are any indication, the strike of truck drivers in Minneapolis is going to be a far-reaching affair. . . . Even before the official start of the strike at 11:30 P.M. Tuesday, the 'General Headquarters' organization set up at 1900 Chicago Avenue was operating with all the precision of a military organization."

Our people had a commissary all fixed up. They didn't wait until the strikers were hungry. They had it organized beforehand in preparation for the strike. They set up an emergency hospital in a garage—the strike headquarters was in a garage—with their own doctor and their own nurses before the strike even broke. Why? Because they knew that the bosses, their cops, and thugs and deputies would try in this case, as in every other, to beat the strike down. They were prepared to take care of their own people and not let them be sent, if injured, to a city hospital and then placed under arrest and put out of commission. When a fellow worker was injured on the picket line they brought him to their own headquarters and doctored him up there.

They took a leaf from the Progressive Miners of America and organized a Women's Auxiliary to help make trouble for the bosses. And I tell you, the women made lots of trouble, running around protesting and scandalizing the bosses and the city authorities, which is one of the most important political weapons. The strike leadership organized picketing on a mass basis. This business of appointing or hiring a few people, one or two, to watch and count and report how many scabs have been hired, doesn't work in a real struggle. They sent a squad to keep any scabs from going in. I mentioned that they had their strike headquarters in a garage. This was because the picketing was put on wheels. They not only organized the pickets, they mobilized a fleet of picketing cars. Every striking worker, sympathizer, and trade unionist in town was called upon to donate the use of his car or truck. The strike committee thus had a whole fleet at its disposal. Flying squads of pickets on wheels were stationed at strategic points throughout the town.

Whenever a report came in of a truck being operated or any attempt to move trucks, the "dispatcher" called through the loudspeaker in the garage for as many cars, loaded with pickets, as were needed to go out there and give the operators of the scab trucks an argument.

The "dispatcher" in the May strike was a young man named Farrell Dobbs. He came out of a coal yard in Minneapolis into the union and the strike, and then into the party. He first became known to us as a dispatcher who shot out the squad cars and the pickets. At first the pickets went out barehanded, but they came back with broken heads and injuries of various kinds. Then they equipped themselves with shillalahs for the next trips. A shillalah, as any Irishman can tell you, is a blackthorn stick you lean on in case you suddenly go lame. Of course, it is handy for other purposes too. The attempt of the bosses and the police to crush the strike by force culminated in the famous "Battle of the Market." Several thousand special deputies in addition to the whole police force were mobilized to make one supreme effort to open up a strategic part of the town, the wholesale market, for the operation of trucks.

Those deputies, recruited from the petty-bourgeois and the employing classes of the town, and the professions, came to the market in a sort of gala holiday spirit. They were going to have fun down there just beating up strikers. One of the special deputies wore his polo hat. He was going to have one hell of a time down there, knocking strikers' heads around like polo balls. The ill-advised sportsman was mistaken; it was no polo game this time. He and the whole mob of deputies and cops ran into a mass of determined, organized pickets of the union supplemented by sympathetic unionists from other trades and by members of the unemployed organizations. The attempt to drive the pickets from the market place ended in failure. The counterattack of the workers put them to flight. The battle has gone down in Minneapolis history as "The Battle of Deputies Run." There were two casualties, and they were both on the other side. That was one of the features of the strike that lifted Minneapolis high in the estimation of the workers everywhere. In strike after strike of those days the same story had been monotonously repeated in the press: Two strikers killed; four strikers shot; twenty strikers arrested, etc. Here was a strike where it wasn't all one-sided. There was one universal burst of applause, from one end of the labor movement to the other, for the militancy and resoluteness of the Minneapolis fighters. They had reversed the trend of things, and worker militants everywhere praised their name.

As the organizing campaign developed, our National Committee in New York was informed of everything and collaborated as much as possible by mail. But when the strike broke out we were fully conscious that this was the time for us to do more, to do all that we possibly could to help. I was sent to Minneapolis by airplane to assist the comrades, especially in the negotiations for a settlement. This was the time, you will recall, when we were still so poor that we couldn't afford a telephone in the office. We had absolutely no financial basis for such extravagant expenses as airplane fares. But the consciousness of our movement was expressed very graphically in the fact that in the moment of necessity we found the means to pay for an airplane trip to save a few hours time. This action, taken at an expense far beyond what our budget could normally carry, was designed to give the local comrades involved in the fight the benefit of all the advice and assistance we could offer, and to which, as members of the League, they were entitled. But there was another aspect, just as important. In sending a representative of the NC to Minneapolis our League meant to take responsibility for what they were doing. If things went wrong—and there is always the possibility that things will go wrong in a strike—we meant to take responsibility for it and not leave the local comrades to hold the sack. That has always been our procedure. When any section of our movement is involved in action, the local comrades are not left to their own resources. The national leadership must help and in the final analysis take the responsibility.

The May strike lasted only six days and a quick settlement was reached. The bosses were swept off their feet, the whole country was clamoring to get the thing settled. There was pressure from Washington and from Governor Olson. The settlement was severely attacked by the Stalinist press, which was very radical at that time, because it was not a sweeping victory, but a compromise; a partial victory that gave recognition to the union. We took full responsibility for the settlement our comrades had made, and took up the challenge of the Stalinists. Our press simply chased the Stalinists off the field in this controversy. We defended the settlement of the Minneapolis strike and frustrated their campaign to discredit it and thereby to discredit our work in the unions. The radical labor movement was given a complete picture of this strike. We published a special issue of the *Militant* which described in detail all the different aspects of the strike and the preparations leading up to it. This issue was written almost entirely by the leading comrades in the strike.

The main point around which we wove the explanation of the compromise settlement was: What are the aims of a new union in this period? We pointed out that the American working class is still unorganized, atomized. Only a part of the skilled workers are organized into craft unions, and these do not represent the great mass of American labor. The American workers are an unorganized mass and their first impulse and need is to take the first elementary step before they can do anything else; that is, to form a union and compel the bosses to recognize that union. Thus we formulated the problem.

We maintained—and I think with full justice—that a group of workers, who in their first battle gained the recognition of their union, and on that basis could build and strengthen their position, had accomplished the objectives of the occasion and should not overtax their strength and run the danger of demoralization and defeat. The settlement proved to be correct because it was enough to build on. The union remained stable. It was not a flash in the pan. The union began to forge ahead, began to recruit new members and educate a cadre of new leaders. As the weeks went by it became clear to the bosses that their scheme to trick the truck drivers out of the fruits of their struggle was not working out so well.

Then the bosses came to the conclusion that they had made a mistake; that they should have fought longer and broken the union, so as to teach the workers of Minneapolis the lesson that unions could not exist there; that Minneapolis was an open-shop slave town and should remain that way. Somebody gave them some bad advice. The Citizens Alliance, the general organization of the employers and labor haters, kept needling and inciting the bosses in the trucking industry to break the agreement, to chisel and stall on the concessions they had agreed to give, and whittle away the gains that had been made by the workers.

The leadership of the union understood the situation. The bosses had not been sufficiently convinced by the first test of strength with the union and needed another demonstration. They began to prepare another strike. Again the workers in the industry were prepared for action. Again the whole labor movement of Minneapolis was mobilized to support them, this time in the most impressive, the most dramatic fashion. The campaign for the adoption of resolutions in the Central Labor Union and its affiliated unions in support of Local 574 was pointed toward a great parade of organized labor. The members of the various unions turned out in force and marched in solid ranks to a huge mass meeting in the City Auditorium, to back up the truck drivers and pledge them support in the impending struggle. It was an imposing demonstration of labor solidarity and of the new militancy which had taken hold of the workers.

The bosses remained obdurate. They raised the "Red Scare" in a big way, denouncing the "Trotsky Communists" in screaming advertisements in the newspapers. On the union side, preparations went ahead as in the May strike, but on an even more highly organized plane. When it became clear that another strike could not be avoided without sacrificing the union, our National Committee decided that the whole Communist League of America would have to go all out in its support. We knew that the real test was here, that we dared not dabble with the issue. We sensed that here was a battle that could make or break us for years to come; if we gave half-hearted support, or withheld this or that aid which we could give, it might tip the balance between victory and defeat. We knew that we had plenty to give to our Minneapolis comrades.

In our movement we never played with the absurd idea that only those directly connected with a union are capable of giving assistance. Modern strikes need political direction more than anything else. If our party, our League as we called it then, deserved to exist it would have come to the aid of the local comrades. As is always the case with trade union leaders, especially in strike times, they were under the weight and stress of a thousand pressing details. A political party, on the other hand, rises above the details and generalizes from the main issues. A trade union leader who rejects the idea of political advice in the struggle against the bosses and their government, with its cunning devices, traps, and methods of exerting pressure, is deaf, dumb, and blind. Our Minneapolis comrades were not of this type. They turned to us for help.

We sent quite a few forces into the situation. I went there about two weeks before the outbreak of the second strike.

After I had been there a few days, we agreed to call in more aid—a whole staff, in fact. Two additional people were brought from New York for journalistic work: Shachtman and Herbert Solow, an experienced and talented journalist who was a sort of sympathizer of our movement at that time. Borrowing an idea from the Toledo Auto-Lite strike, we called in another comrade whose specific task was to organize the unemployed to assist the strike. That was Hugo Oehler who was a very capable mass worker and trade unionist. His work in Minneapolis was the last bit of good he ever did for us. Soon afterwards he caught the sectarian sickness. But up to then Oehler was all right, and he contributed something to the strike. On top of this, we imported a general attorney for the union, Albert Goldman. We knew from previous experience that a lawyer is very important in a strike, if you can get a good one. It is very important to have your own "mouthpiece" and legal front who gives you honest advice and protects your legal interests. There are all kinds of ups and downs in a hard-fought strike. Sometimes things get too hot for the "disreputable" strike leaders. Then you can always push a lawyer forward and he says calmly: "Let us reason together and see what the law says." Very handy, especially when you have such a brilliant lawyer and loyal man as Al Goldman.

We gave all we could to the strike from our center in New York, on the same principle as I mentioned before, which should serve as the guiding line for every kind of activity of a serious party, or a serious person for that matter. This is the principle: If you are going to do anything, for heaven's sake do it properly, do it right. Never dabble, never do anything halfway. Woe to the lukewarm! "Because thou art lukewarm, and neither cold nor hot, I will spew thee out of my mouth."

The strike began July 16, 1934, and lasted five weeks. I think I can say without the slightest exaggeration, without fear of any contradiction, that the July–August strike of the Minneapolis truck drivers and helpers has entered into the annals of the history of the American labor movement as one of its greatest, most heroic, and best organized struggles. Moreover: the strike and the union forged in its fires are identified forever in the labor movement, not only here but all over the world, with Trotskyism in action in the mass movement of the workers. Trotskyism made a number of specific contributions to this strike which made all the difference between the Minneapolis strike and a hundred others of the period, some of which involved more workers in more socially important localities and industries. Trotskyism made the contribution of organization and preparations down to the last detail. That is something new, that is something specifically Trotskyist. Second, Trotskyism introduced into all the plans and preparations of the union and the strike, from beginning to end, the class line of militancy; not as a subjective reaction—that is seen in every strike—but as a deliberate policy based on the theory of the class struggle, that you can't win anything from the bosses unless you have the will to fight for it and the strength to take it.

The third contribution of Trotskyism to the Minneapolis strike—the most interesting and perhaps the most decisive— was that we met the government mediators on their own ground. I tell you, one of the most pathetic things observable in that period was to see how in one strike after another the workers were outmaneuvered and cut to pieces, and their strike broken by the "friends of labor" in the guise of federal mediators.

These slick rascals would come in, take advantage of the ignorance and inexperience and political inadequacy of local leaders, and assure them that they were there as friends. Their assignment was to "settle the trouble" by extorting concessions from the weaker side. Inexperienced and politically unschooled strike leaders were their prey. They had a routine, a formula to catch the unwary. "I am not asking you to give any concession to the bosses, but give me a concession so that I can help you." Then, after something had been given away through gullibility: "I tried to get a corresponding concession from the bosses but they refused. I think you had better make more concessions: public sentiment is turning against you." And then pressure and threats: "Roosevelt will issue a statement." Or, "We will feel obligated to publish something in the papers against you if you aren't more reasonable and responsible." Then get the poor greenhorns into conference rooms, keep them there hours and hours on end, and terrorize them. This was the common routine these cynical scoundrels employed.

They came into Minneapolis all greased up for another standard performance. We were sitting there waiting for them. We said, "Come on. You want to negotiate, do you? All right. That is fine." Of course our comrades put it in the more diplomatic language of the negotiations "protocol," but that was the gist of our attitude. Well, they never negotiated two cents out of the Trotskyist leaders of Local 574. They got a dose of negotiations and diplomacy which they are still gagging from.

We wore out three of them before the strike was finally settled.

A favorite trick of the confidence men known as federal mediators in those days was to assemble green strike leaders in a room, play upon their vanity, and induce them to commit themselves to some kind of compromise which they were not authorized to make. The federal mediators would convince the strike leaders that they were "big shots" who must take a "responsible" attitude. The mediators knew that concessions yielded by leaders in negotiations can very rarely be recalled. No matter how much the workers may oppose it, the fact that the leaders have already committed themselves in public compromises the position of the union and creates demoralization in the ranks.

This routine cut many a strike to pieces in that period. It didn't work in Minneapolis. Our people weren't "big shots" in the negotiations at all. They made it clear that their authority was extremely limited, that they were in fact the more moderate and reasonable wing of the union, and that if they took a step out of line they would be replaced on the negotiations committee by other types. This was quite a poser for the strike-butchers who had come to Minneapolis with their knives out for unsuspecting sheep. Every once in a while Grant Dunne would be added to the Committee. He would just sit in a corner saying nothing, but scowling every time there was any talk of concessions. The strike was a hard and bitter fight but we had plenty of fun in planning the sessions of the union negotiations committee with the mediators. We despised them and all their wily artifices and tricks, and their hypocritical pretenses of good fellowship and friendship for the strikers. They were nothing but the agents of the gov-

ernment in Washington, which in turn is the agent of the
employing class as a whole. That was perfectly clear to a
Marxist, and we took it as rather an insult for them to assume
that we could be taken in by the methods they employed with
novices. They tried it though. Apparently they didn't know
any other methods. But they didn't make an inch of headway
until they got down to cases, put pressure on the bosses, and
made concessions to the union. The collective political experience of our movement was very useful in dealing with the
federal mediators. Unlike stupid sectarians, we didn't ignore
them. Sometimes we would initiate discussions. But we didn't
let them use us, and we didn't trust them for one moment.
Our general strategy in the strike was to fight it out, not give
anything away to anybody, to hold on and fight it out. That
was Trotskyist contribution number four. It may appear to
be a very simple and obvious prescription, but that is not the
case. It was not obvious to the great majority of strike leaders
of the time.

The fifth and crowning contribution that Trotskyism made
to the Minneapolis strike was the publication of the daily strike
newspaper, the *Daily Organizer*. For the first time in the history of the American labor movement, strikers were not left
dependent on the capitalist press, were not befuddled and terrorized by it, did not see public sentiment disoriented by the
capitalist monopoly of the press. The Minneapolis strikers
published their own daily newspaper. This was done not by a
half million coal miners, a hundred thousand auto or steel
workers, but by a single local union of 5,000 truck drivers, a
new union in Minneapolis which had Trotskyist leadership.
This leadership understood that publicity and propaganda are

highly important, and that is something very few trade union leaders know. It is almost impossible to convey the tremendous effect of this daily newspaper. It wasn't a big one—just a two-page tabloid. But it completely counteracted the capitalist press. After a day or two we didn't care what the daily papers of the bosses said. They printed all kinds of things but it didn't make that much difference in the ranks of the strikers. They had their own paper and took its reports as gospel. The *Daily Organizer* covered the town like a blanket. Strikers at the headquarters all used to get it straight from the press. The Women's Auxiliary sold it in every tavern in town that had working-class customers. In many saloons in working-class neighborhoods they would leave a bundle of papers on the bar with a slotted collection can beside them for contributions. Many a dollar was collected that way and carefully watched by the friendly bartenders.

Union men used to come from the shops and railroad yards every night to get bundles of the *Organizer* for distribution among the men on their shifts. The power of that little paper, its hold on the workers, is indescribable. They believed the *Organizer* and no other paper. Occasionally a story would appear in the capitalist press about some new development in the strike. The workers wouldn't believe it. They would wait for the *Organizer* to see what the truth was. Press distortions of strike incidents and outright fabrications—which have destroyed the morale of many a strike—didn't work in Minneapolis. More than once, among a crowd that always surged around strike headquarters when the latest issue of the *Organizer* was delivered, one could hear remarks such as this: "You see what the *Organizer* says. I told you that story in the *Tribune* was a damned lie." That was the general sentiment of the workers toward the voice of labor in the strike, the *Daily Organizer.*

This powerful instrument didn't cost the union a penny. On the contrary, the *Daily Organizer* made a profit from the first day and carried the strike through when there was no money in the treasury. The profits of the *Organizer* paid the daily expenses of the commissary. The paper was distributed free to anyone who wanted it, but nearly every sympathetic worker gave from a nickel to a dollar for a copy. The morale of the strikers was kept up by it, but above all, the role of the *Organizer* was that of an educator. Every day the paper had the news of the strike, some jokes about the bosses, some information about what went on in the labor movement. There was even a daily cartoon drawn by a local comrade. Then there would be an editorial drawing the lessons of the past 24 hours, day after day, and pointing the way ahead. "This is what has happened. This is what is coming next. This is our position." The striking workers were armed and prepared in advance for every move of the mediators or Governor Olson. We would be poor Marxists if we couldn't see 24 hours in advance. We called the turn so many times that the strikers began to take our forecasts as news and to rely upon them as such. The *Daily Organizer* was the greatest of all the weapons in the arsenal of the Minneapolis strike. I can say without any qualification that of all the contributions we made, the most decisive, the one that tipped the scale to victory, was the publication of the daily paper. Without the *Organizer* the strike would not have been won.

All these contributions which I have mentioned were integrated and carried out in the greatest harmony between the staff sent by the National Committee and the local comrades in the leadership of the strike. The lessons of the hotel strike, the lamentable experiences with swelled-headed and disloyal people, were fully assimilated in Minneapolis. There was the closest collaboration from beginning to end.

The strike presented Floyd Olson, Farmer-Labor governor, with a hard nut to crack. We understood the contradictions he was in. He was, on the one hand, supposedly a representative of the workers; on the other hand, he was governor of a bourgeois state, afraid of public opinion and afraid of the employers. He was caught in a squeeze between his obligation to do something, or appear to do something, for the workers and his fear of letting the strike get out of bounds. Our policy was to exploit these contradictions, to demand things of him because he was labor's governor, to take everything we could get and holler every day for more. On the other hand, we criticized and attacked him for every false move and never made the slightest concession to the theory that the strikers should rely on his advice.

Floyd Olson was undoubtedly the leader of the official labor movement in Minnesota, but we did not recognize his leadership. The labor bureaucrats in Minneapolis were under his leadership, just as the present bureaucrats of the CIO and AFL are under the leadership of Roosevelt. Roosevelt is the boss, and Floyd Olson was the boss of the whole labor movement in Minneapolis except Local 574. But he wasn't our boss; we didn't hesitate to attack him in the most ruthless manner. Under these attacks he would flinch a little bit and make a concession or two which the strike leadership would grab on the fly. We had no sentiment for him at all. The local labor bureaucrats were weeping and wailing in fear that his political career would be ruined. We didn't care. That was his affair, not ours. What we wanted was more concessions from him, and we hollered for them day after day. The labor skates were scared to death. "Don't do this; don't push him into this calamity; remember the difficulties of his position." We paid them no mind and went our own way. Pushed and pounded from both sides, afraid to help the strikers and afraid not to, Floyd Olson declared martial law. This is really one of the most fantastic things that ever happened in the history of American labor. A Farmer-Labor governor pro-claimed martial law and stopped the trucks from running. That was supposed to be one on the side of labor. But then he allowed the trucks to run again under special permits. That was one for the bosses. Naturally the pickets undertook to stop the trucks, permit or no permit. Then, a few days later, the Farmer-Labor governor's militia raided the head-quarters of the strike and arrested the leaders.

I am jumping a little ahead of the story. Upon the declara-tion of martial law, the first casualties, the first military prison-ers of Olson and his militia became myself and Max Shacht-man. I don't know how they found out we were there, as we were not very conspicuous in public. But Shachtman was wearing a great big ten-gallon cowboy hat—where he got it, or why in God's name he wore it, I never knew—and that made him conspicuous. I suppose that is how they located us. One evening Shachtman and I came away from the strike headquar-ters, walked downtown, and, being in need of diversion, looked around to see what shows were playing. Toward the lower end of Hennepin Avenue we were confronted with an alternative: in one place a burlesque show, next door a movie. Which to go to? Well, naturally, I said a movie. A couple of detectives, who had been on our trail, followed us in and arrested us there. What a narrow escape from being arrested in a burlesque show. What a scandal it would have been. I would never have lived it down, I am sure.

They kept us in jail for about 48 hours; then took us into court. I never saw so many bayonets in one place in my life as there were in and around the courtroom. All these young, upstate "apple-knockers" and white collar squirts in the militia seemed to be quite eager to get a little bayonet practice. Some of our friends were in the court watching the proceedings. Finally the judge turned us over to the military, and Shachtman and I were marched down the corridors and down the stairs between two rows of bayonet-clutching militiamen. As they were marching us out of the courthouse, we heard a shout overhead. Bill Brown and Mick Dunne were sitting comfortably up in a third-floor window watching the procession, laughing and waving at us. "Look out for those bayonets," Bill shouted. Anything for a laugh in Minneapolis. When a few days later Bill and Mick were arrested by the militia, they took it just as lightheartedly.

They threw us into the guardhouse and kept two or three of these nervous rookies watching us with their hands on their bayonets all the time. Albert Goldman came down, threatening legal action. The militia chiefs seemed to be anxious to get us off their hands and avoid any trouble with this lawyer from Chicago. On our side, we did not care to make a test case of our detention. We wanted, above all, to get out so that we could be of some help to the steering committee of the union. We decided to accept the offer they made. They said, if you agree to leave town you can go. So we said, all right: We moved across the river to St. Paul. There every night we had meetings of the steering committee as long as any of the leading comrades were out of jail. The steering committee of the strike, sometimes with Bill Brown, sometimes without him, would get into a car, drive over there, talk over the day's experiences, and plan the next day. There was never a serious move made during the whole strike that was not planned and prepared for in advance.

Then came the raid on the strike headquarters. One morning the troops of the militia surrounded the headquarters at 4:00 A.M. and arrested hundreds of pickets and all of the strike leaders they could lay their hands on. They arrested Mick Dunne, Vincent Dunne, Bill Brown. They "missed" some of the leaders in their hurry. Farrell Dobbs, Grant Dunne, and some others slipped through their fingers. These simply set up another committee, and substitute headquarters in several friendly garages; the picketing, organized underground, went on with great vigor. The fight continued and the mediators continued their finagling.

A man named Dunnigan was the first one sent into the situation. He was an impressive looking fellow who wore pince-nez glasses, suspended on a black ribbon, and smoked expensive cigars, but he didn't know very much. After trying vainly for a while to push the strike leaders around, he worked out a proposal for a compromise providing for substantial wage increases for the workers without granting their full demands. In the meantime, one of Washington's ace negotiators, a Catholic priest named Father Haas, was sent in. He associated himself with Dunnigan's proposal and it became known as the "Haas-Dunnigan Plan." The strikers immediately accepted it. The bosses stalled, and were put in the position of opposing a government proposal, but that didn't seem to bother them. The strikers exploited the situation effectively in mobilizing public opinion in their favor. Then, after a few weeks had gone by, Father Haas found out that he could not put any pressure on the bosses, so he decided to put the pressure on the strikers. He put the issue baldly to the union's negotiating committee: "The bosses won't give in so you must give in. The strike must be settled; Washington insists."

The strike leaders answered: "No, you can't do that. A bargain's a bargain. We accepted the Haas-Dunnigan plan. We are fighting for your plan. Your honor is involved here." Whereupon Father Haas said—this is another threat they always hold over strike leaders: "We will appeal to the rank and file of the union in the name of the United States government." That threat usually scares the pants off inexperienced labor leaders.

But the Minneapolis strike leaders were not scared. They said: "All right, come on." So they arranged a meeting for him. Oh, he got a meeting that he never bargained for. That meeting, like every other important action taken in the strike, was planned and prepared in advance. Father Haas had no sooner ended his speech than the storm broke over his head. One by one, the rank-and-file strikers got up and showed how well they had memorized the speeches that had been outlined in caucus. They almost drove him out of the meeting. They made him physically sick. He threw up his hands and left town. The strikers voted unanimously to condemn his treacherous attempt to wreck their strike and thereby their union.

Dunnigan was finished, Father Haas was finished. Then they sent in a third federal mediator. He had obviously learned from the sad experiences of the others not to try any shenanigans. Mr. Donaghue, I think that was his name, got right down to business and in a few days worked out a settlement which was a substantial victory for the union.

The name of a new galaxy of labor leaders flashed in the northwestern sky: William S. Brown; the Dunne brothers— Vincent, Miles, and Grant; Carl Skoglund; Farrell Dobbs; Kelly Postal; Harry DeBoer; Ray Rainbolt; George Frosig.

The great strike came to an end after five weeks of bitter struggle during which there hadn't been an hour free from tension and danger. Two workers were killed in that strike, scores injured, shot, beaten on the picket line in the battle to keep the trucks from running without union drivers. A great deal of hardship, a great deal of pressure of every kind was endured, but the union finally came out victorious, firmly established, built on solid rock as a result of those fights. We thought, and we wrote later, that it was a glorious vindication of Trotskyism in the mass movement.

Minneapolis was the highest point of the second strike wave under the NRA. The second wave surged higher than the first, as the third wave was destined to transcend the second and reach the peak of the CIO sit-down strikes. The giant of the American proletariat was beginning to feel its power in those years, was beginning to show what tremendous potentialities, what resources of strength, ingenuity, and courage reside in the American working class.

In July of that year, 1934, I wrote an article about these strikes and the strike waves for the first issue of our magazine, the *New International*. I said:

"The second strike wave under the NRA rises higher than the first and marks a big forward stride of the American working class. The enormous potentialities of future developments are clearly written in this advance. . . .

"In these great struggles the American workers in all parts of the country are displaying the unrestrained militancy of a class that is just beginning to awaken. This is a new generation of a class that has not been defeated. On the contrary, it is only now beginning to find itself and to feel its strength, and in these first tentative conflicts the proletarian giant gives a glorious promise for the future. The present generation remains true to the tradition of American labor; it is boldly aggressive and violent from the start. The American worker is no Quaker. Further developments of the class struggle will bring plenty of fighting in the U.S.A."

The third wave, culminating in the sit-down strikes, confirmed that prediction and gave us ground to look forward with the greatest optimism to still greater, more grandiose demonstrations of the power and militancy of the American workers. In Minneapolis we saw the native militancy of the workers fused with a politically conscious leadership. Minneapolis showed how great can be the role of such leadership. It gave great promise for the party founded on correct political principles and fused and united with the mass of American workers. In that combination one can see the power that will conquer the whole world.

* * *

During that strike, tied up as we were from day to day with innumerable details and under the constant pressure of daily events, we didn't forget the political side of the movement. In the steering committee, on occasion, we discussed not only the day's immediate problem of the strike; as best we could, we kept alive and alert to what was going on in the world outside Minneapolis. At that time Trotsky was elaborating one of his boldest tactical moves. He proposed that the Trotskyists of France should make their way into the revivified left-wing section of the French Social Democracy and work there as a Bolshevik faction. This was the famous "French turn." We discussed this proposal in the heat of the strike at Minneapolis. We translated it for America as an injunction to hasten the amalgamation with the American Workers Party. The AWP was obviously the political group closest to us and moving toward the left. We decided to recommend to the national leadership of our League that it take decisive steps to speed up the unification and to accomplish it before the end of the year. The Musteites had led a great strike in Toledo. The Trotskyists had distinguished themselves in Minneapolis. Toledo and Minneapolis had become linked as twin symbols of the two highest points of proletarian militancy and conscious leadership. These two strikes tended to bring the militants in each battle closer together; to make them more sympathetic to each other, more desirous of close collaboration. It was obvious, by all the circumstances, that it was time to give the signal for the unification of these two forces. We returned from Minneapolis with this goal in view and moved decisively to the fusion of the Trotskyists and the American Workers Party, to the launching of a new party—the American section of the Fourth International.

9

The Fusion with
the Musteites

At the end of the last lecture we left Minneapolis and were on our way back to New York, looking for new worlds to conquer. The great strike wave of 1934, the second under the Roosevelt administration, had not yet spent its force. In the numbers of workers involved, but in no other respect, it reached its crest in September with the general strike of the textile workers. 750,000 cotton mill workers went on strike September 1, 1934. The *Militant* reported the strike with full editorial suggestions as to what the strikers should do in order to make the most of their situation. Riding on the wave of the workers mass movement, our political organization was moving forward. Our march of progress, however, at that time was interrupted for a moment by a slight obstacle, namely financial embarrassment. The same issue of the *Militant* which reported the strike of 750,000 textile workers, with a few articles on the aftermath of the Minneapolis strike, carried the following notice on the front page. I copied it to-day so as to give you the flavor of the situation as it appeared to us at that moment:

"We are in a crisis. . . . Our activities in Minneapolis have drained our resources to the very bottom. . . . Here are the facts: It is only a matter of days when the marshal will appear at our shop and move our printing equipment into the street. A dispossess notice has already been served. And even if the landlord should be merciful for a few days, then we probably will be forced to stop operating anyway. An electric bill is long overdue; the lights and power will be turned off. The gas company, the paper company, and a host of other bill collectors are on our necks demanding payments. Send con-tributions—Act Now!"

Thus equipped and accoutred, we addressed the American Workers Party with another proposal for unity. We called on them to unite with us to form a new party to con-quer the world. We reopened negotiations with a letter of September 7, requesting the AWP to take a positive stand in favor of unification and appoint a committee to discuss with us the program and the organization details. This time we re-ceived a prompt reply from the American Workers Party. It was a two-sided letter. On the one hand, under the influence of the rank-and-file activists at the Pittsburgh conference, who had spoken rather emphatically in favor of unity, the letter of the AWP, signed by Muste, the National Secretary, was conciliatory in tone and spoke in favor of unity if we could come to an agreement. This expressed the sentiments of the honest, active elements, the field workers of the AWP. I believe Muste himself was of the same disposition at that time. The same letter, however, had another side containing a provocative reference to the Soviet Union. This represented the influence of Salutsky and Budenz, who were bitterly hostile to unity with the Trotskyists.

The AWP was not a homogeneous organization. Its progressive character was determined by two factors: (1) through its energetic activities in the mass movement, in the trade unions, and in the unemployed field, it had attracted some rank-and-file militant workers who were in dead earnest about fighting capitalism; (2) the general direction in which the American Workers Party was moving at the time was clearly to the left, toward a revolutionary position. These two factors determined the progressive character of the Muste movement as a whole and attracted us toward it. At the same time, as I have said, we realized that it was not a homogeneous organization. In fact, it could be properly described as a political menagerie which had within it every type of political species. Put another way, the membership of the AWP included everything from proletarian revolutionists to reactionary scoundrels and fakers.

The outstanding personality in the American Workers Party was A. J. Muste, a remarkable man who was always extremely interesting to me and for whom I always had the most friendly feelings. He was an able and energetic man, obviously sincere and devoted to the cause, to his work. His handicap was his background. Muste had started out in life as a preacher. That put two strikes on him to start with. Because it is very hard to make anything out of a preacher. I say this not in jest, and more in sorrow than in anger. I have seen it tried many times, but never successfully. Muste was, you may say, the last chance and the best chance; and even he, the best prospect of all, couldn't come through in the end because of that terrible background of the church, which had marred him in his formative years. To take the opium of religion is very bad in itself—Marx correctly defined it as opium. But to peddle the opium of religion, as preachers do—that is far worse. It is an occupation that deforms the human mind. Not a single preacher, of the many who have come to the radical labor movement of America, throughout its history—not a single one of them turned out good and became a genuine revolutionist in the end. Not one. But despite the handicap of this background, Muste gave promise because of his exceptional personal qualities, and because of the great influence he had over the people associated with him; his prestige and his good reputation. Muste gave promise of becoming a real force as a leader in the new party.

Muste wasn't the only leader of the AWP. He was, one might say, the one in the middle, the moderator, the central leader who balanced everything between the contending sides.

There was another extremely able man in the National Committee of the American Workers Party. I mentioned him in a previous lecture: his name was Salutsky. That is the name we knew him by in the Socialist Party and the first years of American Communism. He goes now by the name of J. B. S. Hardman, the editor of *Advance,* official organ of the Amalgamated Clothing Workers, and has held this post for the past twenty years. Salutsky was a half-and-half man. Intellectually he was a socialist. His background was in the Russian socialist movement, the Jewish Bund. He had been the outstanding leader of the Jewish Socialist Federation of the

American Socialist Party. For years he was the editor of the organ of the Jewish Federation and by far its most capable man, standing head and shoulders above such people as Olgin and others also prominent in the movement. Morally, Salutsky was a weakling, an opportunist waverer who could never quite make up his mind to go the whole way. He wanted to and he didn't want to. Salutsky was always divided in his allegiance, and every move he made in one direction was arrested by that contradiction within himself, that double personality, that pulled him in another direction. He lived a double life. On Sundays he wanted to belong to a party, give lectures, discuss theory, associate with people of ideas. But on weekdays he was J. B. S. Hardman, flunkey editor of the *Advance,* intellectual sharpshooter who did all kinds of dirty work for that ignorant boor and trickster who was the boss of the Amalgamated Clothing Workers, Sidney Hillman.

I knew Salutsky personally quite well. When I encountered him in 1934, in the course of the negotiations with the American Workers Party, it was for the second time in a similar relationship. Thirteen years before, in 1921, he and I—on opposite sides—participated in the joint negotiating committee of the "Workers Council" and the underground Communist Party. The "Workers Council" was the name of a short-lived grouping of Left Socialists who split in 1921 from the Socialist Party; that is, two years after the big, decisive split of 1919, and sought unity with us on the basis of a legal Communist Party. His position then was characteristic of the man. In 1919, when the main split took place, when the whole movement was divided into Communists on one side and Social Democrats on the other, Salutsky rejected the

Communists and remained with the Socialist Party. But his leftist tendencies and his knowledge of socialism were such that he could not reconcile himself entirely to the right wing, and he began to play with the organization of a new left group in the Socialist Party. This was a group of second-line, second-grade Communists. By 1921 Salutsky, his friends, and similars had gone through a new split from the Socialist Party and formed another organization, the "Workers Council."

It was characteristic of Salutsky that he didn't join the Communist Party outright and forthright, either in 1919 or 1921. He didn't want to join the underground CP but only to form, together with us, a new party with a moderate, strictly "legal" program. He joined, so to speak, through the back door in 1921, through this fusion we made with the "Workers Council" to form our legal party, the Workers Party. That fusion happened to coincide with our purposes at the time. The Communist Party of the United States was underground and we were trying to force it back into the open by degrees, as I have already related. At that time we wanted to form a legal organization, not as a self-sufficient party, but as a cover for the underground movement and as one step in our fight for legality. It served our purposes very well to effect a unification with half-and-half groups such as Salutsky's organization, the "Workers Council," and to launch a legal party in which the Communist majority was firmly assured. This legal party—known as the Workers Party—was completely under the domination of the Communist Party. Everybody knew that it was the legal expression of the Communist Party. Salutsky, and other people such as Engdahl, Lore, and Olgin, were willing to join this legal organization, but not the underground Communist Party. It was a sort of shamefaced adhesion to the Communist movement that Salutsky made. But he didn't stay long. When the Workers Party, under the direction and the influence of the Communist Party, opened up a campaign against the labor bureaucracy, he began to slink away. Salutsky had no stomach for that sort of thing.

It is one thing to make a lecture on Sunday about socialism and the class struggle; to explain the contradictions of capitalism and the inevitability of the revolution. It is another thing to engage in practical revolutionary action which brings you into conflict with the labor fakers, thereby endangering your chance to serve them in well-rewarded positions. Salutsky presently quit the Workers Party, or was thrown out—I don't remember which. It doesn't matter. Salutsky, however, could not quit playing with the ideas of socialism and revolution. He joined the Conference for Progressive Labor Action, the predecessor of the American Workers Party. He helped give the CPLA a certain political direction, and sponsored the idea of transforming it into a party, but he wanted a pseudorevolutionary party, not a real one. He wanted no clash with the labor bureaucrats. Above everything else he feared a union with the Trotskyists. Nothing that Salutsky could do to sabotage the unification was left undone. He knew, as many others knew, that characteristic of our movement which I have mentioned in previous lectures: Trotskyists mean business. Salutsky knew that once a fusion of the AWP with the Trotskyists took place, all further possibilities of masquerading as a socialist with a pseudoradical party would be lost for him.

In the negotiations we met with Salutsky as enemies, polite, of course, as is the prevailing custom for negotiators, passing the time of day, making a few jokes, and concealing your knife—at least in the beginning. I recall the first day that we—Shachtman and myself, and I think Abern, or Oehler—I am not sure which—walked into the office of the American Workers Party to meet by appointment with Muste, Salutsky, and Sidney Hook, the New York University professor then dabbling with socialism. As we were exchanging pleasantries before the meeting came to order, Salutsky said to me, with that mirthless smile he seemed permanently to wear: "I always read the *Militant*. I like to see what Trotsky has to say."

It was on the tip of my tongue to answer that I always read the *Advance* because I like to see what Hillman has to say. But I let it pass. We were on our best behavior, determined to accomplish the unity with as little friction over incidentals as possible. Salutsky tried to sabotage the unity by every means, but he lost the game in the end. Instead of his pulling the American Workers Party away from the Trotskyists, we pulled it towards us, into an eventual unification, and he was thrown aside like an old dishcloth. That ended Salutsky's activities as a "socialist." He quit the party, and radical politics altogether. Now he is in the Roosevelt camp—and that is where he belongs.

Another outstanding leader of the American Workers Party at that time was a man named Louis Budenz. He had been a social worker to begin with. His interest in the labor movement for years was that of student-observer and publisher of a subsidized magazine which gave advice to the workers but represented no organized movement. Eventually, through the medium of the Conference for Progressive Labor Action, he became engaged for the first time in the

mass movement for which he unquestionably had considerable talents.

Mass work is hard work and it devours many people. By
1934 Budenz, who had no socialist background or education,
was a 100 percent patriot, three-fourths a Stalinist, tired and
somewhat sick, and looking for a chance to sell out. He was a
vicious opponent of the unification. Budenz was already
looking toward the Stalinist party, as indeed, a considerable
section of the AWP organization had been. Only the vigor-
ous intervention of the Trotskyists and the pressure of our
unity negotiations prevented the Stalinist party from gob-
bling up a large section of the AWP at that time. I might add
that Budenz eventually found his opportunity to sell out, is
today the editor of the *Daily Worker*, and for years has been
doing all the dirty work they pay him to do.

And then there was Ludwig Lore, well known to us from
the old days of the Communist Party. Lore, one of the original Communists in the United States; one of the editors of
Class Struggle, the first Communist magazine in this country;
a Left Socialist rather than a Communist at heart, who had
slipped backwards, was then passing through the AWP on
his way to complete reconciliation with bourgeois democracy. He finally landed a job on the *New York Evening Post* as
a superpatriotic columnist. Lore was against the unification.

These were some of the leading figures in the AWP. In
discussing in our ranks the question of unifying with the
Musteites, we encountered an opposition, the beginning of a
sectarian faction in our movement headed by Oehler and
Stamm. We heard the old familiar arguments of sectarians
who see only the official leaders of organizations, not the

membership, and who judge accordingly. They asked: "How can we unite with Salutsky, with Lore, and so on?" If there were nothing to the American Workers Party but Salutsky, Lore, and Company there would have been some logic in their opposition.

Behind these fakers and renegades we saw some serious people, some proletarian militants. I have previously mentioned the comrades who led the Toledo strike. They had numerous elements of this type throughout Pennsylvania and the Middle West. They had built up an unemployed organization of considerable size. These proletarian activists in the AWP were the types that interested us; these together with Muste who we thought could be made into a Bolshevik. Besides Muste, who was a type by himself; besides Budenz, Salutsky, Lore, there were others in this heterogeneous mass called the American Workers Party: the Toledo people, the rank-and-file militants in the unemployed movement, and some rank-and-file trade unionists. In addition, to round out the roll call of the American Workers Party, there were some YWCA girls, Bible students, assorted intellectuals, college professors, and some nondescripts who had just wandered in through the open door.

Our political task was to prevent the Stalinists from swallowing up this movement, and to remove a centrist obstacle from our path by effecting a unity with the proletarian activists and the serious people, isolating the frauds and fakers, and discarding the unassimilable elements. That was quite a large order but in the end we succeeded, not without great effort and difficulty.

I mentioned that the AWP letter, which had been sent in

reply to our second proposal for negotiation, contained a provocation on the Russian question, unquestionably inspired by Salutsky and Budenz. I quote a few sentences from that letter to give you an idea of what the provocation consisted. It said: "We must take care that our criticism of CI and CP policies not only is not, but is free from any appearance of being, an attack upon the Soviet Union. However justified the CLA criticisms of certain policies of the Soviet Union may have been, they have stood out in the public mind as an expression of an antagonistic attitude toward the Soviet Union."

They went on to say in the letter that there must be a clear understanding that, in uniting with us, they were not going to be anti-Soviet. When we read this letter in our National Committee meeting we hit the ceiling. Here, we felt—this was our subjective reaction—we have been defending the Soviet Union since 1917. These people for the most part have just discovered it and yet they presume to lecture us on our duties in regard to the Soviet Union. In white heat we sat down and knocked out a blistering reply to get it out of our system. After we had written this reply, telling them where to get off at, we cooled off. We recognized it for what it was: a provocation. It would be foolish for us to be caught in a trap like that and lose sight of our political aims and tasks. We thereupon outlined in the committee meeting another reply which would: (1) state our position on the Soviet Union firmly; (2) pretend not to notice the provocation; and (3) again emphasize the necessity of unity. This kind of reply was designed to make it harder for the provocateurs to halt the trend towards unity in the ranks of the AWP.

While we were sitting at the meeting in our headquarters

on Second Avenue, discussing the points of this outline and deciding who should draft the statement, we received a visit at the headquarters from Professors Hook and Burnham, who were both members of this fantastic national committee of the American Workers Party. They were for the fusion. That was very advantageous for us—to have a couple of professors on the AWP committee in favor of fusion regardless of what their real motives might be. Hook wanted the fusion in order to get the AWP off his hands and end his brief adventure in party politics. He wanted to retire to the sidelines, the only place where he has ever felt at home, and which he ought never to have left. Burnham, as later events showed, wanted unification with the Trotskyists because he was then taking a step forward, getting a little bit more radical; he wanted to put his toe a little deeper into the icy water of proletarian politics while firmly bracing himself, with his other foot, on the bourgeois shore. The two doughty professors warned us of the provocation. They were afraid that we would reply in kind and that this would upset the applecart. That is why they had come to visit us. They were greatly pleased and relieved when we gave them the second outline of the draft of our reply.

While all this was going on in our camp, things were stirring everywhere, in all organizations, under the impact of the developments of the mass movement. We were beginning to attract small groups of people from the Lovestoneites and other circles at that time. There was a notice in the *Militant* of September 8: "Lovestone group cracks in Detroit. Five join the League." The same issue of the *Militant* reported that Herbert Zam had quit the Lovestone organization, and that Zam and Gitlow were going to join the Socialist Party. The *Militant* of September 29 reported: "The French Bolshevik-Leninists have joined the Socialist Party of France as a faction." This was the first big action taken in carrying out the line of Trotsky's "French turn" which directed that our comrades join, wherever possible, those reformist socialist organizations which might be open to them in order to establish contact with the developing Left Wing and, thereby, lay the basis for a new party.

Our organizational proposals, which we submitted to the American Workers Party in our third meeting, went a long way to facilitate the unification. We always believed that the program decides everything. A group which is assured of the adoption of the Marxist program does not need to fight too hard over every organizational detail. It is a common error made by inexperienced militants in politics to exaggerate the organization question and deprecate the decisive role of the program. In the early days of the American Communist movement many of the fights and even splits were unnecessarily caused by an exaggerated concern of the different factions for organizational positions which were considered posts of vantage for the faction. We had learned something from that experience, which now served us in good stead.

When, in the course of the negotiations, we found the Musteites coming closer to us on the question of the program, we came forward with a complete set of proposals for the organizational side of the fusion, a side which concerned a number of them very much. We offered them a fifty-fifty arrangement all up and down the line. By that time we were stronger than the Musteites numerically. When you came to a showdown of the dues-paying members of the organization, we had more forces. They had perhaps a bigger movement in a nebulous form, perhaps more general sympathizers, but we had more actual members. Our organization was more compact. But we disregarded all that and offered them an arrangement whereby the official positions in the party would be divided equally between the two sides. Moreover, in each case where there were two posts of relatively equal importance, we offered them the choice. For example, in the two leading positions we proposed that Muste should be national secretary, and that I should be editor of the paper. Or, if they wished it, the other way around, I would be national secretary and Muste, the editor. It was very hard for them to object. We knew what it meant to them, with their overemphasis on purely organizational matters, to have the secretaryship because the secretary, theoretically at least, controls the party machine. We were more interested in the editorship because that shapes more directly the ideology of the movement. Similarly, with the posts of labor secretary and educational director. We proposed to take the latter and give them the former, or vice versa, as they saw fit.

The National Committee was to have an equal number from each side and all other organization questions which might arise were to be settled on a parity basis. Such was our proposal. Its obvious fairness, even generosity, strongly impressed Muste and his friends. Our "organization proposals," instead of precipitating conflicts and deadlock, as has so often been the case, greatly facilitated the unity. As I said, we were able to do this, and to eliminate at one stroke what has so often been an insuperable obstacle, because we had learned the lessons of the organization struggles of the past in the Communist Party.

We took a liberal and conciliatory attitude on the organization question, reserving our intransigence for the question of the program. A joint committee was selected to draft the program. After two or three drafts had been drawn up, discussed, and amended; after a little pressure and conflict, a program was finally agreed upon. This became after ratification by the joint convention, the "Declaration of Principles" of the Workers Party of the United States, which was characterized by Comrade Trotsky as a rigidly principled program.

Meantime we got some advice from the Stalinists who had been sleeping on the sidelines while the despised little "sectarian" group of Trotskyists had entered a field which they thought properly belonged to them. They had fully intended to absorb the Muste organization and had more right to expect success than we had. But we had beaten them to the punch; we had acted at the right time—time is of the essence in politics—and were deep in the unity negotiations with the AWP before the Stalinists realized what was going on. When they woke up they broke out in their press with both warnings and advice. The headline of the *Militant* of October 20 reports: "Stalinist Press 'Warns' AWP Against Unity With Us." The reference was to an article in the *Daily Worker* by the notorious Bittleman, who, under the title "Does the American Workers Party Know With What It Is Uniting?" gave a free-hearted warning to both sides. To the Musteites the Stalinists said: "We must warn the workers who follow Muste and his American Workers Party against a trap that is being laid for them by their leaders, the trap of counterrevolutionary Trotskyism." And then, to show their impartiality, in the same article they turned around and said: "To the few misguided workers who still follow the Trotskyists: Cannon, Shachtman, and Company are leading you into unity with Muste, the champion of bourgeois nationalism."

We answered them: "If the Trotskyists are counterrevolutionists and the Musteites are bourgeois nationalists, you might as well throw them all together in one sack. No harm can come from it because neither one can be made any worse for the fusion." We thanked them for their impartial, two-sided, double-acting advice—and went on with the fusion. The two organizations began to collaborate in practical activities. We held joint meetings before the fusion. The *Militant* of October 6 reports that Muste and Cannon spoke at a joint mass meeting of the CLA and AWP in Paterson, New Jersey, to 300 silk workers, discussing the lessons of the strike.

About that time, in October 1934, I was sent abroad by the National Committee to the meeting of the Plenum of the Executive Committee of the International Communist League in Paris. From there I went to visit Comrade Trotsky in Grenoble, in the south of France. It was the first time I had seen Comrade Trotsky personally since his exile from the USSR years back. Numerous other American comrades had been abroad, but this was my first trip. Shachtman had been there twice and several other individual members of the organization, who were able to finance personal trips to Europe, had seen him. At that time Comrade Trotsky was being hounded by the French fascists.

Some of you remember that at that time, 1934, the French fascist press began a big hue and cry about the presence of

Trotsky in France. They created such an agitation—in which they were joined by the Stalinists under the joint slogan: "Drive Trotsky out of France"—that they terrorized the Daladier government into revoking his visa. He was ordered to leave France, deprived of his right to stay. But they could not find one single capitalist country in the entire world that would give him an entrance visa, so they had to keep him in France. But he was there under the most uncertain and dangerous circumstances, without any real protection, any legal rights, while the fascist press and the Stalinists kept hounding him all the time. He was then hiding in the house of a sympathizer in Grenoble. He had no assistants, no secretariat, no typist, because he was living on a day-to-day basis. He was obliged to do all his work in longhand. The hounds of reaction kept him on the go: Hunted from one place to another, he would just get settled in the house of a sympathizer, and get started to work, when the local fascists would discover his presence in the new place of refuge. The next morning there would appear a screaming headline in the newspaper: "What Is the Russian Murderer, Trotsky, Doing in this Town?" Then there would be a hue and cry, and he would have to leave in the dead of night, as quickly as possible, in order to save his life, and find another place of safety. The same thing was repeated over and over again. During that time Trotsky's health was very bad and he almost succumbed. Those were the days of the greatest anxiety for all of us.

It was a very, very happy moment for me, early in the morning—about seven—after riding all night from Paris, to be able to walk into his house in the country, to see and know that he was still alive. I met him before breakfast, but he wanted to sit down and begin a political discussion right away. His first questions were, "What happened at the Plenum? Did they pass the resolution?" I politely raised the question of a little sustenance. So I had breakfast with Trotsky and Natalia, and broke one of the house rules, which I later regretted very much. I did it through ignorance. I had heard that he did not allow smoking in his presence. Glotzer and others had come back with fierce tales of the scoldings they had received on this score. I had thought it only an idiosyncracy on Trotsky's part, not to be taken too seriously. I am accustomed to smoking after breakfast, and, as coffee was served—that is the time when a smoke tastes best—I pulled out my cigar and after the fact was about one-half accomplished, I said facetiously: "I hear some people get expelled for smoking. Is that correct?" He said, "No, no, go ahead and smoke." He added: "For boys like Glotzer I don't allow it, but for a solid comrade it is all right." So I smoked all the time in his presence during my visit. Only in later years I learned that smoking was physically repugnant to him, even made him ill, and I deeply regretted doing it.

In the afternoon Trotsky's host took us on a trip in his automobile to the top of the French Alps. On the mountaintop we had a long discussion on the projected fusion with the Musteites. The Old Man approved everything we had done, including our evasion of the provocation on the USSR. We came to an agreement on one or two points which we had held in abeyance awaiting his advice; measures to facilitate our unity with the Musteites. He was fully in favor of it, and he also was greatly interested in the personality of Muste, asked me questions about him and entertained some hopes that Muste would develop into a real Bolshevik later.

The Plenum of the International Communist League was held in Paris, October 1934. The purpose of this Plenum was to put the capstone on the decision that had already been agreed upon by the International Executive Committee and endorsed by referendum of the national sections: the decision to carry out the "French turn"; that is, the turn taken by our French organization to join the Socialist Party of France as a body in order to work within this reformist party as a faction, to come into contact with its Left Wing, seek to influence it and to fuse with it, and thereby to broaden the basis for the eventual construction of a new revolutionary party in France. The Plenum supported this line, which meant a reorientation of our tactics throughout the world. The action was taken under the general slogan which I mentioned before: Turn from a propaganda circle, such as we had been for five years, to mass work, to contact with the living movement of workers traveling in the direction of revolutionary Marxism.

When I returned from Paris to report on the Plenum to our organization in New York, we encountered an opposition headed by Oehler and Stamm and reinforced by a voluble, left-sick German emigre named Eiffel. They objected in principle to our joining any section of the Second International. Their arguments, like all the arguments of sectarians, were strictly formalistic, sterile, defiant of the reality of the day. "The Second International," they said—and quite correctly—"betrayed the proletariat in the World War. It was denounced by Rosa Luxemburg as a 'stinking corpse.' The Communist International was formed in 1919 in struggle against the Second International. And now, in 1934, you want to go back into this reformist, traitor organization. That means a betrayal of principle."

In vain we explained to them that the Second International of 1934 wasn't exactly the same organization that it had been in 1914 or in 1919. That the bureaucratization of the Comintern had pushed into the Socialist parties, with their looser, more democratic form of organization, a new stratum of awakening workers, of militants. That there had grown up a new generation of young socialists who had no part in the betrayal of 1914–1918. Since we were barred from any participation in the Comintern, we should recognize the new force. That if we wanted to build a new revolutionary party we should direct our forces into the Second International and establish contact with this new Left Wing.

Then the sectarian opposition came forward with a new argument. "Isn't it one of the principles of Marxism, and one of the conditions for admission into the Trotskyist movement, that we must stand for the unconditional independence of the revolutionary party at all times and under every circumstance? Isn't that a principle?"

"Yes," we answered, "that is a principle. That is the great lesson of the Anglo-Russian Committee. That is the fundamental lesson of the Chinese revolution. We have published pamphlets and books to prove that the revolutionary party must never merge itself with another political organization, never mix up the banners, but remain independent even in isolation. The Hungarian revolution was destroyed in part because of the falsely-motivated fusion of the Communists and Social Democrats.

"All that is correct," we said, "but there is just one small screw loose in your argument. *We are not yet a party*. We are only a propaganda group. Our problem is to *become* a party. Our problem, as Trotsky put it, is to get some flesh on our bones. If our French comrades can penetrate the political mass movement of the Socialist Party, attract the viable Left Wing and fuse with it, then they can constitute a party in the real sense of the word, not a caricature. Then they can apply the principle of the independence of the party under all conditions, and the principle will have some meaning. You set up the principle in such a way as to make it a barrier against the tactical moves necessary to make the creation of a real party possible."

We couldn't budge them. Formalistic-mindedness, that is the trait of sectarianism; lack of a sense of proportion; disregard of reality; sterile hairsplitting in a closed circle. We began to fight out the question of the "French turn" in our League a year before it had to be applied here in the same way as in France. The projected fusion with the Musteites was the same thing in different form, but the Oehlerites didn't recognize it— precisely because the *form* was different. They forgave us the fusion with the Musteites, but with great trepidation, fear, and prophecies of bad things to come from mixing with strange people. As one of our lads—Larry Turner—expressed it in a letter the other day, the sectarians are always afraid of their own suppressed desires to be opportunists. They are afraid of coming into contact with opportunists lest the opportunists corrupt them. But we, being sure of our virtue, went confidently forward. In the 1934 discussion of the French turn, a division grew up in our organization. The contending tendencies eventually hardened into factions. The dispute of 1934 over the action of our French comrades was the dress rehearsal for the knockdown, drag-out definitive fight against Oehlerite sectarianism in our ranks the following year. Our victory in that fight was the precondition for all our further advances.

We were moving rapidly toward the fusion, negotiating day after day. We were cooperating with the Musteites in various practical activities, and the whole trend was toward unification of the two organizations. We finally came to an agreement on the draft program; that is, the two committees came to an agreement. We came to an agreement on the organizational proposals. Nothing remained then except to submit the matter to the conventions of the respective organizations for ratification. There was still some doubt on both sides as to what the rank and file would do. We did not know how strong the Oehlerites might turn out to be outside New York; and Abern, as always, was maneuvering furtively in the dark, monkey wrench in hand. Muste, by this time, had become a firm advocate of the fusion, but he wasn't sure of his majority. Consequently, instead of calling a joint convention, we first held separate conventions of the two organizations. The conventions met separately November 26–30, 1934, and thrashed out all the internal affairs of each side. Each convention finally ratified the Declaration of Principles that had been drawn up by the joint committees, and ratified the organization proposals. Then, on the basis of these separate decisions, we called the two conventions into joint session on Saturday and Sunday, December 1–2, 1934. The *Militant*, reporting that joint convention in its next issue, said: "The Workers Party of the United States has been formed. . . . The unity convention of the American Workers Party and the Communist League of America completed its historic task Sunday afternoon in Stuyvesant Casino. . . . Minneapolis and Toledo, exemplifying the new militancy of the American working class, were the stars that presided over its birth. . . . New party launched into its tremendous undertaking: The overthrow of capitalist rule in America and the creation of a workers state."

10

The Struggle against Sectarianism

The formal unification of the Communist League and the American Workers Party, the Musteites, was the first unification of forces that had taken place in the American movement for more than a decade.

The revolutionary labor movement doesn't develop along a straight line or a smooth path. It grows through a continuous process of internal struggle. Both splits and unifications are methods of developing the revolutionary party. Each, under given circumstances, can be either progressive or reactionary in its consequences. The general popular sentiment for unification all the time has no more political value than a preference for a continual process of splitting which you see taking place interminably in the purist sectarian groups. Moralistic views on the question of splits, and so forth, are simply stupid. Splits are sometimes absolutely necessary for the clarification of programmatic ideas and for the selection of forces in order to make a new start on a clear basis. On the other hand, in given circumstances, unifications of two or more groups which approach programmatic agreement are absolutely indispensable for the regroupment and consolidation of the forces of the workers vanguard.

Unity between the Trotskyist organization—Communist League of America—and the Musteite organization was unquestionably a progressive action. It brought together two groups with different origins and experiences which, nevertheless, had approached, at least in the formal sense of the word, an agreement on the program. The only way to test out whether this agreement was real and thoroughgoing or only formal; the only way to learn which elements in each of the groups were capable of contributing to the further progressive development of the movement, was by unification, by bringing them together and testing these questions out in the course of common experience.

As throughout the world since 1928, there had been a continuous and uninterrupted series of splits in the American movement. The basic cause of this, of course, was the degeneration of the Communist International under the pressure of the world encirclement of the Russian revolution and the attempt of the Stalinist bureaucracy to adapt itself to this encirclement by deserting the program of internationalism. The degeneration of the Communist International could not fail to produce disruptions and splits. In all the parties the defenders of unfalsified Marxism within this degenerating organization were a source of irritation and conflict which the bureaucracy found no way to remove except by bureaucratic expulsions. We were expelled from the American Communist Party in October 1928. Six months later, in the spring of 1929, the Lovestoneites were expelled and set up a third Communistic organization in this country. Little sects and cliques of individuals and their friends, representing quirks and vagaries of various kinds, were a common feature of the times. The movement was going through a period of pulverization, of pulling apart, until a new rise in the class struggle and a new verification of programs on the basis of world experiences could lay the ground for integration once again.

There was our faction and the Lovestone faction. There was the little group of Weisbord which at one time reached the total of 12 or 13 members, but made enough noise to make one think they represented a great historical tendency. Moreover, the Weisbordites, not satisfied with forming an independent organization, insisted—under what appears to be the compulsion of a natural law for such arbitrarily created groups—on going through a couple of splits within their own ranks. The Fieldites—Field and a few of his personal associates and friends and family connections whom we threw out of our movement for treachery during the hotel strike—naturally formed an organization of their own, published a paper, and spoke in the name of the entire working class.

The Lovestoneites suffered a split of the Gitlow forces, and a few months later of a little group represented by Zam. There had existed in this country since 1919 still another Communistic group called the Proletarian Party, which had also maintained an isolated existence and also produced periodic splits.

The demoralization of the movement during that period was reflected in this trend to dispersal, this continuous process of splitting. This sickness had to run its course. Throughout that period we Trotskyists were never unity shouters, especially in the first five years of our separate existence. We concentrated on the work of clarifying the program and rejected all talk about improvised unifications with groups not sufficiently close to us in what we considered then, and what we consider now, the question of all questions—that of the program. The fusion that we entered into in December 1934 was the first unification to take place in this entire period. Just as the bona fide Trotskyist group was the first one to be expelled from the Communist Party when the Stalinists were completely bureaucratizing the Third International and stifling revolutionary and critical thought, so also was the Trotskyist group the first to take the initiative to begin a new process of regroupment and unification when the political prerequisites for such a step were at hand. It was the first positive sign of a counterprocess to the trend of disintegration, dispersal, and split.

The unification of the Trotskyists and the Musteites, the formation of the Workers Party, indubitably represented a great forward step, but only a step. It soon became apparent to us—at least to the most influential leaders of the former Communist League—that the regroupment of revolutionary forces had only begun. We were obliged to take this realistic attitude because, as has been remarked in previous lectures, simultaneously with the radical development of the Musteites, important changes had taken place in the Socialist Party of the United States, as in the Social Democratic movements throughout the world.

Fresh workers and younger elements, untainted by responsibility for the betrayals of the past, had been shaken and awakened by the tremendous impact of world events, especially the crushing of the German labor movement with the coming of fascism to power. A new wind was blowing in this old decrepit organization of Social Democracy. A Left Wing was forming there, manifesting the impulse of large numbers of people to find a revolutionary program. We thought this could not be disregarded because it was a fact, an element of American political reality. Even though we had formed a new party, and had proclaimed it as the unification of the vanguard, we realized that we could not ignore or arbitrarily shut off from participation in this new movement these new elements of strength and health and revolutionary vitality. On the contrary, we had an obligation to help this inchoate movement in the Socialist Party to find the right road. We were convinced that without our help they could not do it, because they had no Marxist leaders, they had no tradition, they were beset on every side by influences and forces and pressures that blocked off their road to a clear view of the revolutionary program. Their ultimate fate, the possibility of their development on the revolutionary road, rested with the more experienced and tested cadres of Marxism represented in the newly founded Workers Party. The leaders of the nebulous Left Wing in the Socialist Party called themselves the "Militants." Why, we have never been able to ascertain. The *Militant* was the name of the official organ of the American Trotskyists from the very beginning, and everybody recognized that it was the right name for our paper. The *Militant* signified the party worker, the party activist, the party fighter. But why the leaders of the Left Wing of the Socialist Party at that time, who were philistines to the marrow of their bones, without tradition, without serious knowledge, without anything at all, could call themselves "Militants"—that remains a problem to be solved by the students of historical research who are yet to come in our movement. The reason hasn't been discovered yet. At least I never learned it.

This wretched leadership, these accidental figures, pretenders, windbags, incapable of any real sacrifice or serious struggle for an idea, without serious devotion to the movement—most of them are working for the government at various war jobs today—these "knights for an hour" didn't interest us very much. What interested us was the fact that beneath the froth on the top there was a quite live youth movement in the Socialist Party and a considerable number of activist worker elements, trade unionists, and fighters in the unemployed field, who constituted good raw material for the revolutionary party. There is a big difference. You can't do much with the type of leader which the Socialist Party in any of its wings had then or now. But out of serious rank-and-file militants, trade union activists, and radical youth, you can make a party which can lead a revolution. We wanted to find a road to them. At that time nobody knew, and least of all did the young Socialists know, which way their movement was going to go. They were stifled by the conservative bureaucracy in the Socialist Party, and time and time again their worthless leaders—the so-called "Militants"—showed tendencies to capitulate to the Right Wing bureaucracy.

On the other hand, they were beset by the Stalinists who had a powerful press and apparatus and plenty of money to corrupt, and who didn't hesitate to use money for just that purpose. At that time the Stalinists were exerting extraordinary pressure on the Socialists in order to lay hold of this progressive left-wing movement and turn it back in the direction of reformism by way of Stalinism. They had succeeded in doing this in Spain and many other European countries. The young Socialist movement in Spain, which had on its own initiative announced its support of the idea of a Fourth International, was neglected by the Trotskyists of Spain who, sterilized in sectarian purity, eschewed any kind of maneuvers in the direction of the young Socialists. They were satisfied to recite the ritual of the split between the Social Democracy and the Comintern in 1914–19, with the result that the Stalinists cut right in ahead of them, took over this grandly promising Socialist youth organization, and made it into an appendage of Stalinism. That was one of the decisive factors in the destruction of the Spanish revolution. We didn't want that to happen here. The Stalinists had the edge on us to begin with. In the Socialist Left Wing there were already strong sentiments of conciliation with Stalinism, and the Stalinists were working the demagogic "unity" slogan for all it was worth. We recognized the problem and realized that if we did not bestir ourselves, what had happened in Spain would happen again here.

We had barely started our work under the independent banner of the Workers Party, but this problem would not wait. We began to insist that more and more attention be paid to the Socialist Party and its developing Left Wing. We argued along the following lines: We must frustrate the Stalinists. We must cut in between the Stalinists and this developing movement of Left Socialism and turn it in the direction of genuine Marxism. And in order to accomplish this we must lay aside all organizational fetishism. We cannot content ourselves with saying: "Here is the Workers Party. It has a correct program. Come and join it!" That is the attitude of sectarians. This Left Wing is a loose grouping of thousands of people in the Socialist Party, somewhat hazy in their conceptions, confused, and badly led, but very valuable for the future if they receive the proper fertilization of Marxist ideas.

Our position was formulated in the Cannon-Shachtman resolution. We met determined resistance in the party from Oehler, and also from Muste. The Oehlerites took their stand on dogmatic sectarian grounds. Not only would they have nothing to do with any present orientation toward the Socialist Party, but they insisted, as a matter of principle, that we specifically exclude this from any future consideration. We have formed the party, said the Oehlerites. Here it is. Let the Left Socialists join us if they accept the program. We are Mohammed and they are the mountain, and the mountain must come to us. That was their whole prescription for those confused young Left Socialists who had never shown the slightest inclination to join our party. We said: "No, that is too simple. Bolsheviks must have sufficient political initiative to help the Left Socialists find their way to the right program. If we do this, the problem of uniting with them in a common organization can be worked out easily."

Muste opposed this—not on principled grounds, but on grounds of organizational fetishism, perhaps personal pride. Such sentiments are fatal in politics. Pride, anger, spite—any kind of subjectivity which influences a political course leads only to the defeat and destruction of those who give way to it. You know, in the prize-fighting profession—"the manly art of self-defense"—one of the first lessons the young boxer learns from the case-hardened trainer is to keep cool when facing an antagonist in the ring. "Don't ever get mad in the ring. Don't ever lose your head, because if you do you will wake up on the canvas." Boxers have to fight calculatingly, not subjectively. The same thing is doubly true in politics. Muste couldn't bear the thought that after we had founded a party and proclaimed it the one and only party, we should then pay any attention to any other party. We should go on in our own way, keep our heads up, and see what happens. If they failed to join us, well, that would be their own fault. Muste's position was not sufficiently thought out, not reasoned with the necessary objectivity. It would not do in the situation. If we had stood aside, the Stalinists would have gobbled up the Socialist Left Wing and it would have been used as another club against us, as in Spain.

Before the Socialist Party question could be solved, and thereby another obstacle removed from the path of the development of the American party of the vanguard, we had to fight the question out in the ranks of the Workers Party. We had to fight out the question of principle with the sectarians; and when they remained stubborn and became undisciplined we had to drive them out of the party. I said that with a little emphasis because that was the way we had to deal with the Oehlerites—with emphasis. If we had failed to do that in 1935, if we had yielded to any kind of sentimentalism toward people who were ruining our political prospects with their stupid formalism, our movement would have been wrecked in 1935. We would have been cut off from the possibility of further development. An inevitable disintegration would have taken place. The movement would have ended in the blind alley of sectarian futility.

Sectarianism is not an interesting idiosyncracy. Sectarianism is a political disease that will destroy any organization where it takes firm hold and isn't rooted out in time. Our party is living today and is quite healthy thanks to the medicinal and surgical treatment that sectarianism received in 1935. Medicinal treatment is the more important and must always come first in any case. Ours consisted of sound education on Marxist principles and their sectarian caricatures; thorough discussion, patient explanation. By these methods we cleared away the miasma and, although we were in a minority at the start, eventually gained a large majority and isolated the Oehlerites. This was not done in a day. It took many months. Surgical treatment followed only when the defeated Oehlerites began to violate party discipline systematically and to prepare a split. In the course of discussion and explanation, we educated the great majority of the party. The body of the party had been cured and was in good health. The tip of the little finger remained infected and began to turn gangrenous, so we just chopped it off. That is why the party lives today and is able to talk about that time.

After we finished with the Oehlerites we had to go through a rather prolonged faction struggle with the Musteites—two internal struggles in the first year of the existence of the Workers Party—before the way was clear to solve this problem of the Left Wing of the Socialist Party. These internal struggles, which consumed the energies of the new party almost from its inception, were certainly very inconvenient. We should have had a year or two of constructive work, uninterrupted by differences, conflicts, and internal fights. But history didn't work that way. We had no sooner launched the new party than we were confronted with the problem of the Left Wing of the Socialist Party. We could not agree on what to do, so we had to spend a year fighting it out.

Of course, these conflicts didn't begin immediately. The new party, organized in early December 1934 began its work quite auspiciously. One of the party's first demonstrations of political activity, which was also intended to symbolize the unification of the two currents, was a joint cross-country speaking tour of Muste and myself. We were received with enthusiasm along the way. One could notice in the radical labor movement a general spirit of appreciation of the fact that a process of unification had begun after the long period of disintegration and splits. We had very good meetings in most places, and the tour reached its high point at Minneapolis. This was six months or so following the great strike victories; we were received there very well. The comrades in Minneapolis were highly pleased that we had not allowed ourselves to become so completely absorbed in economic strikes as to neglect opportunities of the purely political party field. Our unification with another group, whose militants they valued very highly because of the work they had done in the unemployed movement, the Toledo strike, etc., was warmly applauded by the Minneapolis comrades. They gave us a good reception and laid themselves out to celebrate our visit by a well-planned series of meetings and conferences, culminating in a banquet in honor of the National Secretary of their party and the editor of the paper that was so dear to their hearts—the *Militant*. They always do things right in Minneapolis. In the course of our stay there, they decided to dress us up in a manner befitting the dignity of our positions. The leading comrades came down from the union hall, picked up Muste and me—who, I must admit, were looking a bit seedy at the time—and took us on a tour of clothiers and haberdashers. They rigged us out in new outfits from head to foot. It was a very fine gesture. I was sharply reminded of that suit of clothes long after I had worn it out. In the summer of 1936 Muste, disoriented by all the complications and difficulties, and overwhelmed by the blood and violence in the Spanish civil war and Moscow trials, reverted as you know, to his original position as a religionist and went back to the church. Vincent Dunne got the news through a private letter and he passed the information on to Bill Brown. "Bill," he said, "What do you think? Muste has gone back to the church." Bill was flabbergasted. "Well, I'll be damned," he said. Then, a moment later: "Say, Vincent, we ought to get that suit back!" But he should have known better. Preachers never give anything back.

We parted at Minneapolis. Muste went on further South to cover other parts of the country. I went on to California to finish the tour. This was at the time of the Sacramento "criminal-syndicalism" trial of Communist Party members. One of our comrades—Norman Mini—was among the defendants, and because he had turned Trotskyist, not only did the Stalinists refuse to defend him, but they denounced him in their press as a "stool pigeon" while he was on trial. We came to his aid. The Non-Partisan Labor Defense, a non-Stalinist defense committee, did very distinguished work in providing defense for Comrade Mini. We exploited to the

THE STRUGGLE AGAINST SECTARIANISM   239

full all the political aspects of this situation.

While this tour was in process, lasting a couple of months, we began to hear the first rumbling of trouble with the sectarian phrasemongers back in New York. They always begin it in New York. They didn't let the party rest, they wouldn't let it get a good start in its work. Consider the situation. Here was a newly formed organization, representing a unification of people with entirely different experiences and backgrounds. This party required a little time to work together, and to have peace in common work. That was the most reasonable, the most realistic program for the first period. But you can never get reasonableness or realism from sectarians. They came tearing into this united organization in New York with a "Bolshevization" program. They were going to take these centrist Musteites and make Bolsheviks out of them, whether they liked it or not. And quick too. Discussions! They scared some of these Musteites out of their wits with their discussions, theses, and clarifications till all hours of the night. They went about searching for "issues," hounding all who might be deviating from the straight and narrow path of doctrine. No peace, no fraternal common work, no education in a calm atmosphere, no will to let the young party develop naturally and organically. An irresponsible factional struggle was the contribution of the sectarians almost from the very beginning.

This ruction in New York was preparing the way for an explosion at the famous Active Workers Conference, called by the party to meet in Pittsburgh in March 1935. The Active Workers Conference was an excellent institution which had been brought over from the experiences of the American

Workers Party. The idea is to invite all the party activists in a given area, or the whole country over, to pick up and come to a central place to discuss practical work, report on experiences, get acquainted with one another, etc. It is a marvelous institution, as we found out in our experiences at Chicago in 1940 and again in 1941. It works out beautifully when there is harmony in the party and you are able to come together to transact business and get it over with. But when there are serious disputes in the party, which nothing but a formal convention can settle, especially if an irresponsible faction is on the loose, it is best to dispense with informal Active Workers Conferences which have no constitutional powers to decide the disputes. In such a situation informal gatherings only feed the flames of factionalism. We found that out at Pittsburgh.

The Active Workers Conference we tried at Pittsburgh was a horrible fizzle because, from the very opening of it, the Oehlerites used it as a sounding board for their factional struggle against the "opportunism" of the leadership. The Musteite comrades, new to the experience of political party life, came in from the field with the naive idea that they were going to hear each others' reports on party mass work and discuss how they could step it up a little. Instead of that, they were confronted with an unrestrained free-for-all factional fight from the very beginning. The Oehlerites started the fight over the selection of the chairman, and thereafter continued it—in a fanatical, life-and-death, do-or-die manner—on every question. It was a factional shambles such as I had never seen before in such a setting. Forty or fifty innocent field workers, with little or no experience in party politics or caucuses, who had come there looking for some inspiration from this new party and some sensible guidance in their practical work, were treated to discussions and arguments and factional denunciation, lasting all day and night. I imagine many of them said to themselves in alarm: "What have we got into? We always heard the Trotskyists were crazy theses sharks and professional factionalists. Perhaps the stories had some truth in them." They saw factionalism in the worst version there.

The mass work activist, as a rule, is inclined to want only a very little discussion, to settle a few very necessary details, and then proceed to action. At Pittsburgh they—and we too —wanted to get down to business and have an exchange of experiences in the practical work of the party: trade union activity, the unemployed leagues, the functioning of party branches, finances, etc. The sectarians weren't interested in such humdrum matters. They insisted on discussing Ethiopia, China, "the French turn," and other "principled questions," which were very important, to be sure, but not on the agenda of the conference.

Oehler, Stamm, and Zack were the three leaders. I don't know how many of you know the famous Joseph Zack. He had recently come over to us from Stalinism but was only bivouacking in our camp on his way to other destinations. He had been one of the inside bureaucrats of the Stalinist party, and had contributed a full share to the corruption and bureaucratic degeneration of the party. Then he became a Trotskyist for a few weeks—at the most a few months. He had no sooner got his feet wet in our organization, than he turned and began to attack us from the "left." We tolerated him for a while, but when he began to disrupt party discipline we chucked him out. He fell off into space and finally landed in the anti-Communist "democratic" camp, as a contributor to the *New Leader* —you know that Social Democratic newspaper over there on Fifteenth Street; that Old Renegades Home, where all the political cripples and lepers live.

At Pittsburgh, Muste united with Shachtman and Cannon to beat back this assault of the sectarians. He was able to recognize that their conduct was disruptive. Muste was always extremely responsible and constructive in his attitude toward the organization. He was very glad to have our cooperation and help in handling these wild men, beating them down, and making it impossible for them to disrupt the party work. And he certainly needed our help. Muste was far too much of a gentleman ever to deal with them the way they needed to be dealt with. We pushed them back a little bit at Pittsburgh, but we settled nothing. We realized that the decisive fight lay ahead and that it had to be settled theoretically and politically. All our hopes of letting the party breathe freely for a while, our hopes of maintaining harmony for the sake of developing the party's mass work, were blasted by the irresponsible sectarians.

We came back to New York determined to take our coats off and give them a fight to the finish. It is a good thing for the party that we did. The party owes us something for that —that we didn't trifle with sectarianism turned virulent. We mapped out a whole campaign of offensive operations against the Oehlerites. They wanted discussion? We proposed to give them—and the party—a thoroughgoing discussion which would leave not a single question at issue unclarified. Our objective was to reeducate the party members who had become infected with the sectarian sickness, and if it proved impossible to reform the leaders, to so isolate them in the party that they could not hamper its movements or disrupt its work. The high hopes we had entertained at the fusion convention naturally began to sag a little bit when we ran into all these difficulties.

But you never get a straight road in politics. People who are easily discouraged, whose hearts sink when they encounter conflicts and setbacks, shouldn't go into revolutionary politics. It is hard fighting all the time, there is never any assurance of smooth sailing. How can that be expected? The whole weight of bourgeois society presses down upon a few hundred or a few thousand people. If these people are not united in their own conceptions, if they fall to quarreling among themselves, that is also a sign of the tremendous pressure of the bourgeois world on the vanguard of the proletariat, and even more on the vanguard of the vanguard. The influence of bourgeois society finds an expression at times even in sections of a revolutionary workers party. Therein is the real source of serious factional fights. One ought, if he goes into politics, to try to understand all these things; try to estimate them clearly from the political point of view and find a political solution for them. That is what we did with the Oehlerites. We did not become discouraged and downhearted. We analyzed the question politically and decided to solve it politically.

The internal fight was paralyzing the new party. The objective factors of the workers mass movement were not favorable enough to help us to drown out the internal factionalism with a big flood of new recruits. The rise of the Left Wing in the Socialist Party was fatal to our further development along the line of a purely independent movement, ignoring the Socialist Party. The very fact that a Left Wing was arising in the Socialist Party made it more attractive to the radical-minded workers than it had been for years. The Socialist Party was a much bigger organization than our party. And we, watching every sign and symptom, began to notice that workers who were awakening to radical ideas and other workers who had dropped out of the political movement and wanted to rejoin, were joining the Socialist Party, not our party. They had the idea that the SP was eventually going to become a genuine revolutionary party, thanks to the development of the Left Wing. This cut off recruiting to the Workers Party. It was the warning signal to us that we must not let ourselves become isolated from the Left Wing of the Socialist Party.

Difficulties of a financial nature beset us in the midst of these difficulties and complications. One of the major factors in the development of the American Workers Party, as in the Conference for Progressive Labor Action before it, had been the personal contacts and associations of Muste, and the financial resources accruing therefrom. Upon his entry into the labor movement in 1917—in the Lawrence strike—Muste joined the textile workers union and became one of its outstanding leaders. Then he founded the Brookwood Labor College at Katonah, New York—ran it for years at a great expenditure of money. While still at Brookwood, he founded the Conference for Progressive Labor Action (in 1929). Later he abandoned the Brookwood Labor College and devoted himself entirely to politics. During all that time he had been able to raise considerable sums of money from various kinds of individuals of means who had confidence in him personally and wanted to support his work. He had been able to retain this support through his various activities. That had been a decisive feature in the financing of the Conference for Progressive Labor Action and the American Workers Party. But when Muste joined with the Trotskyists to form the Workers Party, these contributors began to drift away. Many of his contacts, friends, and associates were churchmen, Christian social workers, and do-gooders in general—people from that theological underworld from which Muste himself had come. They were willing to support a union, give money for the unemployed, finance a workers college where the poor workers could get an education, help a "Conference" to do something "progressive"— whatever that might mean. But give money—even to Muste— for Trotskyism? No, that was going too far. Trotskyism is entirely too serious a matter; the Trotskyists mean business. One by one, Muste's most generous contributors, on whom he had counted to help finance the expanded activities of the united party, fell away.

We had begun with quite an ambitious program of party activity. The enthusiasm of the unity convention had brought in contributions of various kinds, and there was money on hand to start with. The boys in New York, while Muste and I were out on the road, decided that the least we could do was have a presentable headquarters. They rented a grand place on the corner of Fifteenth Street and Fifth Avenue. I think the rent was $150 or $175 a month. There were offices of all kinds for the different officials and dignitaries. They installed a switchboard—not a single telephone but a switchboard, with a girl sitting there plugging it in, while the various officials, editors, and functionaries would pick up their phones—I don't know whom they were talking to. It looked good while it lasted. But it was a St. Martin's summer, not a real one. In the summer of 1935 we were evicted for nonpayment of rent. We had to make the best of it and rent a rather unprepossessing old loft on Eleventh Street. We cut out the switchboard and decided to have one telephone—and even that was cut off after a few months for nonpayment of bills. But we survived.

We tried our best during that period to develop the mass work of the party. The National Unemployed League, created by the old Muste organization, had flourishing branches in many parts of the country, especially in Ohio, Pennsylvania, and parts of West Virginia. We gave, I think, some real help to the field workers who had done that great job. We reached thousands of workers through these unemployed organizations. But further experience also taught us an instructive lesson in the field of mass work too. Unemployed organizations can be built and expanded rapidly in times of economic crisis and it is quite possible for one to get illusory ideas of their stability and revolutionary potentialities. At the very best they are loose and easily scattered formations; they slip through your fingers like sand. The minute the average unemployed worker gets a job he wants to forget about the unemployed organization. He doesn't want to be reminded of the misery of the former time. Besides that, chronically unemployed workers very often give way to demoralization and despair. I don't know of any task in the revolutionary movement more discouraging and disheartening than the task of trying to keep an organization like this together. It is a hard job to stick to, month after month and year after year, in the hope of crystallizing something firm and stable for the revolutionary movement.

One sure lesson, I think, to be drawn from the experience of that time, is that the employed workers in the factories are the real base of the revolutionary party. That is where the power is, the vitality and the confidence in the future. The unemployed masses, the unemployed organizations, can never be substituted for a base in the employed factory workers.

In that period there were rumblings of an approaching strike in the rubber factories in Akron. We went out there, several of us, to try to find a way to enter it through some contacts. Nothing happened. The strike was postponed. I mention the incident only to show that we were oriented always in the direction of mass activity, trying to overlook no opportunities. In that summer the strike of the Chevrolet workers in Toledo broke out. Our comrades were extremely active in the strike. Muste went out there and exerted considerable influence on the rank-and-file leaders of the strike. We got a lot of publicity from his activity, but nothing tangible in the way of organization. That was one of the weaknesses, it seemed to me, of Muste's methods, after I had had a chance to observe his personal traits over a period of time. He was a good administrator, and a good mass worker, gaining the confidence of workers very quickly. But he tended to adapt himself to the masses more than a real political leader can afford to do, with the result that he was seldom able to crystallize a firm nucleus on a programmatic basis for permanent functioning. In practically every case Muste in his mass work did a good job which some other political tendency, less generous and easy-going than Muste, eventually profited by.

In this period of party depression and internal difficulty Budenz began to show his hand. Budenz, as one of the leaders of the American Workers Party, had automatically come over into the new party—but without any enthusiasm. He had been opposed to the fusion. He was sick at the time and never participated in the work. After a few months of grumbling, he began an open opposition on his own account. He accused us of not carrying out the "American approach." That had been one of the emphasized points of the American Workers Party: that we should approach the American workers in understandable terms, talk their language, and emphasize those events in American history which could be interpreted in a revolutionary way, etc. We Trotskyists had always emphasized internationalism in our fight against the nationalistic degeneration of Stalinism. When they first began to discuss with us, the Musteites were greatly surprised to learn that we were perfectly willing to accept the "American approach." As a matter of fact, years back in the Communist Party, our faction had waged a fight along this very line. We demanded that the Communist Party, which had been inspired by the Russian revolution and kept its eyes all the time on Russia, look homeward. We said the party should Americanize itself, adapt itself in every way possible to the psychology, habits, and traditions of the American workers, illustrate its propaganda, whenever possible, by events of American history. We were fully agreed with that. I don't know if any of you noticed that we tried to apply it a little bit in the recent Minneapolis trial. In cross-examination, Mr. Schweinhaut was trying to get me to say what we would do if the army and navy turned against the workers and farmers government. I gave him the illustration of the American Civil War, what Lincoln did.

We were all for that kind of Americanization, that is, adaptation of our propaganda technique to the country. That is good Leninism too. But Budenz very quickly showed that by Americanism he meant a crude version of jingoism. He came to the National Committee of our party with a proposal that our whole program should be an amendment to the Constitution; that our revolutionary program be whittled down to one parliamentary project. It was a terribly capitulatory, a philistine program of the crudest kind. Budenz tried to make some trouble in the ranks, hoping to exploit ignorance and prejudice. There we had to be very careful about repercussions, because he had been a field worker and was known to the workers in the field. The word had been assiduously spread that the Trotskyists were theses sharks and hairsplitters, who understood nothing of the realities of the mass movement, and that no mass worker could have anything to do with them. We had to be very careful of this prejudice that had been spread against us. We didn't care about Budenz. We had his number. But we were greatly interested in his friends among the field workers who had come from the American Workers Party. We moved very carefully against Budenz. We didn't expel him, didn't threaten him. We simply opened a very cautious discussion. We began a very patient explanation, a political discussion, a political education.

I think the political education which we conducted on the Budenz question in that period was a model in our movement. The results of it were shown when Budenz later drew the logical conclusions from his philistine "Americanization" program and sold out to the Stalinists who at that time were waving the Star-Spangled Banner with both hands. He had expected to split the party and carry with him all these experienced and valuable militants in the field. He counted without his host. He underestimated what had been accomplished in the preceding patient discussion and cooperation in common work. At the showdown Budenz found himself isolated and went over to the Stalinists virtually alone. The field workers remained loyal to the party, and were gradually transforming themselves from militant mass field workers into genuine Bolsheviks. That takes time. Nobody is born a Bolshevik. It has to be learned. And it cannot be learned solely from books either. It is learned, over a long time, by a combination of field work, struggle, personal sacrifices, tests, study, and discussion. The making of a Bolshevik is a long, drawn-out process. But in compensation, when you get a Bolshevik, you have got something. When you get enough of them you can do anything you want to do, including making a revolution.

We had various difficulties and internal squabbles, all of which were simply sparks from the main fight over the question of the Socialist Party Left Wing. That was the focal point of all interest. At the National Committee Plenum of June 1935 we had a grand battle over the issue. This "June Plenum" is outstanding in the history of our party. This was no longer a disorganized scramble as at Pittsburgh in March. We came to the June Plenum ready for a fight. We came organized and determined, prepared with resolutions, to make the plenum discussions the springboard for an open fight in the party which would clarify the issue and educate the membership.

We demanded more emphasis on the Socialist Party. Evidence was accumulating before our eyes that our party was not attracting the unaffiliated radical workers, as we had hoped. We gained a few, but the bulk of them were joining the Socialist Party, under the impression that the future revolutionary party would take shape out of its Left Wing. Workers don't like to join a small party if they can belong to a bigger one. They can't be blamed for that; there is no virtue in smallness in and of itself. We saw that the Socialist Party was attracting such workers and barring the door to recruitment for the Workers Party. Even though the Socialist Party Left Wing wasn't consciously competing with us, by weight of their larger numbers they were drawing prospective recruits to the Socialist Party, and away from us. The Socialist Party was in our way. We had to remove that obstacle from our path.

At the June Plenum the old alignments were broken up. Burnham joined us in support of the Cannon-Shachtman resolution on the question of the Socialist Party. Muste and Oehler found themselves together on the other side. At the March Active Workers Conference, Muste had been in a bloc with us, but the political issues there had not been clearly drawn. By the time of the June Plenum Muste had become more and more suspicious that we might possibly have some ideas about the Socialist Party that would infringe upon the integrity of the Workers Party as an organization. He was dead set against that, and he entered into a virtual, though informal, bloc with the Oehlerites. In part, he was pushed into this ill-advised combination by Abern and his little clique; they do not deserve the dignity of the name of faction because they had no principles. These unprincipled internal clique fighters jumped into the situation, and the combination—Musteites, Oehlerites, and Abernites—constituted a majority at the June Plenum.

We began the great struggle against sectarianism as a minority—both in the leadership and in the membership. Our program in brief was this: major attention to the Left Wing and all developments in the Socialist Party. How was that major attention to be expressed? (1) By numerous articles in our press analyzing the developments in the Socialist Party addressing ourselves to the Left Wing workers, offering them advice and criticism in a friendly way. That would facilitate our approach to them. (2) By instructing our members to establish personal contacts among the Left Socialists, and try to get them interested in questions of principle, political discussions, joint meetings with us, etc. (3) Form Trotskyist fractions in the Socialist Party. Send in a group—30 or 40 members—to join the Socialist Party, and work inside it in the interests of the Bolshevik education of the Left Wing. These three points constituted the first half of our program. The second half was to leave organization perspectives open for the present. This apparently put us in a somewhat defensive position. We didn't say, "Let us join the Socialist Party." On the other hand, we didn't say that we would never under any conditions join the SP. We said: "Let us keep the door open on this point. Let us maintain the Workers Party, try to build it up by independent work. But let us establish close relations with the Left Wing in the SP, aim to fuse with them, and wait to see what the future developments will bring on the organizational side of the question."

In fact, we could not have joined the Socialist Party at that time even if the whole party had wanted to. The Right Wing, in control in New York, would not have permitted it. But we realized that the SP was in great ferment and that things might change radically on short notice. We wanted to be prepared for any developments which might occur. We said: "It may be that the Left Wing will be expelled from the Socialist Party and come to join us or unite with us in a new party. It may be that the Right Wing will split away and so open up the situation in the Socialist Party that we will have to join it in order to keep the Stalinists from grabbing the movement. Let us keep the question open and await developments."

That would not do for our opponents. The Oehlerites came forward with an absolutely positive and definite proposal, as sectarians always do. They said: "Don't join the Socialist Party, now or ever, as a matter of principle." Why must we mortgage the future in June 1935? Why? "Because the Socialist Party is affiliated with the Second International which became bankrupt in 1914 and was denounced by Rosa Luxemburg and by Lenin. The Communist International was organized because of the bankruptcy of the Second International. If we join the Socialist Party—now or in the future—we will be bolstering up the Social Democracy, and giving new credit to the Scheidemanns and Noskes who killed Karl Liebknecht and Rosa Luxemburg." That is about the essence of Oehlerism, fairly stated. Explain to them that there have been tremendous changes, new people, new factors, new political alignments? It is very difficult to explain anything to sectarians. They demanded that our party repudiate in principle the "French turn," the name given to the decision of the French Trotskyists to join the Socialist Party of France. The Oehlerites rejected that policy for all countries of the world. We fought them on the line of principle. We defended the "French turn." We said that under similar circumstances we would do the same thing in America.

They accused us of deliberately planning to join the Socialist Party, of concealing our aims in order to maneuver the membership in stages. Many party members believed this accusation for a time but there was no truth in it. It was impossible at that time, as we understood the situation in the SP, to take a more definite position. We did not propose to join the SP at that time but we refused to bar the way to such future decision by a declaration in principle against it. A party cannot be maneuvered; it must be educated—that is, if you have in mind the building of a revolutionary party. I would say that a leadership that plays that kind of game does not deserve any confidence at all. I never would identify myself with that kind of politics. If you believe in something, the thing to do is to begin propagandizing it right away so as to get the education abroad as quickly as possible. A party that does not act consciously, with the full knowledge of what it is doing, and why it is doing it, isn't worth much. To keep quiet and hope that some way or another you can smuggle a program through—that is not Marxist politics; that is petty-bourgeois politics, of which the moralistic Professor Burnham later gave us several examples. The whole purpose of any faction fight, from a Trotskyist standpoint, is not simply to gain the advantage and win a majority for the day. That is a perverted conception; it belongs to another world than ours.

This June Plenum was thrown open to the membership.

The discussion grew so hot we couldn't keep it within four walls. The whole membership was seething with interest. They were all at the door anyway. We went at it, debating night and day. There is some peculiar physical quality about Trotskyists—I don't know what it is. Normally they have no greater physical endurance than other people, sometimes not as much. But I have noticed more than once that in political fights, when it is a question of fighting for some political idea, Trotskyists can stay awake longer and speak longer and more frequently than people of any other political type. A part of our advantage at the plenum was a physical one. We simply wore them out. Finally, at about four o'clock of the third morning, exhausted, the majority shut off debate. They presented the motion to end the discussion at three o'clock. Then we talked for another hour on the ground that this violated democracy. By that time they were so tired they didn't care if it was democratic or not, but we were fresh as daisies. They closed the plenum with us in the minority but on the offensive to the last moment.

From the plenum the discussion was taken to the ranks. We were determined to defeat the sectarian policy and to isolate the sectarian faction. After four months of internal discussion it was evident that we had succeeded. The Muste-Oehler bloc was broken under the hammer-blows of the discussion, and the Oehlerites were isolated. In the course of further developments, the disloyalty of the left sectarians became manifest. They began to break the discipline of the party, distributing their own publications at public meetings despite the prohibition of the party. They came in with theses demanding the right to set up a press of their own as an independent faction. At the October Plenum we passed a resolution explaining that their demand was impossible to grant from a practical point of view and false in principle from the point of view of Bolshevism. Shachtman wrote this resolution showing why their demand was wrong and why we could not grant it. Later on, in the fight with the petty-bourgeois opposition, Shachtman wrote another resolution showing how it was correct in principle and necessary for his faction to have an independent, dual organ. That contradiction was nothing strange or new to us. Shachtman was always distinguished not only by an extraordinary literary facility, but also by a no less extraordinary literary versatility, which enabled him to write equally well on both sides of a question. I believe in giving every man his due, and Shachtman is entitled to that compliment.

The October Plenum rejected the demands of the Oehlerites, and on the motion of Muste, gave them a stern warning to cease and desist from further violations of party discipline. They disregarded the warning and continued with systematic violations of party discipline. On that ground they were expelled from the party shortly after the October Plenum.

In the meantime, while all this was going on in our ranks, things were rapidly coming to a head in the Socialist Party. The Right Wing, which was concentrated in New York around the Rand School, the *Daily Forward,* and the trade union bureaucracy, grew more and more aggressive in the fight, and finding themselves in a minority, split away on their own initiative in December 1935. This created an entirely new situation in the Socialist Party. The split-off of the Right Wing gave us the opportunity we needed to establish direct contact with this developing Left Wing. Thanks to the definitive settlement of the score with the sectarians, our hands were free by that time and we were ready to grasp the opportunity.

11

The 'French Turn' in America

The last lecture brought us up to the conclusion of the internal struggle with the Oehlerite sectarians at the October Plenum, 1935. The relation of forces at the June Plenum had radically changed after four months of discussion and factional struggle. The minority at the June Plenum had gained the majority in the ranks of the party. In addition to that, the tacit bloc of the ultraleft Oehlerites and the Musteite forces which had confronted us at the June Plenum, had been broken by the time of the plenum in October. There Muste himself found it necessary to introduce the resolution, which the Muste faction and the Cannon-Shachtman faction had drawn up jointly, laying down the conditions under which the Oehlerites could remain in the party. In view of the disloyal attitude they had taken, it was understood that this would signalize their departure from the party. That was the case. Their failure to comply with the disciplinary regulations of the October Plenum resulted in their expulsion.

One could draw a certain political lesson from the experience of Muste in his ill-starred bloc with Oehler. Combinations which cut across the lines of principle inevitably result in disaster for a political group. Such blocs cannot be maintained. Muste's error in playing with the Oehlerites at the June Plenum, and afterward, had greatly weakened his position in the party among those who took political programs seriously. But it must be said that he extracted himself from his untenable position in a much more creditable manner than Shachtman did later in his unprincipled bloc with Burnham. Muste, as soon as it became clear to him that the Oehler faction was disloyal to the party and was breaking with us, unceremoniously broke his relations with them. Then he joined hands with us to push them aside and eventually to expel them from the party. Shachtman hung onto Burnham's coattails till the very end—until Burnham shook him loose.

Following the departure of the sectarians, an uneasy truce prevailed in the party between the two factions: the Muste faction, which had the support of the Abernites, and the Cannon-Shachtman faction which by this time had become a majority both in the National Committee and in the ranks of the membership. It was an uneasy truce based on a sort of pseudo-agreement on what the practical tasks of the party should be. The specter of the Socialist Party Left Wing still hovered over the Workers Party. The problem was still there, but the means of solving that problem had not yet matured. Even after the October Plenum, 1935, we still made no proposal to enter the SP. This was not—as we were accused so often, and perhaps as some comrades are still inclined to believe—because we were dissimulating and trying to maneuver the party into the SP without the knowledge and consent of the membership. It was because the situation in the Socialist Party at that time did not permit the possibility of our group joining it. So long as the Right Wing "Old-Guard" had control of the organization in New York, the entry of the Trotskyists was mechanically excluded. The "Old-Guard" would never have permitted it. Consequently, we made no such proposal.

Just about that time, in fact, there had been a meeting of the National Committee of the Socialist Party where the weak-kneed "Militants" disgracefully capitulated to the Right Wing. The rank and file of the "Militant" caucus rose up against the action and their pressure pushed the leadership to the left again. It was not yet possible to say with assurance what would be the outcome of the fight in the Socialist Party. We could only wait and see. The fundamental problem of the Socialist Party remained unsolved on our part because the situation in the Socialist Party had not yet jelled.

During all this time the attention of the advanced workers, the unaffiliated but more or less radical and class-conscious workers, was concentrated on the Socialist Party because it was a bigger party. They said: "Let us wait and see whether it is going to be the Socialist Party or the Workers Party which will really be the heir to the radical movement of the United States. Let us see if the Socialist Party will really turn to the left. In that case we can join a revolutionary party that is bigger than the Workers Party." Under such conditions it was extremely difficult to recruit into the Workers Party.

There was continual friction inside the Workers Party over the Socialist Party question despite the fact that at that time there were no proposals of one faction as against the other. All of us presumably were going along building up the WP, conducting our independent agitation, and so on. We said we had no proposal about joining the Socialist Party. They could not have opposed such a proposal from a principled standpoint, since they had endorsed the "French turn." Nevertheless, there was a difference in the way the problem was viewed by the two factions. They looked upon the ferment in the Socialist Party as a bothersome question, something to be avoided. Every time something of interest drew new attention to the factional fight within the SP, they would resent it because it distracted attention from our own organization. They regarded the Socialist Party as only a rival organization, and didn't see the conflicting currents and tendencies, some of whom would be destined to march together with us. It was an organizational approach. That is, I think, the proper way to characterize the attitude of Muste at that time. "Pay no attention to the SP; it is a rival organization." Formally that was the case. But the Socialist Party was not a homogeneous body. Some of its elements were irreconcilable enemies of the socialist revolution; others were capable of becoming Bolsheviks. Organizational loyalty and pride is an absolutely indispensable quality in a revolutionary movement. But organizational fetishism, especially on the part of a small organization which has yet to justify its right to leadership, can become a disorienting tendency. So it was in this case.

We approached the problem from another standpoint, not so much from the organizational side as from the political side. We saw in the ferment in the Socialist Party not a troublesome diversion from the work of building up our own party. We saw it rather as an opportunity to be seized upon for the advancement of our movement regardless of what organizational form it might eventually take. Our inclination was to turn toward it, to try to influence it in some way. As I said, the practical proposals at the moment were not very different between the two factions, but the difference in attitude toward the problem of the Socialist Party was fundamental, and bound sooner or later to bring us to a clash. The organizational question is important, but the political line is decisive. No one can succeed in creating a revolutionary organization who does not understand that politics is superior to organizational questions. Organization questions are important only insofar as they serve a political line, a political aim. Independently they have no merit whatsoever. During the particular period, while the issue in the Socialist Party remained undecided, the Muste position appeared to be more positive and clear-cut than ours. The simple prescription of Muste was appealing to some comrades. "Stay away from the Socialist Party, build our own party"—clear-cut and positive. But the superiority of the Muste formula was only the superficial appearance of things. The minute something new happened in the SP—and this was the everlasting bedevilment of the Musteites; something was always happening in that boiling cauldron—we would have to turn our attention to it and write about it in our press.

And something happened this time. A new turn of events resolved all doubts on our part and put the issue of entry or nonentry into the SP very squarely. The faction-ridden Socialist Party began to split wide open in December 1935. The Right Wing, which was in control of the apparatus in New

York, was confronted at the City Central Committee—a body of delegates from branches—with the growing strength of the Left Wing and its majority there. The Right Wing, instead of recognizing this majority and letting democratic processes operate, showed their teeth as professional Socialist "democrats" always do in such situations. As a matter of course, they turned around, expelled and reorganized a number of the "Militant" branches, and the split was precipitated. In this case, as in past instances, we see revealed the real essence of the so-called democracy of the Socialist Party and of all petty-bourgeois groups who holler to heaven about the dictatorial methods and harshness of Bolshevism. All their talk about democracy is shown up as a pretense and sham the minute it is put to a test. They speak against Bolshevism in the name of democracy, but when their interests and their control are at stake, they never yield to the democratic majority of the rank and file. These organizations have a pseudodemocracy which permits a great deal of talk and criticism as long as this talk and criticism doesn't in any way menace the control of the organization. But the moment their rule is challenged, they come down every time with the most brutal bureaucratic repressions against the majority. This is true of all of them, of all kinds and colors of opponents of Bolshevism in the field of organization. Even the sanctified Norman Thomas was no exception, as I will demonstrate later on. Incidentally, this is also true of all the sectarian groups without exception who split away from the Fourth International, who raised a great hue and cry about the lack of democracy in the Trotskyist movement. The moment they set up their own organizations, they established real despotisms. The

Oehler group, for example, was no sooner constituted as an independent organization than the people who had been lured by his appeals against the terrible bureaucratism of the Trotskyist organization got a rude shock. They encountered the most rigid and despotic caricature of bureaucratism.

The split in New York of the Right Wing of the Socialist Party heralded the national split—that was clear to us. The Right Wing of the Socialist Party was determined, for reasons of their own, to disconnect themselves from the militant rank and file and youth elements in the SP who were talking about revolution. They considered this out of date. They were looking toward the 1936 national elections and already in their own minds had undoubtedly arrived at the position of supporting Roosevelt. They were only looking for a good pretense to break their relations with the rank-and-file militants and youth who were still taking Socialism seriously. This split in New York showed us that the time had come to act without delay. It happened that I was in Minneapolis when the explosion took place in the New York organization of the SP. Here was a striking repetition of the procedure of 1934. The impulsion to speed up the fusion with the American Workers Party came from a discussion held there during the strike. Now, for the second time, the initiative for a sharp political turn came from an informal conference which I had with leading comrades in Minneapolis.

We came to the conclusion that we must move, without one day's unnecessary delay, to get into the Socialist Party while it remained in a state of flux, before a new bureaucracy would have time to crystallize and before the influence of the Stalinists could be consolidated. The whole leadership of our faction, the Cannon-Shachtman faction, was agreed upon this line. The rank and file of the faction had been well prepared and educated in the long internal fight and had entirely assimilated the political line of the leadership. They supported this plan unanimously. They had overcome all prejudices about the "French turn," about the principle of "independence," and all other shibboleths of the sectarian phrasemongers. When the opportunity arose to take a turn which offered the prospect of political advantage they were ready to move. The moment had come to act.

Then everything hung on the question of acting without too much delay, without playing around, without indecision or hesitation. Routine propaganda, which is carried on all the time, is by no means sufficient in itself to build a party and enable it to grow rapidly. The routine exposition of principles is not enough. A political party must know what to do next, and do it before it is too late. In this particular case the thing we had to do next, if we wanted to take advantage of a great fluid situation in the vanguard of the workers movement, was to move forthwith into the SP, seize the opportunity before it slipped away, take a step forward by effecting a fusion of the Trotskyist workers with the militant rank and file and young people in the Socialist Party who had at least the subjective desire to be revolutionists and who were moving in our direction. There is an expression, a good American motto, about striking while the iron is hot. I don't know how many of you realize how vivid that expression can appear to one who understands its meaning in the mechanical sense. It has always been a favorite motto of mine in politics, and it always calls up the vision of the blacksmith shop back home where we boys used to stand around, fascinated by the blacksmith, a heroic figure in our eyes. He took his time, smoked his pipe very leisurely, talked to people about the weather and local politics. When a horse was brought around to be shod, the blacksmith slowly pumped up the bellows under the forge, still taking it easy until the fire reached a certain white heat and the horseshoe became red hot. Then, at the decisive moment, the blacksmith became transformed. All his lassitude thrown off, he seized the horseshoe with his great pincers, lifted it onto the anvil and began to pound it with his hammer while it was red hot. Otherwise the horseshoe would lose its malleability and he could not fashion it into the proper shape. If we had allowed the opportunity in the SP to cool, we would have missed our chance. We had to strike while the iron was hot. There was danger that the Stalinists, who were pressing upon the SP very heavily, would get in ahead of us and repeat their feat in Spain. There was danger that the Lovestoneites who were certainly closer in political affinity to the American Socialists than we were because they were nothing more than centrists themselves, would learn what their next cue was and step ahead of us into the Socialist Party.

We had two small hurdles to jump over before we could effect the entry. First, we had to have a party convention to get the sanction for such an action. Second, we had to get permission from the heads of the Socialist Party before we could join it. Prior to our convention we had to go through one more fierce factional struggle with the Musteites who summoned their cohorts for a last stand to save the "independence" and "integrity" of the Workers Party. They fought with holy zeal against our proposal to dissolve the church of the Lord and go and join the heretic Socialists. They defended the "independence" of the Workers Party as though it were the Ark of the Covenant and we were laying profane hands upon it. It was certainly a furious fight that had in it elements of semireligious fanaticism. But it availed them nothing. The large majority of the party members were clearly on our side from the start.

We began negotiations with the leaders of the "Militants" over the terms and conditions of our entry into the Socialist Party. The negotiations with these *papier-mâché* heroes were a spectacle for gods and men. I will never forget them. I believe that in all my long and somewhat checkered experience, which has ranged from the sublime to the ridiculous, and vice versa, I never encountered anything so fabulous and fantastic as the negotiations with the chiefs of the "Militants" caucus in the Socialist Party. They were all transient figures, important for a day. But they didn't know it. They saw themselves in a distorting mirror, and for a brief period imagined themselves to be revolutionary leaders. Outside their own imagination there was hardly any basis whatever for their assumption that they were at all qualified to lead anything or anybody, least of all a revolutionary party which requires qualities and traits of character somewhat different from the leadership of other movements. They were inexperienced and untested. They were ignorant, untalented, petty-minded, weak, cowardly, treacherous, and vain. And they had other faults too. They were in a quandary over our application for admission to their party. They wanted to have us in the party, most of them, to counterbalance the Right Wing and to help ward off the Stalinists whom they mortally feared on one side and tended to approach on the other. They wanted us in the party and were afraid of what we might do after we came in. They didn't know for sure, from the beginning until the very end, what they really wanted. In addition to everything else, we had to help them make up their minds.

There was Zam, ex-Lovestoneite and renegade Communist who was turning back to Social Democracy. On his way to the right he ran into some young Socialists who were traveling to the left, and for the moment they seemed to be in agreement. But it wasn't really so; they had merely met at the crossroad.

There was Gus Tyler, a very smart young chap whose only trouble was that he had no character. He could stand up and debate the war question from the standpoint of Lenin with one of the Stalinist leaders—and state the Leninist position quite correctly—and then go to work for the Needle Trades fakers, doing "educational work" for their program, including their war program, and then wonder why anybody should be surprised or indignant about it. People without character are like people without intelligence. They don't understand why anybody should think it strange.

There was Murry Baron, a bright young college boy who also got a job as a trade union leader on the sufferance of Dubinsky. He lived well and considered it important that he continue to do so. At the same time, he was dabbling with the task of leading a revolutionary movement, like someone who takes up a hobby on the side.

There were Biemiller and Porter from Wisconsin, young fellows who at the age of thirty had acquired all the senile qualities of the European Social Democrats. Having lost the flame of idealism, if they were ever touched by it, they were already settling down to the business of labor faking on week-days and pretending to be radical on Sunday. They were nearly all of the same type, and it was a very poor type. Yet they were the leaders of the Left Wing of the Socialist Party and we had to negotiate with them all, including Norman Thomas who was head of the party nominally, and who, as Trotsky very well explained, called himself a Socialist as the result of a misunderstanding.

Our problem was to make an agreement with this rabble to admit us to the Socialist Party. In order to do that we had to negotiate. It was a difficult and sticky job, very disagreeable. But that did not deter us. A Trotskyist will do anything for the party, even if he has to crawl on his belly in the mud. We got them into negotiations and eventually gained admission by all sorts of devices and at a heavy cost. It was not simply a question of calling them on the phone and saying, "Let's meet at two o'clock on Tuesday and discuss matters." It was a long, involved, and torturous process. While we were ne-gotiating formally and collectively, we also had several sepa-rate, individual angles working. One of them was Zam, the renegade Communist who seemed to think, because we wanted to join the Socialist Party, that we were going to do a little renegading too. He had personal reasons for wanting us in the SP and he facilitated our admission. He was mortally afraid of the Stalinists, and thought we would be a counter-balance and antidote to them. Private discussions with him always preceded the formal discussion with the leaders. We always knew beforehand what they were planning to do.

270 History of American Trotskyism

In addition to all the other things, they had no internal solidarity or respect for each other and we naturally took advantage of that. Another independent sideline operation, preceding the entry, was with Thomas himself. The arrangement of the rendezvous between Thomas and the Trotskyists was the last progressive act in the life and career of Sidney Hook. Perhaps he felt that he owed us one more favor. Possibly he was moved by sentimental reminiscences of his youth when he had thought the revolution was a pretty good thing. Be that as it may, he arranged a meeting with Thomas which increased the pressure on the "Militants" caucus. They finally agreed to admit us, but they made us pay.

They made very hard conditions. We had to give up our press despite the fact that it had been the tradition of the Socialist Party to let any faction have its own press, and despite the fact that the Socialist *Call* had started as a faction organ of the "Militants." Any section or state or local organization in the SP that wanted its own press had been free to have it. They demanded special conditions of us, that we should have no press. They made us give up the *Militant* and our magazine, the *New International*. They wouldn't allow us the honor and dignity of joining as a body and being received as a body. No, we had to join as individuals, leaving every local Socialist Party branch the option of refusing to admit us. We had to join individually because they wanted to humiliate us, to make it appear that we were simply dissolving our party, humbly breaking with our past, and starting anew as pupils of the "Militants" caucus of the SP. It was rather irritating, but we were not deflected from our course by personal feelings. We had been too long in the Lenin school for that. We were out to serve political aims. That is why, despite the most onerous conditions, we never broke negotiations and never gave them an excuse to shut negotiations off from their side. Whenever they showed signs of indifference, of evasiveness, we kept after them and kept the negotiations alive.

Meantime our own party was moving toward its convention. It was soon revealed that the decisive majority of the party supported the proposals of the Cannon-Shachtman caucus for entry into the Socialist Party. Our proposal also had the support of Trotsky. This was a considerable factor in reassuring the rank and file of the party that it was a good tactical step, not to be construed in any way as a repudiation of principles, as the Oehlerites had represented it. The convention of March 1936 which had to put the seal on the decision was a formality. The majority in favor of the proposal to enter the Socialist Party was overwhelming. The opposition was reduced to such a small group that they had virtually no alternative but to accept the decision, submit to discipline, and go along with us into the Socialist Party.

At this convention there was a kickback from some unprincipled politics that had taken place in the summer, a cruel penalty for unprincipled combinationism. In this case it was the aftermath of the Allentown incident which is quite famous in the history of our party, and is still alive in the memories of those who went through the struggles of those days. Allentown had been one of the main centers of the American Workers Party. The entire organization there, which was quite large, and which was in the leadership of a very substantial movement of unemployed workers organized in the National Unemployed Leagues, was composed of former Musteites. Most of the Allentown members had been in the movement only a short time. They had come into the American Workers Party through the unemployed activities and were in need of Marxist political education, in order that the fruits of their mass work could eventually be transformed into political gains and a firm political party nucleus established there. We sent in some comrades to assist them in this respect. For the youth a young comrade named Stiler was sent in. For the adult movement, Sam Gordon was sent. Their function, while participating in the mass activities, was to assist in the Marxist education of these Allentown comrades who showed a strong will to become completely fused with us in ideology as well as organization. The faction fight arrested these plans and Allentown was a center of infection all through the period.

One of the worst complications arose from the treachery of Stiler. He was sent in there with the trust of the party, but he succumbed to the backward environment. He became an instrument and defender of the worst elements in the American Workers Party who had a center there in Allentown. A man named Reich, another named Hallett were closely connected with one of the Musteite national leaders, named Arnold Johnson. They used Allentown as a base for opposition to every progressive trend in the party. Time and time again, the Allentown organization would deviate from the party line in the mass work, in the direction of Stalinism. Sam Gordon would intervene and a big fight would take place locally. Then, either the National Committee representatives would go to Allentown, or a delegation would come in to New York, for a discussion of the issue. We would speak and explain for hours on end in an effort to clarify the question and educate the Allentown comrades. We suspected nothing at first, but as one incident followed another, we couldn't help noticing that every flare-up had one and the same distinguishing characteristic.

No matter how each fracas started, or what the immediate dispute might be over, there was always a taint of Stalinist ideology in the position of the Allentown comrades. We thought it probable, in the beginning, that the deviations were only tendencies, the expression of the pressure of the Stalinist movement weighing upon them, and not the deliberate work of real Stalinist agents in our ranks. We continued to give them the benefit of the doubt, even when they began to manifest organizational disloyalty, breaking the discipline and unity of action of the Workers Party and working in unison with the Stalinist caucus even against their own comrades in the Unemployed Leagues. We kept fighting it out with them, but our aim was purely educational.

It has always been the policy in our movement to use incidents like this, errors and deviations from party principle, not for the purpose of staging manhunts but as the occasion to explain concretely and in detail the doctrines of Marxism and thus aid the education of the comrades. Many comrades in the party have received their real education in the meaning of Bolshevism from these educational discussions conducted on the basis of some concrete incident or other. We tried the method in this case.

We tried to educate not only the comrades involved in Allentown, but the whole party on what conciliation with Stalinism means in a revolutionary sense. But this work was hampered by the fact that these people were personal friends of Muste and that Muste protected them. For factional reasons he protected his friends against those, who he admitted, were defending a correct political line. Instead of taking a clear stand with us, and joining with us to put pressure on the Allentown people, he would step in between us and them, blur the issue, and prevent any kind of disciplinary action even in the most flagrant violations. Blinded by the intensity of the factional fight, Muste put the thing on a factional basis, protecting his friends. That is one of the gravest offenses against the revolutionary party. What has to be protected in the party, first of all, are the principles of Bolshevism. If one has friends, the best thing he can do for them is to teach them the principles of Bolshevism, not to protect them in their error. If you do that, not only do your friends go to the devil, but you go with them. The friendship business is all right for Tammany Hall, which is based on the exchange of personal favors. But friendship, which is a very good thing in personal life, must always be subordinated to principles and the interests of the movement. I said to Muste after one of those exhibitions: "You are going to be terribly shocked some morning when you wake up and discover a Stalinist nucleus in Allentown trying to betray the party."

He wouldn't listen, but persisted in his fatal course. And he was assisted in this crime by those who knew better. Muste was not a man of long experience in the tradition and the doctrines of Bolshevism. That might be said in his extenuation. But Muste was supported and egged on in this shielding of Stalinist tendencies and elements for factional reasons by Abern and his little clique. And I won't say anything more about these people here because I have said all that need be said about them in my book, *The Struggle for a Proletarian Party.*

This adventure of Muste and Abern had a terrific kickback in the convention in March 1936. Then, in return for his coddling and covering up and protecting of the Stalinist tendencies in Allentown, Muste was rewarded by the announcement in the *Daily Worker,* on the day our convention opened, that Reich, Hallett, and Johnson had joined the Communist Party! Muste's "friends" issued a statement denouncing the "counterrevolutionary Trotskyists," on the very morning that our convention opened. This was the final devastating blow to the Muste-Abern faction, which had already been discredited enough. They had to suffer the final disgrace of seeing a group of people, whom they had protected for factional reasons, turning out to be Stalinist agents trying to demoralize and split our convention on the day it opened. Fortunately, the traitors were completely isolated; their action remained only a personal episode, and did not disturb the convention or the party in any way whatever. It only discredited the faction that had covered them up so blindly in the preceding months. By the same token, this denouement reinforced the authority of the majority faction, which had followed a clearly principled line and was in no way involved in the scandal.

We had an overwhelming majority at the convention. The minority, which was a very small minority by then, accepted the decision. There was nothing else they could do. At the Socialist Party convention in Cleveland a few weeks later, the split with the Right Wing was completed on a national scale, and our members all over the country began joining the Socialist Party as individuals under the direction of the national leadership. We suspected a double cross even at that late date. Our advice to our comrades everywhere was: "Hurry, don't delay. Don't dicker for terms but get into the Socialist Party while there is time. Don't hold out for formal concessions which will give them a pretext for reopening the question and changing their minds."

We received no welcome, no friendly salute, no notice in the press of the Socialist Party. Nothing was offered to us. Not one of the leaders of our party was offered so much as a post as branch organizer by these cheapskates—not one. The Stalinists were howling at the top of their voices: "You will never be able to digest these Trotskyists." They were warning them what would happen when the Trotskyists came in. And this was scaring the "Militants" blue in the face. It was a shabby business—the way they received us. If we had been subjective people standing on our honor, we might have said, "To hell with it!" and walked away. But we didn't, because we were serving political ends.

We didn't construe all these humiliating concessions we had made as conciliation with the centrists. We just said to ourselves: that is blackmail we are paying for the privilege of carrying out a historically important political task.

We went into the Socialist Party confidently because we knew that we had a disciplined group and a program that was bound in the end to prevail. When, a little later, the leaders of the Socialist Party began to repent of the whole business, wishing they had never heard the name of Trotskyism, wishing to reconsider their decision to admit us, it was already too late. Our people were already inside the Socialist

Party and beginning their work of integrating themselves in the local organizations. We issued a declaration in the last number of the *Militant,* published in June 1936, announcing that we were joining the Socialist Party and suspending the *Militant.* We stated our position very clearly, so that nobody could misunderstand us; no one could have any ground to believe that we were joining as capitulators, as renegades from Communism. We said: "We enter the Socialist Party as we are, with our ideas." These world-conquering ideas once again were on the march. And there was a fruitful year of work ahead of us in the Socialist Party.

12

The Trotskyists in the Socialist Party

The last lecture in this series deals with the period of approximately one year that we spent inside the Socialist Party and the six months during which we were neither in nor out, but on our way to another destination. In the course of these lectures I have emphasized repeatedly that the tactics of a party are imposed upon it by political and economic factors beyond its control. The task of political leadership is to understand what is possible and necessary in a given situation, and what is not possible and not necessary. This may be said to be the gist of political leadership. The activities of a revolutionary party, that is, a Marxist Party, are conditioned by objective circumstances. These circumstances sometimes impose defeat and isolation upon the party despite anything that can be done by the leadership and the membership. In other situations the objective circumstances create possibilities for successes and advances, but at the same time limit them. The party always moves within a set of social factors not made by itself. They are features of the process of the development of society.

There are times when the best leadership cannot move the party forward by a single inch. For example, Marx and Engels, the greatest of all the teachers and leaders of our movement, remained isolated practically throughout their entire lives. They could not even create a substantial group in England where they lived and worked during the period of their maturity. This was not due to errors on their part and certainly not to incapacity, but to external factors beyond their control. The British workers were not yet ready to hear the revolutionary word.

During the long period of reaction and stagnation, which gripped the world labor movement in the first years of our existence as a Trotskyist movement in this country, namely from 1928 until 1934, we could not avoid isolation. That was the time when the whole weight of the world seemed to bear down upon a small group, a small handful of irreconcilables. That was the time when fainthearted people, especially those without a theoretical grasp of the nature of modern society and the laws working within it in favor of crises leading to revolution, fell by the wayside. That was the time when only the Trotskyists, the bona fide Marxists, foresaw, in the period of darkest reaction and isolation, that a new rise was bound to come and consciously prepared for it in two ways: first, by elaborating the program which would equip the party for the new time; and, secondly, by assembling the preliminary cadres of the future revolutionary party and inspiring them to hold on with faith in the future. This faith in the

future was justified as we have seen in some of the preceding
lectures. When the logjam in the world labor movement began to break up, especially beginning with 1934, a new
movement of the masses was to be seen in this country, and
all over the world. When that new situation began to reveal
itself we were put to the test and given our opportunity. That
was no longer the time to remain contentedly in isolation,
clarifying principles. That was the time to bestir ourselves
and apply those principles in action in the life of the surging
class struggle. Our determination to do this, our recognition
that the opportunity was before us, and our determination to
grasp that opportunity, brought us into conflict with the
sectarians, the ultraleftists. We had to fight them, we had to
defeat them, in order to go forward. We did that. In the Minneapolis strike we took a step forward in the economic mass
movement. The fusion with the American Workers Party was
another important step along the road toward the development of a serious Marxist party in the United States. But
these progressive actions were only steps, and we had to recognize the limitedness of the accomplishments. Political initiative and resolute actions in more complicated situations
were still required of us.

The entry of our group into the Socialist Party of the
United States was a still more important step along the
complicated, winding, long, drawn-out path toward the
creation of a party that will eventually lead the proletariat of
America to victory in the socialist revolution. That step, the
entry into the Socialist Party, was taken by us at just the right
time. Time is always an important consideration in politics.
Time does not wait. Alas for the political leader who forgets

it. There is a legal expression: "Time is of the essence of the contract." Ten times, a thousand times more does that apply in politics. It is not only what you do that decides, but when you do it; whether you do it at the right moment.

It was not possible for us to join the Socialist Party earlier than we did, and if we had tried it later, it would have been too late. The heterogeneous Socialist Party that was attracting so much of our attention in those days, this centrist mishmash, this headless, helpless party, was buffeted by external events and squeezed by all kinds of pressures. The party itself was not viable. It was already in the stage of violent ferment and disintegration in 1936 at the time of our entry. The Socialist Party was destined, in any case, to be torn apart. The only question was how and along what lines the disintegration and eventual destruction of the historically unviable party would take place.

There was a powerful, though not yet fully conscious movement in the Socialist Party toward reconciliation with the Roosevelt administration, and thereby with bourgeois society. The propaganda and material resources of the well-heeled apparatus of the Communist Party pressed heavily upon the leaderless Socialist workers. The question was: Would the potentially revolutionary element of the centrist party—the worker activists and rebellious youth—be engulfed by these forces? Or, would they be fused with the cadres of Trotskyism and brought over to the road of the proletarian revolution? This could be tested only by our entry into the Socialist Party. It was not possible for the Trotskyists to come into contact with these potentially revolutionary elements of the Socialist Party otherwise than by joining the Socialist Party, for the simple reason that they showed no disposition to join our party. Organizational fetishism had to be cast aside. It had to give place to the demands of political necessity, which always stand above organizational considerations.

Our entry into the Socialist Party took place against a background of great events which were in process of unfolding, both at home and on a world scale. The sit-down strikes in France, a veritable revolution, were taking place at the very moment we were arranging to join the Socialist Party. The second big upsurge of the CIO, destined to carry this tremendous movement to greater heights than the organized labor movement of America had ever known—in numerical strength, in mass militancy, and in its composition of the basic lower strata of the proletariat—this second big upsurge was in the beginning of its development at that time, in the spring of 1936. The CIO rebellion was partly influenced, undoubtedly, by the sit-down strikes in France. The Spanish civil war was about to break out in full force; and to raise once again, in the most acute manner, the prospect of a second victory of the proletarian revolution in Europe. The Spanish revolution had within it the possibility of changing the whole face of Europe if it should succeed.

A few months afterwards the Moscow trials were to shake the whole world.

This great panorama of world-shaking events—and the rise of the CIO was not less important than the others in my judgment, from a world historical point of view—created the most favorable auspices for a forward march of the Marxist vanguard. There was no lack of political interest, no lack of mass activities, no lack of an adequate field for the operation of Marxist revolutionists at the time when we were conducting our activity within the framework of the Socialist Party. If we were worth our salt under such objective conditions, we were bound to gain. We would have had to be the worst kind of leadership; we would almost have had to set out consciously to defeat ourselves in order to fail to gain in such favorable circumstances as those.

Our work in the Socialist Party, when viewed in retrospect, was by no means free from errors and neglected opportunities. There is no doubt at all that the leaders of our movement adapted themselves a little too much to the centrist officialdom of the Socialist Party. A certain amount of formal adaptation was absolutely necessary in order to gain the possibilities of normal work in the organization. But this adaptation undoubtedly was carried too far in some cases and led to illusions and fostered deviations on the part of some members of our movement. There is no doubt at all that after the entry too much time was spent in negotiations and palaver with the leaders of the New York "Militants" group—Zam, Tyler, and other Lilliputians of this type, who had absolutely no real power in the party, and whose strategic position was a transitory one rather than that of real influence over the ranks of the party. There is no doubt that in carrying out the political maneuver of entry into the Socialist Party and concentration on the political problems raised within the Socialist Party, we neglected to do as much mass work as might have been done. There is no doubt that such errors and neglected opportunities can be charged against us. But, on the whole, with the advice and the guidance of Trotsky—a decisive factor in all this work—we accomplished our main task.

We accumulated invaluable political experience, and we more than doubled our forces as a result of the entry and one year's work in the Socialist Party. We began our work very modestly and according to plan. Our first prescription for our people was: Penetrate the organization, become integrated into the party, plunge into practical work, and thus establish a certain moral authority with the rank and file of the party; establish friendly personal relations, especially with those elements of the party who are activists and therefore potentially of some use. Our plan was to let the political issues develop normally, as we were sure they would. We didn't have to force discussion or to initiate the faction struggle artificially. We could well afford to let the political issues unfold under the impact of world events. And we didn't have long to wait.

The situation was vastly different from that of our early years when the general reaction and stagnation held us down. Now objective factors worked in favor of the revolutionists and created the conditions and opportunities they needed to move forward. The Spanish civil war began in July 1936 with the insurrection led by Franco and the great counterattack of the workers. The Moscow trials broke over a startled world in August, a few months after we had joined the Socialist Party. These were issues of world significance, and consequently they became known as "Trotskyist" issues. As far back as 1928 it had been recognized by our enemies, even by the most ignorant, that Trotskyism is no provincial dogma. Trotskyism is a movement of world scope and world perspective. Trotskyism proceeds from the standpoint of internationalism and concerns itself with the problems of the proletariat in all parts of the world.

The general recognition of this fundamental quality of Trotskyism was ironically illustrated during the time we were on trial before the Political Committee and the Central Control Commission of the Communist Party in October 1928. Up until the end of the long trial, when we read our declaration and put a stop to all ambiguity, they had been trying to "prove" a case of "Trotskyism" against us by any kind of "circumstantial evidence" they could get. (We had not admitted that we were a Trotskyist faction for tactical reasons, as I have already explained.) They brought in a lot of witnesses, very much in the manner of the prosecutors at our recent trial in Minneapolis, to bring corroborative and circumstantial evidence of our guilt. One little stool pigeon would run in and say he heard this, and another would say he heard that. But the star witness was the manager of the Communist Party's bookshop. He said he could swear that Shachtman was a Trotskyist. Why? How did he know? "Because he is always coming into the bookstore, trying to get books on China, and I know China is a Trotskyist question." The little weasel wasn't so far wrong at that. China was indeed a Trotskyist question, as were all questions of world import.

The Spanish civil war, the Moscow trials, and the turmoil in the French labor movement—these questions dominated the whole internal life of the Socialist Party. The most animated discussion revolved around these issues, entirely against the will of the leadership. They wanted to confine themselves to practical business, that is, to routine. "Let us settle down and do a practical job here." But these issues occupied the interests of all those who took the word Socialism seriously, and we organized a deliberate campaign to educate the rank and file of the party on their meaning.

As the Moscow trials were reported from day to day, it became obvious that the real object was once again to implicate Trotsky and if possible to bring about his extradition and his execution in Russia; or, in any case, to discredit him before the labor movement of the world. It must be said that the American Trotskyists did not sleep in this situation. We jumped into the breach, did the best political job we had ever done and rendered our greatest service to the cause of the Fourth International in exposing the Moscow Frame-up Trials. It was owing to the existence of the American section of the Fourth International and to the fact that we were members of the Socialist Party at the time, that a work could be started which eventually blew up and discredited the Moscow trials throughout the whole world.

It was required for us historically, at that crucial moment, to be members of the Socialist Party and by that to have closer access to elements—liberals, intellectuals, and half-radical political people—who were necessary for the great political task of the Trotsky Defense Committee. I don't think Stalin could have arranged those trials as well at any other time to insure their complete discreditment as in the summer of 1936. We were then in the most favorable situation as members of the Socialist Party—and, therefore, surrounded to a certain extent with the protective coloration of a half-way respectable party—and we couldn't be isolated as a small group of Trotskyists, mobbed and lynched, as they planned to do. We conducted a terrific campaign to expose the trials and defend Trotsky. The Stalinists, for all their vast resources of apparatus, press, stooge organizations, and money, were put on the defensive from the start. Our comrades in New York, assisted by those throughout the country, were able to initiate the organization of a rather formidable-appearing committee, with John Dewey as chairman and an imposing list of writers, artists, newspapermen, and professional people of various kinds who sanctioned and sponsored the movement to organize an inquiry into the Moscow trials.

This inquiry, as you know, was eventually held at Mexico City in the spring of 1937. The case was thoroughly sifted; out of it came two great books which are and will remain forever classics of the world labor movement, *The Case of Leon Trotsky,* and the second one, the report of the commission, *Not Guilty.* This tremendous political task, which unquestionably resulted in the heaviest blow that we ever dealt to Stalinism, was made possible by this favorable conjuncture of events I have mentioned. A few months later, at the most a few years later, the majority of those petty-bourgeois elements who carried forward such a historically progressive task in the Trotsky Defense Committee were to succumb entirely to bourgeois society and turn their backs on all its irreconcilable opponents. At least 90 percent of these people would today be physically and morally incapable of actively participating in such a movement as the "American Committee for the Defense of Leon Trotsky." But at that particular conjuncture they were able to serve, and did serve, a great progressive end. The exposure and discreditment of the Moscow trials was one of the great achievements which has to be accredited to our political move of joining the Socialist Party in 1936.

The second big political campaign, carried on while we were in the Socialist Party, was around the events of the Spanish civil war and the Spanish revolution. Substantial reports and even books are the result of this work. I call your attention especially to the book written by Felix Morrow, *Revolution and Counter-Revolution in Spain* and the pamphlet, *The Civil War in Spain.* This pamphlet and book summed up and codified the great political fight we carried on; inside the Socialist Party and publicly wherever we had the opportunity we fought to clarify the affairs taking place in Spain and to educate the cadres of the American party on the meaning of those events. Our entry into the Socialist Party facilitated this campaign, gave us an audience right at hand inside of what was then our own party. We didn't really own it. But we had our dues paid up and this gave us an audience at every branch meeting of the Socialist Party.

In California, where I lived at the time for reasons of health, work was unfolded in the mass movement. There we quickly integrated ourselves in the party and acquired a leading influence by virtue of our activity, our speeches, and political work during the election campaign. As a result, within six months after we had joined the party, a weekly paper was started under the auspices of the Socialist Party of California and I was appointed editor. Circumstances worked very favorably in our behalf. My editorship of the paper and the prominence of our people in the locals and the state organization gave us direct entry, for the first time, into the maritime mass movement.

The great maritime strike of 1936–37 offered us a wide-open field. While our comrades in the East were developing the campaigns around the Moscow trials and the Spanish civil war, we out there in California were supplementing this great political work by intense activity in the mass movement which influenced the course of events in the great maritime strike of 1936–37. The work that was done there and the contacts that were established enabled us to organize the first nucleus of a Trotskyist fraction. This work has paid great dividends to our party and still continues to do so. The Trotskyists became from then on a progressively stronger factor in the maritime movement. That is one of the surest signs of our party's good future—that it has established a firm base in one of the most important and decisive industries of the country.

In Chicago we had another base of support in the *Socialist Appeal*. This was originally a small mimeographed bulletin published by Albert Goldman and a few other individuals. Goldman had joined the Socialist Party a year ahead of us, as an individual. He had refused to wait for a decision by the party, but joined on his own account just prior to our fusion with the Musteites. Sharp words were exchanged because of this action. It soon became manifest, however, that this organizational secession of Goldman was not intended by him as a principled break with us. From the start he worked constantly in the direction of our program. As soon as our party became oriented toward entry into the Socialist Party, we reestablished collaboration so effectively that when we gave up our press in response to the demand of the leaders of the Socialist Party, we already had an agreement with Goldman that the *Socialist Appeal,* which was an authorized and established organ in the Socialist Party, would become an official organ of the Trotskyist faction. Our collaboration was reestablished so quickly and so effectively that some people asked whether the whole thing—Goldman's break with the Trotskyist organization and his joining the Socialist Party as an individual, and the polemics between us and Goldman—weren't all a put-up job. That is not so at all. We are not so devious as all that. It just turned out that way; it turned out very well. The mimeographed bulletin was transformed into a printed magazine. The name, *Socialist Appeal* was continued. Despite the suppression of our old press by the "Militants" we soon had a monthly magazine legitimately established in the Socialist Party, espousing our program. By late autumn we had a weekly paper in California, which we called *Labor Action*—a good name that has not been treated so well in recent years.

Thus, to all intents and purposes, we had our press reestablished—a weekly agitational paper and a monthly magazine. *Labor Action* was published under the auspices of the Socialist Party of California, but if it was not a Trotskyist agitational paper, I will never be able to make one. We tried our best to utilize it in that sense. The *Socialist Appeal* became the medium around which our faction was "legally" reconstituted in the Socialist Party.

In the early part of 1937 we organized a national "Socialist Appeal Conference." Socialist Party members were invited from all parts of the country to come to Chicago to discuss ways and means of advancing the interests of the party. Everybody was welcome regardless of his background or his factional alignment. The sole condition was that he agree with the program of the *Socialist Appeal,* which happened to coincide with the program of the Fourth International. On that basis and in that form we constituted in Chicago in the early winter of 1937 what amounted in effect to a new nationwide Left Wing in the Socialist Party. This time it was a real Left Wing; not a hodgepodge "Militants" caucus, but an organization of party members brought together on the basis of a definite program, with leaders who knew what they wanted and were prepared to fight for it.

During all this time of our activity in the Socialist Party, as the fight was developing and we were gaining, the Stalinists were carrying out a tremendous offensive against us. They spent thousands, and I venture to guess, tens of thousands of dollars, in the effort to prevent us from making further headway in the Socialist Party. They were mortally afraid that we would get a sizable group around us. They knew all the time that the real dagger pointed at the heart of Stalinism is the Trotskyist movement, no matter how small it might be at a given moment. This campaign of the Stalinists was sympathetically echoed by a section of the Socialist leadership. They saw the strength and resources of the Stalinists as representatives of a great state power, the Soviet Union. They were far more impressed by this strength and these resources than by the principled correctness of the Trotsyist program. A section of the "Militants"—not all of them—inclined toward collaboration with the Stalinists, and if we hadn't been in the way, would long since have come into closer relations with them, as in Spain. But we had come in between them and the Stalinists with our criticism and our program, and we had stirred up the rank and file of the Socialist Party against the idea of unity with the Stalinists. This blocked their game and they took it out in increased resentment against us. Another section of the Socialist Party leadership, which was already orienting—perhaps without its full knowledge—towards reconciliation with Roosevelt, organized a real offensive against us: "Drive the Trotskyists out of the party." This campaign had a lot of pressure behind it—the Stalinists on the one side and the pressure of bourgeois influences on the other.

Most of those who led the fight against us later reconciled themselves with the bourgeois class. Jack Altman was one of them. Paul Porter became an agent of the War Labor Board. In that capacity he put through a dirty job of reducing the wages of the shipyard workers below what their contract had called for. He was one of the leaders of the Socialist Party who went to the length of writing a pamphlet demanding our expulsion from the party. People of this sort, who later became nothing but Roosevelt hirelings in the labor movement, were more favorably regarded by Norman Thomas and other top leaders than we were. They engineered a special convention of the party, which was not due under the constitution, for the special purpose of expelling the Trotskyists. They wanted to get rid of all this criticism from the Stalinists by removing the cause. They wanted to do away with the revolutionary coloration which we were imparting to the Socialist Party; they wanted to reestablish it in the good will of bourgeois society. The Socialist Party had always had, except for a brief period during the first World War, a "good reputation." It was regarded as a group of people who are for Socialism but don't mean any harm. That kind of party is always tolerated, but never gains any real serious influence. Throughout the labor movement the leaders and members of the SP were known as people who are for Socialism but who never make any trouble for labor fakers, racketeers, or traitors. All they want is the privilege of speaking a few words for Socialism. Our joining the party had changed that. Speaking in the name of the Socialist Party, we were carrying the fight to the Stalinists, we were carrying the fight to the labor fakers and giving the Socialist Party a different complexion in the public mind than it had before. They determined to get rid of us.

Our strategy in regard to this convention which was held in March 1937 was to delay the issue. We weren't entitled to be delegates, so we could not make much of a floor fight. We felt that we hadn't yet had time enough to educate and win over the maximum number of Socialist workers and Socialist youth who were capable of becoming revolutionists. We needed about six months more time. Therefore our strategy was to delay the showdown at this convention.

In furtherance of that strategy, I was brought from San Francisco, where I was at that time editing *Labor Action,* to New York to assist in the negotiations. We brought Vincent Dunne from Minneapolis. He and I were appointed as a committee of two to discuss matters with the leaders of the "Militants" and with Norman Thomas himself to see if we couldn't find a way of delaying the showdown. We had numerous conferences, one of them in Norman Thomas's house. Comrade Dunne and I, representing the Trotskyists, confronted Thomas and Tyler and Jack Altman and Murry Baron and others of the gang of young incipient labor fakers in a meeting to discuss what was to be done, what were the grievances against the Trotskyists that necessitated such a harsh attitude toward us, and so forth. I remember one of the big complaints that impressed Thomas particularly was the report that the Trotskyists, especially in New York, were talking too much at branch meetings; that they insisted on starting theoretical and political discussions along about eleven o'clock at night and going on endlessly. He wanted to know if something couldn't be done to restrain the Trotskyist caucus, or the Trotskyist faction, as the case might be, to limit these discussions to a reasonable hour. This struck a responsive chord in my heart. I had an accumulated resentment against these two o'clock in the morning debates. We made a broad, sweeping agreement that as far as our influence went, we would favor establishing a rule that branch meetings adjourn by eleven o'clock at night. We made a number of other sweeping concessions of this type. We wanted peace, and we offered quite a few things here and there about the question of positions, and in general we were so conciliatory and inoffensive that we finally got an agreement. Norman Thomas solemnly agreed with us there that no proposals should be made at the convention to suppress internal organs—the *Socialist Appeal* in particular—or to expel anybody for his opinions. That was an agreement made with us by Norman Thomas in the presence of the young "Militants" whom I have mentioned.

Norman Thomas made the agreement, but he didn't keep it. When he got to the convention at Chicago, after we had discussed with him, other pressures were put upon him, especially the pressure from Milwaukee, the seat of Social Democratic conservatism, which was destined to become social-chauvinism in the second World War. The pressure of those self-satisfied, bourgeois-minded Social Democrats from Milwaukee, and from those fledgling labor fakers in New York like Murry Baron was stronger than Norman Thomas's word of honor. He broke his word, double-crossed us. He rose up in the convention, and he himself made the motion to prohibit all internal organs in the party. To prohibit all of them merely meant to prohibit the *Socialist Appeal;* there were no others of any consequence or respect in the organization.

Following the convention, we were put right up against the gun. For the second time we were deprived of our press. We still hesitated to bring things to a head because in addition to our general unreadiness, the work of the Trotsky Defense Committee was still uncompleted and we were afraid of jeopardizing it by a premature split. There again Trotsky showed his complete objectivity. Trotsky, who certainly was concerned from a personal as well as political point of view in the issue of the Moscow trials, wrote us: "Of course, it would be a little bit awkward to have a split now in view of the work of the Commission of Inquiry, but that should not be a consideration. The most important thing is the work of political clarification and you should let nothing stand in your road."

Trotsky encouraged us and even incited us to go forward to meet their challenge and not permit them to push us any further for fear it might lead to disintegration of our own ranks, demoralization of the people whom we had led that far along the road. We proceeded cautiously, "legally," at first. We demonstrated that we could have a press, and a pretty effective one, without violating the ban on publications. We worked out a system of multicopied personal letters and branch resolutions. An ostensibly personal letter, evaluating the convention, was signed by one comrade and addressed to another. The letter was then mimeographed and discreetly distributed in the branches. Every time an issue arose, a new stage of development in the Spanish civil war, a resolution would be introduced in a New York branch by an individual comrade, then mimeographed and sent to our faction groups all over the country as a basis for their own resolutions on the question. We had no press. They had the whole machinery of the party. They had the national secretary, the editor, the labor secretary, the organizers—they had the whole works— but we had a program and a mimeograph machine and that proved to be enough.

Our faction everywhere was better informed, better disciplined, and better organized, and we were making rapid headway in recruiting new members into the faction. Then our moralistic Socialist "democrats" gave the party a real dose of democracy. They passed the "Gag" Law. This was a decision of the National Committee to the effect that no more resolutions could be introduced in branches about disputed questions. They had in mind particularly the Spanish civil war—a little incident in their minds. Then we revolted in earnest and began a campaign all over the country against the "Gag" Law. This took the form of introducing in all branches resolutions protesting against the decision to prohibit the introduction of resolutions. If the Socialist bureaucrats had had too many resolutions before, they were flooded with them after the passing of the "Gag" Law.

We decided to fight, bring the thing to a head, and put up with no more abuse. We had finished our work by that time anyway. Between the convention and the few months leading up to this head-on collision, we had virtually completed our work of educating and organizing those elements of the Left Wing, of the youth, who were really serious and capable of becoming proletarian revolutionists. The composition of the Socialist Party was predominantly petty bourgeois. It became clear that we could not hope to win over a real majority of the party with all the restrictions placed upon us. We had to get our hands free to reestablish our public press and turn our main attention once more to the broad class struggle.

We called a meeting of the National Committee of our faction for June in New York, worked up the resolutions for our fight and organized it on a national scale. They retaliated by wholesale expulsions, beginning in New York.

I never saw more bureaucratic and brutal violations of democratic rights and party constitution than these pious Social Democrats resorted to when they found they couldn't beat us in fair debate. They just framed us up and threw us out. A few days after the expulsion of the first group in New York we answered with the *Socialist Appeal* reappearing now as a printed eight-page tabloid weekly. We set up a "National Committee of the Expelled Branches," and called for a convention of the expelled branches to draw the balance of these experiences. All this work was done, especially in the later months, under the closest cooperation and even under the supervision of Comrade Trotsky.

By that time, you know, he was in Mexico and we had personal contact and communication with him. In the midst of all his troubles, and the preparation of all his material on the Moscow trial, he had time to write us frequently and to show that he had a very close and sensitive understanding of our problem. He did everything he could to help us.

Our campaign led us directly to a convention of the expelled branches of the Socialist Party in Chicago on the last day of December and New Year's Day 1938. There we recorded the results of the year and a half experience in the Socialist Party. It was clear that it had facilitated the organization of the Trotsky Defense Committee which had been the means of revealing the truth about the Moscow trials to the whole world, and enabling us to deal the biggest blow at Stalinism it had ever received up to that time. Our entry into the Socialist Party had facilitated our trade union work. Our work in the maritime strike in California, for example, had been greatly aided by the fact that, at the time, we were members of the Socialist Party. Our comrades had better connections in the automobile workers union where, up to then, we had never had anything more than an occasional contact. The basis had been laid for a powerful fraction of Trotskyists in the automobile workers union.

The great surprise of the convention was the revelation that while we had been concentrating on this inner political work inside the Socialist Party, we had been at the same time developing, practically without any direction from our central leadership, our trade union work on a scale we had never approximated before and had at least begun the proletarianization of the party. We had won over to our side the majority of the Socialist youth and the majority of those Socialist workers really interested in the principles of Socialism and the Socialist revolution.

The convention adopted the program of the Fourth Inter-

national without any opposition. This showed that our educational work had been thoroughgoing. All these accomplishments can be chalked up as evidence of the political
wisdom of our entry into the Socialist Party. And another of
them—and not the least of them—was that when the Socialist
Party expelled us and when we retaliated by forming an independent party of our own, the Socialist Party had dealt itself a death blow. Since then the SP has progressively disin-
tegrated until it has virtually lost any semblance of influence
in any party of the labor movement. Our work in the Socialist
Party contributed to that. Comrade Trotsky remarked about
that later, when we were talking with him about the total result of our entry into the Socialist Party and the pitiful state of
its organization afterward. He said that alone would have
justified the entry into the organization even if we hadn't
gained a single new member.

Partly as a result of our experience in the Socialist Party
and our fight in there, the Socialist Party was put on the
sidelines. This was a great achievement, because it was an
obstacle in the path of building a revolutionary party. The
problem is not merely one of building a revolutionary party,
but of clearing obstacles from its path. Every other party is a
rival. Every other party is an obstacle.

Now just contrast these achievements—and I have not exaggerated them—contrast these results with the results of the
policies of the sectarians. They had renounced the idea of
entry into the Socialist Party on principle. They said their
policy of abstention would build a revolutionary party better
and sooner. A year and a half elapsed, two years elapsed, and
what had happened? We had more than doubled our mem-

bership on top of all the other gains I have mentioned. The Oehlerites had not won over a single Socialist youth or worker. Not one. On the contrary, the only thing they had produced was a couple of splits in their own ranks. I think that contrast is a convincing verification of the political questions that arose in the dispute with them. Always bear in mind that there is a way of verifying political disputes, that is, by subsequent experiences. Politics is not religion; political disputes do not remain forever undecided. Life decides. You can never solve a theological dispute because it takes place outside the life on this earth. It is not influenced by class struggle, by political upheavals, or storms or floods or earthquakes. In the Middle Ages they used to argue about how many angels could dance on the point of a needle. How many? A thousand? Ten thousand? The question was never decided because there is no way of knowing by earthly experience how many angels can dance on such a restricted area as the point of a needle. After it was proved that we had made all these gains and the sectarians had gained nothing, the only argument that could be made in their behalf was: "Yes, you doubled your membership, but at the sacrifice of the program." But that wasn't so. When we held our convention at Chicago at the end of our experience in the Socialist Party, it was shown that we had come out with the same program we had taken in—the program of the Fourth International.

Our "round trip" through the Socialist Party had resulted in gains all along the line. We formed the Socialist Workers Party in Chicago on New Year's Day and began once again an independent struggle with good prospects and good hopes. The extensive discussion that took place in our ranks prior to the convention had revealed differences and weaknesses which later were to come out in the open. We had a great discussion over the Russian question. Overwhelmed by the treachery of Stalinism, the Moscow trials, the assassination of the Spanish revolution—all these terrible experiences—a section of the party, already in the fall of 1937, wanted to give up the idea that Russia was a workers state and renounce its defense. It has always happened, ever since 1917, that whenever anybody went wrong on the Russian question he became lost to the revolutionary movement. It couldn't be otherwise because the Russian question is precisely the question of a revolution that has taken place.

Heading the doubters and skeptics in the fall of 1937 was Burnham. Burnham was still willing to give conditional defense to the Soviet Union, but was already beginning to elaborate what he thought was a new theory, that the workers' state never existed. He was simply adapting himself to the half-baked theories of the anarchists and the Mensheviks which had been expounded since 1917 and are renewed at every crisis of the evolution of the Soviet Union. In addition to that, Burnham led an opposition against us on the organization question. He didn't like the Bolshevik method of organization, Bolshevik discipline and centralization, and Bolshevik morality. These symptoms are well known. Anybody who begins by objecting to Bolshevism on the questions of methods, organization, and "morality" certainly has Menshevism in his blood. The political program is the touchstone, but the disputes on the organization question often reveal the symptoms earlier than the political debates.

These weaknesses, these anti-Bolshevik tendencies shown

by Burnham in that period, had their logical development later. At that time I wrote a long letter to Comrade Trotsky, frankly characterizing the position of Burnham and asking his advice about how to cope with him; that is, how to defend Bolshevism most effectively and still try to save Burnham for the revolution. Shachtman at that time was fighting on the side of Bolshevism. He joined in this characterization of Burnham and helped in the fight. But then, Shachtman being Shachtman, it was only natural that two years later, when the same fight broke out again, in much more violent form, with the World War as a background—it was only natural that Shachtman should then join Burnham to fight against us.

The discussion of 1937 foreshadowed future troubles. We were yet to go through another great internal struggle in the party, the most fundamental and thoroughgoing of all the internal fights in the movement since its inception. We had to go through all of this, on top of all the preceding struggles, before the decks could be cleared and the party prepared for the test of war that was to come. We made that fight and Bolshevism was victorious in it; the Bolshevik party is stronger for it. The history of this fight is recorded in documents, the great political and theoretical contributions of Comrade Trotsky, and on the organization side in some writings of mine. Those who want to follow the history of the party from the point where I leave it here, with the foundation of the Socialist Workers Party on New Year's 1938, can pick it up in these documents. As for what happened after the fight with the petty-bourgeois opposition and the eventual split, it seems that this is recent history, so recent that it does not need to be reviewed in this course. It is known to all of you.

Now, dear Comrades, with your permission, I want to say a word about the great happiness and satisfaction I have had in giving these lectures. If a young comrade, studying public speaking were to ask me, an old campaigner, what a public speaker most needs, I would say: "He needs a good audience." And if he gets the kind of audience that I have had in this series of twelve lectures—so warm, responsive, and appreciative, so interested in the subject and so friendly to the speaker—he will indeed be fortunate.

Index

Abern, Martin, 70, 73-6, 81, 98, 211, 225, 251, 274-5; clique, 251, 274-5

Abernites, 259

Active Workers Conference, 239-240, 251

Advance, 207-8, 211

Adventurism, 44

Agitation, 110-3, 147; defined, 147

Akron strike, 247

Albany unemployment conference, 134

Allentown, 271-5

Alma Ata, 66, 67, 80

Altman, Jack, 292-3

Amalgamated Clothing Workers, 166, 208

"American approach," 248

American Civil War, 249

American Commission, 31, 51

"American Committee for the Defense of Leon Trotsky," 287

American Federation of Labor (AFL), 26, 37, 107, 149-50, 174-6, 195

American Labor Alliance, 29

"American Question," 51

American Workers Party (AWP), 143, 158, 166-8, 171, 202-3, 205-19, 225, 227, 230, 239-40, 244-8, 264, 271, 280; Provisional Organization Committee, 158, 171; fusion with CLA, 166, 205-19, 221, 225-6, 227-8, 230, 245; trade union work, 171-2, 202 3, 206; unemployed work, 171-2, 206, 241, 246-7

"America's Road to Revolution" (Cannon), 142

Amter, 90-1

Amtorg, 75

Anarchists, 301

Anglo-Russian Committee, 63-4, 223

Auto-Lite strike, 171-2, 188, 202, 213, 226, 237

Automobile workers union, 298

Barbers Union, 154
Baron, Murry, 268, 293, 295
Basky, Louis, 94
"Battle of Deputies Run, The," 183
"Battle of the Market," 182
Berger, 42
Biemiller, 268
Bittleman, 218
Bolshevik-Leninist Opposition, 80. *See also* Russian Opposition
Bolshevik revolution, 15–6. *See also* Russian revolution.
Bolsheviks, 32, 135, 250
Bolshevism, 14, 17, 30, 36, 42, 74, 98, 122, 256, 263, 273, 274, 301–2; defined, 14
Bordiga, 75
Bordigists, 89
Boston, 32–3, 90
Brandlerites, 59
Bridgeman, Michigan, 26; 1920 convention, 26; 1922 convention, 26
Bronx, the, 134
Brooklyn, 134, 153
Brookwood Labor College, 244
Brown, William S. (Bill), 176–7, 197–200, 238; arrested, 198
Budenz, Louis F., 206, 211–3, 248–50
Bukharin, 28, 32, 67
Bureaucratic centrism, 106
Burnham, James, 47, 215, 251, 254, 259, 301–2

California, 153, 238, 289–90, 298
Call, 270
Canada, 68, 82

Canadian (Communist) Party, 68
Cannon, James P., 2–3, 30–1, 59, 61–2, 68, 69, 71–5, 81–2, 98, 105–6, 108, 128, 136–7, 151, 154, 162, 175, 182–4, 198, 202; trip to Russia, 30–1; meets Trotsky, 30, 219–21; CI delegate, 65–9; secures Trotsky's criticism of draft program of CI, 67–8; expelled for Trotskyism, 73, 228–9; at hotel workers strike, 157; debates Lovestone, 167; at Minneapolis strikes, 184, 187–8, 196–8; arrested, 196–8
Cannon faction, 46–9, 51–2, 63, 71, 77
Cannon-Shachtman faction, 258–9, 264–5, 271
Cannon-Shachtman resolution, 234, 251
Capitalism, 17
Case of Leon Trotsky, The, 287
Central Labor Union (Minneapolis), 177, 186
Charlie, 120
Chevrolet strike, 247
Chicago, 45, 75, 82, 91, 100, 119, 123, 141–2, 154, 197, 240, 289, 290, 298–9; conference of Left Opposition, 100, 119; convention of expelled SP branches, 298–9
China, 63–4, 122, 129, 223, 241, 285
Chinese revolution, 63–4, 122, 129, 223
CIO, 195, 200, 282
CIO sit-down strikes, 200
City College, 44
Citizens Alliance, 173, 186
Civil War in Spain, The, 288
Class Struggle, 212

Cleveland, 32, 90, 92

Cliques, 119, 251, 274

Colonial question, 64, 129

Commission of Inquiry, 295

Communist International (Comintern, Third International), 14, 27, 30–2, 34, 37–8, 47, 50–3, 60–1, 65–6, 80, 106–9, 127, 129, 136–7, 139, 147–8, 168–9, 222–3, 228, 230, 253; Third World Congress, 27; Fourth Congress, 30–2, 34, 67; Commission on American question, 31, 51; Stalinized, 38; degeneration, 50–3, 135–7, 139, 148, 168, 228; Fifth Congress, 52, 67; campaign against Trotskyism, 52, 61–2; Sixth World Congress, 65–9, 80; program 66–7; ultraleftism, 23–7, 34, 36, 106–7, 149, 174; capitulates in Germany, 135–6, 139, 168; bankruptcy, 139, 148, 228

Communist Labor Party, 22–6; driven underground, 22; boycotts election, 24; antiparliamentary tendency, 24; underground fetishism, 24–5; unites with Ruthenberg faction, 26

Communist League of America (Opposition), 98–110, 114–5, 126–7, 130–4, 141, 143–4, 147–50, 153, 156–63, 166–203, 205–19, 221, 223–7, 230; program and tasks, 98–110, 120, 147–8; isolation, 115, 126–7; public meetings, 122, 134,; internationalism, 124, 248; entry into mass work, 130–2; sectarianism 140–1, 222–5; recruiting, 153, 215; supports hotel workers strike, 156–64, 178, 229; fusion with

AWP, 166, 213–9, 221, 224–7, 230; leads Minneapolis strikes, 165, 169–203. *See also* Trotkyist movement

"Communist League of Struggle," 111

Communist Party of the United States (CP), 14–6, 19–20, 20–4, 26–8, 35–8, 40, 55, 60–65, 76–8, 79, 82, 103, 105–12, 136–9, 142, 146, 149, 152, 167, 172, 174, 208–10, 218, 228–9, 238, 248, 281, 285; origin, 14; Foreign Language Federations, 19–22, 41–2; factional struggles, 8, 20–2, 38–53, 180–1; driven underground, 22–23; ultraleftism, 23–4, 106–7, 113, 149, 174–5; splits, 26, 153–4, 208, 216, 228–9; merges with United Communist Party, 26; leadership, 7–9, 28, 42–4; displaces IWW, 36; growth, 36; trade union policy, 37, 106–7, 174–5; Chicago Convention (1919), 41; composition, 41–2, 46; farmer-labor adventure; 44; petty-bourgeois tendencies, 45–7; Foster-Cannon faction, 46, 52, 71; Ruthenberg-Lovestone-Pepper faction, 44–5; Political Committee, 47; Foster faction, 47–8, 55, 61, 71–3, 87; Lovestone faction, 47–48, 63; Cannon faction, 47–8, 52, 63, 71, 78; national narrow-mindedness, 55, 60, 65, 79, 128; February 1928 plenum, 62, 64; expulsion of Oppositionists, 74–7; Stalinization, 83; gangsterism, 85–95, 152–3; December 1928 plenum, 87; apathy to German events, 136; bureaucratized, 137–8; "Third Period," 106, 113, 149, 174

Conference for Progressive Labor Action (CPLA), 139, 140, 142-3, 152, 158, 171, 210-11, 244-5; Pittsburgh Conference 142, 158
Cook, Comrade, 33
Coover Oscar, 92
"Criminal-syndicalism" trial, 238

Daily Forward, 138, 256
Daily Organizer (Organizer), 192-4
Daily Worker, 83, 212, 218, 275
Daladier, 220
DeBoer, Harry, 200
Debs, Eugene V., 23-4, 42
"Declaration of Principles," 218, 225
Democracy, 117, 263
Detroit, 91, 215
Dewey, John, 287
Dobbs, Farrell, 182, 198, 200
Donaghue, Mr., 200
"Draft Program of the Communist International: A Criticism of Fundamentals" (Trotsky), 67, 69, 71; smuggled out of Russia, 69
Dubinsky, 268
Dunne, Bill, 63
Dunne, Grant, 191, 198, 200
Dunne, Mick, 197-8; arrested, 198
Dunne, Vincent R., 10, 65, 92, 198, 200, 238, 293; arrested, 198
Dunnigan, 198-200

Eastman, Max, 39, 49
Eiffel, 222
Engdahl, 209
Engels, 14, 43, 135, 279
England, 63-4, 279; general strike, 64
English Communist Party, 64
Ethiopia, 241

Europe, 282

Factional struggles, 20-2, 38-53, 74, 216, 251, 274-5; laws of, 39-40; provoked by Comintern, 39-40
Farmer-labor party, 38, 180, 195
Fascism, 128, 132-7, 231; triumphs, 135, 231
Federal Labor Board, 159-62
Field, B. J., 156-64, 178, 229; leads hotel strike, 156-63; violates party discipline, 162; expelled, 164
Fieldites, 229
Fifth Congress (Comintern), 52, 67
Five Year Plan, 114-5
Federal mediation, 159-62, 179-80, 189-91, 198-200, 292
Foreign Language Federations, 19-22, 41-2
Forward, 138, 256
Foster, William Z., 36, 44, 67, 97, 113
Foster-Cannon caucus (faction), 46, 52, 71
Foster faction, 47-8, 55, 61-3, 71
Fourth Congress (Comintern), 30-2, 34, 67
Fourth International, 53-6, 60, 105, 139, 143, 149, 168-9, 203, 233, 263, 286, 298-9; campaign for, 139, 143-4, 149, 169, 203
Fraina, Louis C., 18
France, 202, 219-20, 282-5; sit-down strikes, 282
Franco, 284
French fascists, 219-20; hound Trotsky, 219-20
French Social Democracy, 202
"French turn," 202, 216, 222-4, 233-7, 241, 253-4, 258-302; in Amer-

ica, 258–302
Frosig, George, 200

"Gag" Law, 296
Gebert, B. K., 91
German Communist Party, 128, 135; capitulates, 135–6
Germany, 128, 131–9, 141–2, 144, 147, 231
Germany, *the Key to the International Situation* (Trotsky), 128
Gillespie, Illinois, 131–2
Gitlow, Benjamin, 6–7, 40, 49, 69, 143, 151, 216, 229; leaves Lovestonites, 143, 151
Glotzer, 221
Goldman, Albert, 141–2, 188, 197, 289–90
Goodman, 83
Gordon, Sam, 272
GPU, 69
Greenwich Village, 116
Grenoble 219–20

Haas, Father, 199–200
"Haas-Dunnigan Plan," 199
Hallett, 272, 275
Hardman, J. B. S. (Salutsky, Salutsky-Hardman, J.B.), 166, 206, 207–11
Hathaway, 72
Hillman, Sidney, 208, 211
Hillquit, Morris, 42
Hindenburg, President, 131
Hitler, 131
Hook Sidney, 211, 215, 270
Hotel workers general strike, 155–63, 178, 229
Hungarian Communist Party, 223
Hungarian group, 75, 86, 89, 93–4

Hungarian Hall, 93
Hungarian revolution, 223
Hungarian Socialist Party, 223

Illinois, 131–2
India, 129
Industrial Workers of the World (IWW), 14, 35–6, 83, 90, 92; decline of, 36
Infantile Sickness of Left Communism, The (Lenin), 24, 27
Intellectuals, 44–5; role in CP, 44–5
International Communist League, 169, 219, 222; Plenum of Executive Committee, 219, 222
International Labor Defense (ILD), 48, 65, 70, 74
International Secretariat, 124
Irving Plaza, 169
Italian Oppositionists, 75

Jewish Bund, 207
Jewish (Socialist) Federation, 208
Johnson, Arnold, 272, 275

Kansas City, 18, 82, 151
Karsner, Rose, 70
Katonah, New York, 244
Konikow, Antoinette, 90
Kulaks, 114

Labor Action, 290, 293
Labor defense, 38, 48, 65, 70, 74, 238
Labor Temple, 13, 89, 93, 98
LaGuardia, Mayor, 162
Lawrence strike, 244
Left Opposition, 55, 57–78, 80, 79–101, 106, 113–4, 119, 129, 130–1, 147, 151, 153; beginning, 57–78;

growth, 75–8; Russian, 13, 57, 59, 62, 64–6, 69–70, 73, 75–7, 80, 96–7, 119, 129, ostracised, 83–5; slandered, 83, 85; gangsterism against, 85–95, 152–4; addresses Communist Party, 85, 97, 99, 107–8; appeals expulsion, 87; National Conference, 99–102; International Conference (1933), 151; forms Communist League of America, 100. *See also* Trotskyist movement

Left Socialists, 208

Legal question, 24–5, 51

Lenin, 17–8, 27–8, 30, 50, 137, 253, 268, 270

Leninism, 249

Lenin School, 72

Liebknecht, Karl, 253

Lincoln, 249

"Liquidators," 30–1

Local 574, 176–201; Organizing Committee, 177; May general strike, 169–74, 178–86; July-August strike, 169–72, 187–203

London Bureau, 59

Lore, Ludwig, 166, 209, 212

Lovestone, 29, 38, 44, 46, 67, 97, 167, 215, 229–30; debates Cannon, 167

Lovestone faction, 46, 63

Lovestoneites, 47–8, 55, 61, 63, 69, 73, 76, 87, 103, 113–4, 143, 167, 215, 229, 266; expelled, 113, 229; defections from, 215, 229

Lunatic fringe, 26, 115–6, 126

Luxemburg, Rosa, 222, 253

Lyons, Eugene, 39, 49

Manifesto of the International Communist League, 169

Maritime strike, 288, 298

Marx, 14, 207

Marxism, 13–6, 54, 57, 76, 79–80, 129, 137, 146–7, 222–3, 228, 231, 233–4, 273

"Meaning of the German Events, The," 132

Mediation, 189–91, 198–200

Mensheviks, 30, 301

Menshevism, 301

Mexico, 297

Mexico City, 287

Middle West, 213

Militant, The, 13–6, 78, 81, 86–9, 95–8, 120, 123, 130–4, 139, 142, 143, 150–4, 157–8, 168–9, 174, 185, 204, 215–6, 225, 237, 270, 277; campaign on German events, 132–4; campaign on hotel strike, 157–8

"Militants," 231–2, 260, 263, 267–70, 276–7, 283, 290–1, 293–4

Milwaukee, 295

Mini, Norman, 238

Minneapolis, 9–10, 65, 75, 82, 92–3, 119, 123, 151, 165, 169–205, 226, 237–8, 264, 280, 293; coal yard strike, 165; May strike, 169–74, 178–86; July-August strike, 169–72, 187–203

Minneapolis trial, 248, 285

Minneapolis Tribune, 181

Minnesota, 76, 92, 180

Mooney Congress, 141–2

Moscow, 30, 37, 51–3, 60–1, 65–6, 68–9, 72, 135; *Pravda,* 80

Moscow trials, 238, 282–9, 295, 297, 301

Muste, A. J., 139, 205–7, 211, 217, 218–9, 225, 234–5, 237–8, 242,

244-6, 251, 256, 258-9, 261, 274-5
Muste-Abern faction, 275
Muste faction, 258-9
Musteites, 172, 202, 206, 212, 216-7, 218-9, 225, 227-8, 230, 236, 240, 252, 258-9, 266, 272, 289
Muste–Oehler bloc, 255, 259; unprincipled, 259

Natalia, 221
"National Committee of the Expelled Branches," 297
National Labor Board, 179
National Unemployed Leagues, 171, 241, 246, 272
Needle Trades, 268
New Haven, 89, 90
New International, 201, 270
New Leader, 242
"New Party and the New International, The," 169
New York City, 18, 45, 65-6, 75-6, 83, 89, 93, 95, 102, 111, 113, 116-8, 121, 130-1, 141-2, 155-65, 204, 225, 239, 242, 245, 253, 260, 262-4, 272, 283, 287, 293-7; unemployment conference, 130-1; hotel workers strike, 155-65, 178, 195, 229
New York Evening Post, 212
New York School of Social Science, 120
New York University, 211
Non-Partisan Labor Defense, 238
Northern Minnesota District Federal Court, 92
Norway, 96
Noske, 253
Not Guilty, 287

NRA, 201

October revolution. *See* Russian revolution
Oehler, Hugo, 134, 188, 211-2, 222, 234, 241, 251, 259
Oehlerites, 116, 224-5, 234-6, 240-3, 251-2, 254-9, 271, 300; expelled, 256-9
Ohio, 246
"Old Guard." *See* Socialist Party Right Wing
Old Renegades Home, 242
Olgin, M. J., 208, 209
Olson, Governor Floyd, 184, 194-6; role in Minneapolis strikes, 194-6; arrests strike leaders, 196
Organizational fetishism, 234
Organization question, 62, 234, 262, 301
Organizer, 192-4
"Our Appeal to the Party," 87

Pacific Coast, 65
Paris, 219, 222
Paris Commune, 135
Passaic strike (1926), 39
Paterson silk strike, 151, 219
Pennsylvania, 213, 246
Pepper, 44
Philadelphia, 77-8, 82-3
Pittsburgh, 142, 158, 205, 239-42, 250; CPLA conference, 142, 158, 205
Pivert, 59
"Platform" (Left Opposition), 96-7
Plekhanov, 147
Porter, Paul, 268-9, 292
Postal, Kelly, 200

Problems of the Chinese Revolution, 122, 129

Progressive Miners of America, 131, 181

Proletarian Party, 229

Propaganda, 110–3, 120, 146–8; defined, 146–7

Radek, 28, 32, 59, 114, 121

Rainbolt, Ray, 200

Rakovsky, 59

Rand School, 256

Red Army, 17, 61

"Red Purge," 175

"Red Unions," 107, 174

Reed, John, 18

Reich, 272, 275

Republican Party, 40, 49

Revolution and Counter-Revolution in Spain (Felix Morrow), 288

Revolutionary Age, The, 18

Roosevelt, 147, 170, 180, 190, 195, 204, 211, 264, 281, 292

Russia, 18, 32, 53–4, 57, 67, 69, 80, 96, 99, 105–6, 115, 124, 127, 206, 214, 221, 286, 291, 301

Russian Communist Party, 32, 52–3, 57, 67, 97

Russian Federation, 19

Russian (Left) Opposition, 13, 57–9, 62, 64, 66, 69–70, 73, 75–7, 80–1, 96–7, 119, 129

Russian question, 62–3, 66, 97, 98–9, 104–5, 128, 214, 301

Russian revolution, 13, 16, 28, 41, 49, 54, 74, 108, 228, 248

Russian revolution of 1905, 30, 135

Ruthenberg, 26, 29, 44, 46

Ruthenberg faction, 26

Ruthenberg-Lovestone-Pepper faction, 44–6

Sacramento "criminal-syndicalism" trial, 238

Salutsky-Hardman, J. B. (Salutsky, Hardman, J.B.S.), 9, 166, 206, 207–11

San Francisco, 293

Scheidemann, 253

Schweinhaut, Mr., 248

Second International, 14, 16, 136–7, 148, 149, 169, 222–4, 253, 268

Sectarianism, 37, 140–1, 149, 188, 212, 222–30, 233–42, 251–7, 263–5, 280, 299–300; Spanish, 233

Shachtman, Max, 47, 58, 70, 73–6, 81, 98, 131–2, 134, 169, 188, 196–7, 211, 219, 242, 256, 259, 285, 302; arrested, 196–7

Shachtman-Burnham bloc, 259; unprincipled, 259

Sixth World Congress (Comintern), 65–70, 80

Skoglund, Carl, 65, 92, 200

Social Democracy. *See* Second International

Social Democratic parties, 16, 137–8, 148; leftist development, 138, 148

Social Democrats, 133, 135, 248; reject united front in Germany, 133; capitulate to fascism, 135

Socialism in one country, 97

Socialist Appeal, 289–90, 294–5, 297

"Socialist Appeal Conference," 290

Socialist *Call,* 270

Socialist Labor Party, 77

Socialist Party of California, 288–90

Socialist Party of France, 202, 216,

222-4, 254; entered by Trotsky-ists, 202, 222, 254

Socialist Party of the United States, 14-21, 28, 35, 40, 42, 98, 138-9, 143, 148, 164, 168, 207-8, 216, 231-7, 244-5, 250-4, 256-302; leadership, 16, 28, 164; composi-tion, 16, 261; Foreign Language Federations, 19; splits, 21-2, 138, 262-3, 275, 295; upsurge in, 138; bureaucracy, 263-4; Cleveland convention, 275; entry of Trot-skyists, 258-302; Chicago con-vention, 293-5; expulsion of Trotskyists, 297; disintegration, 299. *See also* Socialist Party Left Wing

Socialist Party Left Wing, 14-6, 18-21, 139, 143, 148, 168, 216, 231-7, 293-4, 250-53, 257, 259-60, 263, 269, 275-6, 291, 297; inspired by Bolshevik revolution, 16, 17-8; formed, 17-8; first National Con-ference, 17-8, 21; composition, 18-9; struggle for native leader-ship, 20-1; splits, 21-2

Socialist Party Right Wing, 138, 232, 253, 256, 260, 262-4, 275

Socialist Workers Party, 14, 24-5, 47, 99, 105, 256, 300-2; petty bour-geois opposition, 47, 99, 105, 256, 301-2; formed, 300-2

Solow, Herbert, 188

Southern Illinois, 83

Soviet Union, 18, 52-3, 57, 67, 80, 83, 96-8, 99, 105-6, 115, 124, 127, 206, 214, 221, 286, 291, 301; Five Year Plan, 114, 127; defense of, 206, 214, 301. *See also* Russian

question

Spanish Civil War, 129, 233, 238, 282, 284, 285, 288-9, 296, 301

Spanish Socialist Party, 233, 235

Spector, Maurice, 68, 82

Splits, 21-2, 26, 138, 153, 208, 216, 227-9, 236-7, 262, 275, 295

Stalin, 51, 54-5, 62, 67, 69-71, 86, 106, 113-4, 135, 137, 153, 241

Stalinism, 13, 49, 57, 64, 72, 83-9, 99, 114-5, 127, 133, 136-7, 142, 168, 228, 233, 241, 248, 272-5, 287, 291-3, 298, 301; destroys CI, 137

Stalinist "left turn," 113

"Stalinist Press 'Warns' AWP Against Unity With Us," 218

Stalinists, 13, 49, 64, 85-95, 133-4, 152-3, 266, 268-9, 272-5, 291-3; gangsterism by, 85-95, 152-3; re-ject united front in Germany, 133

Stamm, 212, 222, 241

Stiler, 272

St. Louis, 83

St. Paul, 198

Strikes, 38-9, 127, 151, 155-65, 169-204, 213, 219, 266, 229, 237, 244, 247, 288-9, 298

Struggle for a Proletarian Party, The (James P. Cannon), 275

Stuyvesant Casino, 132, 151, 226

Tactics, 98-113, 146, 278-82, 284

Tammany Hall, 40, 49, 274

Teamsters Joint Council, 176

Teamsters Union, 176

"Tenacity! Tenacity! Tenacity!" (Trotsky), 124

Ten Days that Shook the World (John Reed), 18

Textile workers general strike, 204

Textile workers union, 244

Third International. *See* Communist International

Third Period, 106-7, 113-4, 149, 174

Third World Congress (Comintern), 27

Thomas, Norman, 263, 269-70, 292-5

"Three Generals Without an Army," 81-2, 87, 99

Toledo Auto-Lite strike, 171-2, 188, 202-3, 213, 226, 237

Toledo Chevrolet strike, 247

Trade union question, 26, 37, 44, 51, 62, 97, 106-7, 149-50, 154-5, 158, 163-4, 241, 298

Trade unions, 36-8, 44, 46, 48, 131, 138-9, 141, 147-50, 152, 154-5, 163-5, 173, 232, 241, 298

"Tragedy of the German Proletariat, The" (Cannon), 142

Tribune. See Minneapolis Tribune

Trotsky, Leon, 13, 17, 18, 27-8, 30-1, 50-1, 52, 54, 59, 61-2, 65-6, 67-70, 72-3, 77-8, 80, 89-90, 95-6, 98, 100, 119, 122, 123-4, 124, 127-9, 133, 135-7, 139, 141, 151, 202, 211, 216, 218-21, 224, 269, 271, 283, 286, 295, 297-9, 302; deported, 59, 96, 98

Trotsky, Natalia, 221

Trotsky Defense Committee, 286-7, 295, 298

Trotskyism, 13-14, 52, 56, 58, 61-2, 68-70, 72-3, 76-8, 79, 132, 151-2, 158, 169, 172, 189, 200, 245, 276, 281, 284-5; defined, 13; campaign against, 52, 61-2

Trotskyist caucus, 294

Trotskyist faction, 290, 294, 296

Trotskyist movement, 13, 55-6, 59-60, 70-1, 89-95, 97-8, 118-23, 126-7, 133-4, 143-4, 279; origin, 55-6, 70-1; public meetings, 89-95, 98, 134; growth 95; poverty, 118-23, 126; isolation, 279-80. *See also* Left Opposition (Communist League of America), Workers Party, Socialist Workers Party

"Truth About Trotsky and the Russian Opposition, The," 89

Turkey, 96

Turner, Larry, 224

Tyler, Gus, 268, 283, 293

Ultraleftism, 23-7, 34, 36, 106-7, 114, 149, 174, 280

Unemployed League, 171-2, 241, 246, 272-3

Unemployed movement, 130, 171-2, 206, 213, 232, 237, 241, 246-7, 271-3

Unemployment, 130-1, 171

Unifications, 227-8

Union Square, 86, 120, 134

United Communist Party, 26, 29-32; formed, 26; boycotts AFL, 26; struggle for legality, 29-32; replaced by Workers Party, 32

United front, 130-1, 133, 142, 152-3

"United Front Against Hooliganism," 152

United Front of the Workers' Organizations and Battle to the Death!, The, 133

United front workers guard, 153

United States, 114; depression, 114

USSR. *See* Russia, Soviet Union

War Labor Board, 292
Washington, 184, 198
Webster, Ben, 119, 150–2
Weisbord, Albert, 110–3, 229
Weisbordites, 229
West Virginia, 246
Wolfe, Bertram D., 62–3
Women's Auxiliary, 181, 193
Workers and Farmers government, 248
"Workers Council," 209
Workers Defense Guard, 92–3, 153
Workers Party (Third International), 29–30, 32, 209–10; formed, 29; program, 16; replaces underground CP, 32
Workers Party of the United States, 225–30, 244–5, 250–8, 260–1, 267–71, 271–5, 280–1; formed, 225; finances, 244–5; June (1935) plenum, 250–5; October (1935) plenum, 256, 258; negotiates with "Militants," 267–71; Stalinist agents in, 271–5; enters Socialist Party, 281–2
World War I, 14, 84, 292
World War II, 85, 294, 302

Yipsels. *See* Young Peoples Socialist League
Young Peoples Socialist League (YPSL, Yipsels), 140, 143, 168

Zack, Joseph, 241–2
Zam, Herbert, 215–6, 229, 268–9, 283
Zinoviev, 28, 31, 59, 61–2, 65

Their Trotsky and Ours: Communist Continuity Today
by Jack Barnes

New International
A MAGAZINE OF MARXIST POLITICS AND THEORY

Their Trotsky and ours
COMMUNIST CONTINUITY TODAY
by Jack Barnes

LENIN AND THE COLONIAL QUESTION
—— *by Carlos Rafael Rodríguez*

The 1916 Easter rebellion in Ireland: Two views
—— *by V. I. Lenin and Leon Trotsky*

—— 1 ——

"We need to view ourselves and our contributions in the way explained forty years ago by James P. Cannon, a founding leader of our movement in the United States," says Socialist Workers Party national secretary Jack Barnes in this December 1982 talk.

"In the very second paragraph of his *History of American Trotskyism,* Cannon stressed that, 'We have no new revelation: Trotskyism is not a new movement, a new doctrine, but the restoration, the revival, of genuine Marxism as it was expounded and practiced in the Russian revolution and in the early days of the Communist International.'

"If we follow this advice from Cannon, then we can make progress in reconquering our political continuity with Bolshevism and the Communist International under the leadership of Lenin's team. That is the foundation on which we must build."

In *New International* no. 1
Available from Pathfinder. $8.00

Related Reading . . .

The Left Opposition in the U.S.

Writings and Speeches, 1928-31

James P. Cannon

Supporters of the fight to continue Lenin's revolutionary course begin to rebuild the Marxist movement in the United States. $22.95

The Communist League of America

Writings and Speeches, 1932-34

James P. Cannon

The communist movement's turn toward new openings in the unions as the industrial working class begins to recover from the initial blows of the Great Depression. $22.95

The Struggle for a Proletarian Party

James P. Cannon

In a political struggle in the late 1930s with a petty-bourgeois current in the Socialist Workers Party, Cannon and other SWP leaders defended the political and organizational principles of Marxism. The debate unfolded as Washington prepared to drag U.S. working people into the slaughter of World War II. A companion to *In Defense of Marxism* by Leon Trotsky. $19.95

NEW FROM PATHFINDER

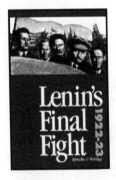

Lenin's Final Fight
Speeches and Writings, 1922-23

V. I. LENIN The record of Lenin's last battle to maintain the proletarian course with which the Bolshevik Party led the workers and peasants to take power over the landlords and capitalists of the former tsarist empire and initiate a world communist movement. Includes several items appearing in English for the first time. $19.95

The Changing Face of U.S. Politics
Working-Class Politics and the Trade Unions

JACK BARNES A handbook for workers coming into the factories, mines, and mills, as they react to the uncertain life, ceaseless turmoil, and brutality of capitalism in the closing years of the twentieth century. It shows how millions of workers, as political resistance grows, will revolutionize themselves, their unions, and all of society. $19.95

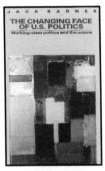

The Bolivian Diary of Ernesto Che Guevara

Guevara's account, newly translated, of the 1966-67 guerrilla struggle in Bolivia. A day-by-day chronicle by one of the central leaders of the Cuban revolution of the campaign to forge a continent-wide revolutionary movement of workers and peasants capable of contending for power. Includes excerpts from the diaries and accounts of other combatants, including —for the first time in English—*My Campaign with Che* by Bolivian leader Inti Peredo. Introduction by Mary-Alice Waters. $21.95

ALSO FROM PATHFINDER

In Defense of Marxism
The Social and Political Contradictions of the Soviet Union

LEON TROTSKY   During the buildup toward U.S. entry in World War II, Trotsky explains why workers have a stake in opposing imperialist war and in combating assaults on the degenerated Soviet workers state by either the fascist or "democratic" capitalist powers. Also available in Spanish. $24.95

Ireland and the Irish Question

KARL MARX AND FREDERICK ENGELS   For workers in Britain, Marx and Engels explain, "the national emancipation of Ireland is no question of abstract justice or humanitarian sentiment, but the first condition of their own social emancipation." $19.95

Cosmetics, Fashions, and the Exploitation of Women

JOSEPH HANSEN, EVELYN REED, AND MARY-ALICE WATERS   How big business promotes cosmetics to generate profits and perpetuate the oppression of women. In her introduction, Mary-Alice Waters explains how the entry of millions of women into the workforce during and after World War II irreversibly changed U.S. society and laid the basis for a renewed rise of struggles for women's equality. $12.95

Why Is Mark Curtis Still in Prison?
The Political Frame-up of a Unionist and Socialist and the Campaign to Free Him

NAOMI CRAINE   Tells the story of Mark Curtis, a packinghouse worker and political activist who was framed up and sentenced in 1988 to twenty-five years in prison for rape and burglary, describes what happened to Curtis on the day of his arrest, the fight to defend immigrant rights he was a part of, and the ongoing international campaign to free him from prison. Booklet $6.00

Write for a free catalog

February 1965: The Final Speeches

MALCOLM X Speeches from the last three weeks of Malcolm X's life, presenting the accelerating evolution of his political views. A large part is material previously unavailable, with some in print for the first time. The inaugural volume in Pathfinder's selected works of Malcolm X. $17.95

Teamster Rebellion

FARRELL DOBBS The 1934 strikes that built a fighting union movement in Minneapolis, recounted by a leader of that battle. The first in a four-volume series on the Teamster-led strikes and organizing drives in the Midwest that helped pave the way for the CIO and pointed a road toward independent labor political action. $16.95

Left-Wing Communism: An Infantile Disorder

V.I. LENIN Drawing on the experience of the Bolshevik Party in Russia, Lenin explains why ultraleftism is a deadly obstacle to building communist parties rooted in the working class. Booklet $4.95

On the Paris Commune

KARL MARX AND FREDERICK ENGELS "Storming heaven," Marx wrote, the "proletariat for the first time held political power" in Paris for three months in 1871 and the international workers struggle "entered upon a new stage." Writings, letters, and speeches on the Paris Commune. $15.95

To Speak the Truth
Why Washington's 'Cold War' against Cuba Doesn't End

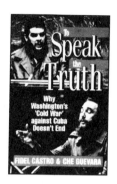

FIDEL CASTRO AND CHE GUEVARA   In historic speeches before the United Nations and its bodies, Guevara and Castro address the workers of the world, explaining why the U.S. government is determined to destroy the example set by the socialist revolution in Cuba and why its effort will fail. $16.95

The Communist Manifesto
KARL MARX AND FREDERICK ENGELS   Founding document of the modern working-class movement, published in 1848. Explains how capitalism arose as a specific stage in the economic development of class society and how it will be superseded by socialism through worldwide revolutionary action by the working class. Booklet $2.50

The Revolution Betrayed
What Is the Soviet Union and Where Is It Going?

LEON TROTSKY   Classic study of the Soviet workers state and its degeneration under the brutal domination of the privileged social caste whose spokesman was Stalin. Illuminates the roots of the Russian crisis of the 1990s. Also available in Russian and Spanish. $19.95

Nelson Mandela Speaks
Forging a Democratic, Nonracial South Africa

Mandela's speeches from 1990 through 1993 recount the course of struggle that put an end to apartheid and opened the fight for a deep-going political, economic, and social transformation in South Africa. $18.95

See front of book for addresses

New International
A MAGAZINE OF MARXIST POLITICS AND THEORY

New International no. 10
Imperialism's March toward Fascism and War *by Jack Barnes* • What the 1987 Stock Market Crash Foretold • Defending Cuba, Defending Cuba's Socialist Revolution *by Mary-Alice Waters* • The Curve of Capitalist Development *by Leon Trotsky* $14.00

New International no. 9
The Triumph of the Nicaraguan Revolution • Washington's Contra War and the Challenge of Forging Proletarian Leadership • The Political Degeneration of the FSLN and the Demise of the Workers and Farmers Government $14.00

New International no. 8
The Politics of Economics: Che Guevara and Marxist Continuity *by Steve Clark and Jack Barnes* • Che's Contribution to the Cuban Economy *by Carlos Rafael Rodríguez* • On the Concept of Value *and* The Meaning of Socialist Planning *two articles by Ernesto Che Guevara* $10.00

New International no. 7

Opening Guns of World War III: Washington's Assault on Iraq *by Jack Barnes* • Communist Policy in Wartime as well as in Peacetime *by Mary-Alice Waters* • Lessons from the Iran-Iraq War *by Samad Sharif* $12.00

New International no. 6

The Second Assassination of Maurice Bishop *by Steve Clark* • Washington's 50-year Domestic Contra Operation *by Larry Seigle* • Land, Labor, and the Canadian Revolution *by Michel Dugré* • Renewal or Death: Cuba's Rectification Process *two speeches by Fidel Castro* $10.00

New International no. 5

The Coming Revolution in South Africa *by Jack Barnes* • The Future Belongs to the Majority *by Oliver Tambo* • Why Cuban Volunteers Are in Angola *two speeches by Fidel Castro* $9.00

New International no. 4

The Fight for a Workers and Farmers Government in the United States *by Jack Barnes* • The Crisis Facing Working Farmers *by Doug Jenness* • Land Reform and Farm Cooperatives in Cuba *two speeches by Fidel Castro* $9.00

New International no. 3

Communism and the Fight for a Popular Revolutionary Government: 1848 to Today *by Mary-Alice Waters* • 'A Nose for Power': Preparing the Nicaraguan Revolution *by Tomás Borge* • National Liberation and Socialism in the Americas *by Manuel Piñeiro* $8.00

New International no. 2

The Aristocracy of Labor: Development of the Marxist Position *by Steve Clark* • The Working-Class Fight for Peace *by Brian Grogan* • The Social Roots of Opportunism *by Gregory Zinoviev* $8.00

Distributed by Pathfinder

Many of the articles that appear in *New International* are also available in Spanish in *Nueva Internacional,* in French in *Nouvelle Internationale,* and in Swedish in *Ny International.*